Bloom's Shakespeare Through the Ages

Bloom's Shakespeare Through the Ages

THE TAMING
OF THE SHREW

Edited and with an introduction by
Harold Bloom
Sterling Professor of the Humanities
Yale University

Volume Editor
Pamela Loos

BLOOM'S
LITERARY CRITICISM
An imprint of Infobase Publishing

Bloom's Shakespeare Through the Ages: The Taming of the Shrew

Copyright ©2008 by Infobase Publishing

Introduction ©2008 by Harold Bloom

Bloom's Literary Criticism
An imprint of Infobase Publishing
132 West 31st Street
New York NY 10001

Library of Congress Cataloging-in-Publication Data
The taming of the shrew / edited and with an introduction by Harold Bloom ; volume editor, Pamela Loos.
      p. cm. — (Bloom's Shakespeare through the ages)
   Includes bibliographical references and index.
   ISBN-13: 978-0-7910-9598-0 (acid-free paper)
   ISBN-10: 0-7910-9598-3
   1. Shakespeare, William, 1564-1616. Taming of the shrew. I. Bloom, Harold.
   II. Loos, Pamela. III. Shakespeare, William, 1564–1616. Taming of the shrew.
   PR2832.T37 2008
   822.3'3—dc22   2007026817

Bloom's Literary Criticism books are available at special discounts when purchased in bulk quantities for businesses, associations, institutions, or sales promotions. Please call our Special Sales Department in New York at (212) 967-8800 or (800) 322-8755.

You can find Bloom's Literary Criticism on the World Wide Web at
http://www.chelseahouse.com

Series design by Erika K. Arroyo
Cover design by Ben Peterson
Cover photo © The Granger Collection, New York

Printed in the United States of America

Bang EJB 10 9 8 7 6 5 4 3 2 1

This book is printed on acid-free paper.

CONTENTS

❧

SERIES INTRODUCTION

❧

Shakespeare Through the Ages presents not the most current of Shakespeare criticism, but the best of Shakespeare criticism, from the seventeenth century to today. In the process, each volume also charts the flow over time of critical discussion of a particular play. Other useful and fascinating collections of historical Shakespearean criticism exist, but no collection that we know of contains such a range of commentary on each of Shakespeare's greatest plays and at the same time emphasizes the greatest critics in our literary tradition: from John Dryden in the seventeenth century, to Samuel Johnson in the eighteenth century, to William Hazlitt and Samuel Coleridge in the nineteenth century, to A.C. Bradley and William Empson in the twentieth century, to the most perceptive critics of our own day. This canon of Shakespearean criticism emphasizes aesthetic rather than political or social analysis.

Some of the pieces included here are full-length essays; others are excerpts designed to present a key point. Much (but not all) of the earliest criticism consists only of brief mentions of specific plays. In addition to the classics of criticism, some pieces of mainly historical importance have been included, often to provide background for important reactions from future critics.

These volumes are intended for students, particularly those just beginning their explorations of Shakespeare. We have therefore also included basic materials designed to provide a solid grounding in each play: a biography of Shakespeare, a synopsis of the play, a list of characters, and an explication of key passages. In addition, each selection of the criticism of a particular century begins with an introductory essay discussing the general nature of that century's commentary and the particular issues and controversies addressed by critics presented in the volume.

Shakespeare was "not of an age, but for all time," but much Shakespeare criticism is decidedly for its own age, of lasting importance only to the scholar who wrote it. Students today read the criticism most readily available to them, which means essays printed in recent books and journals, especially those journals made available on the Internet. Older criticism is too often buried in out-of-print books on forgotten shelves of libraries or in defunct periodicals. Therefore, many students, particularly younger students, have no way of knowing that some of the most profound criticism of Shakespeare's plays was written decades or centuries ago. We hope this series remedies that problem, and, more importantly, we hope it infuses students with the enthusiasm of the critics in these volumes for the beauty and power of Shakespeare's plays.

Introduction by Harold Bloom

૪૭

In just two months, I will commence my fifty-third consecutive year on the Yale faculty. For the last 25 of those years I have taught courses on Shakespeare. I intend to continue until I retire, and I never will retire. Doubtless, being mortal, I will fall apart, in body or mind or both, though I expect someday to be carried out of my very last Shakespeare seminar in a large body bag, *still talking*.

This is preamble to my reflections upon the change in my students' reactions to *The Shrew* during the last quarter-century. The early 1980s were the heyday of the School of Resentment, my amiable name for academic Political Correctness. Now, in 2007, Resentment abides in various persons and locales, but I never encounter it among my own students.

Something of this transition can be found in some of the following essays, particularly those that represent, respectively, the twentieth and the twenty-first centuries. But modifications between a Feminist view of Katherine as a Patriarchal victim and as a "subversive" shrew themselves will join the realm of Period Pieces. Some years back I was sent a "casebook" on the *Shrew*, which contained extracts from English Renaissance tracts on wife beating! Of course, Petruchio is too good-natured, and in the process of falling in love, ever to strike Katherine. She hits him once, and he warns her not to do it again, but I doubt he would retaliate.

Harold C. Goddard, William Empson, and Ruth Nevo share the critical laurels in this book. All of them see what should be seen, and what Cole Porter saw so well: This is a play about a happy marriage, with a free-for-all farce leading on to it.

I tend to start any class on the *Shrew* with the lovely street-exchange between the recently married Kate and Petruchio (Act V, Scene I, lines 130–38):

Kath. Husband, let's follow, to see the end of this ado.
Pet. First kiss me, Kate, and we will.
Kath. What, in the midst of the street?
Pet. What, art thou ashamed of me?
Kath. No sir, God forbid; but ashamed to kiss.

Pet. Why then, let's home again. Come, sirrah, let's away.
Kath. Nay, I will give thee a kiss. Now pray thee, love, stay.
Pet. Is not this well? Come, my sweet Kate.
        Better once than never, for never too late.
                                    Exeunt.

It may be one of Shakespeare's subtly ironic jokes that the two best marriages in all his work turn out to be between the roaring-boy Petruchio and the not-at-all-shrewish Kate, and—in shattering contrast—the Macbeths! Both couples are conspiring against all the rest of us, but the comedic pair's marriage is as benign as that of the Macbeths is malign. Shakespeare, perhaps on the basis of personal experience as well as observation, was not exactly an idealizer of the blessed state of matrimony.

I stay away firmly from *all* current performances of *The Taming of the Shrew*, just as I will not go near any new production of *The Tempest*. The last *Shrew* I walked out on was a fusion of parodistic feminism and sadomasochism. Each *Tempest*, from George Wolfe's fiasco in Central Park some years ago (from which I departed in high vocal fury) to one or two recent Resentment rallies, has featured Caliban and Ariel as heroic rebel slaves, with Prospero as a kind of Simon Legree.

All fashions vanish (as we too must) but *The Taming of the Shrew* is a permanent delight of a comedy, and will survive Cultural Correctness. My students initially blink when I tell them that Petruchio and Kate fall forever in love at first sight, but my observation is merely true.

Biography of
William Shakespeare

&

WILLIAM SHAKESPEARE was born in Stratford-on-Avon in April 1564 into a family of some prominence. His father, John Shakespeare, was a glover and merchant of leather goods who earned enough to marry Mary Arden, the daughter of his father's landlord, in 1557. John Shakespeare was a prominent citizen in Stratford, and at one point, he served as an alderman and bailiff.

Shakespeare presumably attended the Stratford grammar school, where he would have received an education in Latin, but he did not go on to either Oxford or Cambridge universities. Little is recorded about Shakespeare's early life; indeed, the first record of his life after his christening is of his marriage to Anne Hathaway in 1582 in the church at Temple Grafton, near Stratford. He would have been required to obtain a special license from the bishop as security that there was no impediment to the marriage. Peter Alexander states in his book *Shakespeare's Life and Art* that marriage at this time in England required neither a church nor a priest or, for that matter, even a document—only a declaration of the contracting parties in the presence of witnesses. Thus, it was customary, though not mandatory, to follow the marriage with a church ceremony.

Little is known about William and Anne Shakespeare's marriage. Their first child, Susanna, was born in May 1583 and twins, Hamnet and Judith, in 1585. Later on, Susanna married Dr. John Hall, but the younger daughter, Judith, remained unmarried. When Hamnet died in Stratford in 1596, the boy was only 11 years old.

We have no record of Shakespeare's activities for the seven years after the birth of his twins, but by 1592 he was in London working as an actor. He was also apparently well known as a playwright, for reference is made of him by his contemporary Robert Greene in *A Groatsworth of Wit*, as "an upstart crow."

Several companies of actors were in London at this time. Shakespeare may have had connection with one or more of them before 1592, but we have no record that tells us definitely. However, we do know of his long association with the most famous and successful troupe, the Lord Chamberlain's Men. (When James I came to the throne in 1603, after Elizabeth's death, the troupe's name changed to the King's Men.) In 1599 the Lord Chamberlain's Men provided the financial backing for the construction of their own theater, the Globe.

The Globe was begun by a carpenter named James Burbage and finished by his two sons, Cuthbert and Robert. To escape the jurisdiction of the Corporation of London, which was composed of conservative Puritans who opposed the theater's "licentiousness," James Burbage built the Globe just outside London, in the Liberty of Holywell, beside Finsbury Fields. This also meant that the Globe was safer from the threats that lurked in London's crowded streets, like plague and other diseases, as well as rioting mobs. When James Burbage died in 1597, his sons completed the Globe's construction. Shakespeare played a vital role, financially and otherwise, in the construction of the theater, which was finally occupied sometime before May 16, 1599.

Shakespeare not only acted with the Globe's company of actors; he was also a shareholder and eventually became the troupe's most important playwright. The company included London's most famous actors, who inspired the creation of some of Shakespeare's best-known characters, such as Hamlet and Lear, as well as his clowns and fools.

In his early years, however, Shakespeare did not confine himself to the theater. He also composed some mythological-erotic poetry, such as *Venus and Adonis* and *The Rape of Lucrece*, both of which were dedicated to the earl of Southampton. Shakespeare was successful enough that in 1597 he was able to purchase his own home in Stratford, which he called New Place. He could even call himself a gentleman, for his father had been granted a coat of arms.

By 1598 Shakespeare had written some of his most famous works, *Romeo and Juliet*, *The Comedy of Errors*, *A Midsummer Night's Dream*, *The Merchant of Venice*, *Two Gentlemen of Verona*, and *Love's Labour's Lost*, as well as his historical plays *Richard II*, *Richard III*, *Henry IV*, and *King John*. Somewhere around the turn of the century, Shakespeare wrote his romantic comedies *As You Like It*, *Twelfth Night*, and *Much Ado About Nothing*, as well as *Henry V*, the last of his history plays in the Prince Hal series. During the next 10 years he wrote his great tragedies, *Hamlet*, *Macbeth*, *Othello*, *King Lear*, and *Antony and Cleopatra*.

At this time, the theater was burgeoning in London; the public took an avid interest in drama, the audiences were large, the plays demonstrated an enormous range of subjects, and playwrights competed for approval. By 1613, however, the rising tide of Puritanism had changed the theater. With the desertion of the theaters by the middle classes, the acting companies were compelled to depend more on the aristocracy, which also meant that they now had to cater to a more sophisticated audience.

Perhaps this change in London's artistic atmosphere contributed to Shakespeare's reasons for leaving London after 1612. His retirement from the theater is sometimes thought to be evidence that his artistic skills were waning. During this time, however, he wrote *The Tempest* and *Henry VIII*. He also wrote the "tragicomedies," *Pericles, Cymbeline*, and *The Winter's Tale*. These were thought to be inspired by Shakespeare's personal problems and have sometimes been considered proof of his greatly diminished abilities.

However, so far as biographical facts indicate, the circumstances of his life at this time do not imply any personal problems. He was in good health and financially secure, and he enjoyed an excellent reputation. Indeed, although he was settled in Stratford at this time, he made frequent visits to London, enjoying and participating in events at the royal court, directing rehearsals, and attending to other business matters.

In addition to his brilliant and enormous contributions to the theater, Shakespeare remained a poetic genius throughout the years, publishing a renowned and critically acclaimed sonnet cycle in 1609 (most of the sonnets were written many years earlier). Shakespeare's contribution to this popular poetic genre are all the more amazing in his break with contemporary notions of subject matter. Shakespeare idealized the beauty of man as an object of praise and devotion (rather than the Petrarchan tradition of the idealized, unattainable woman). In the same spirit of breaking with tradition, Shakespeare also treated themes previously considered off limits—the dark, sexual side of a woman as opposed to the Petrarchan ideal of a chaste and remote love object. He also expanded the sonnet's emotional range, including such emotions as delight, pride, shame, disgust, sadness, and fear.

When Shakespeare died in 1616, no collected edition of his works had ever been published, although some of his plays had been printed in separate unauthorized editions. (Some of these were taken from his manuscripts, some from the actors' prompt books, and others were reconstructed from memory by actors or spectators.) In 1623 two members of the King's Men, John Hemings and Henry Condell, published a collection of all the plays they considered to be authentic, the First Folio.

Included in the First Folio is a poem by Shakespeare's contemporary Ben Jonson, an outstanding playwright and critic in his own right. Jonson paid tribute to Shakespeare's genius, proclaiming his superiority to what previously had been held as the models for literary excellence—the Greek and Latin writers. "Triumph, my Britain, thou hast one to show / To whom all scenes of Europe homage owe. / He was not of an age, but for all time!"

Jonson was the first to state what has been said so many times since. Having captured what is permanent and universal to all human beings at all times, Shakespeare's genius continues to inspire us—and the critical debate about his works never ceases.

Summary of
The Taming of the Shrew
❧

Induction

Induction is a Latinate word for "introduction." Here Shakespeare describes events that occur outside of the main action of *The Taming of the Shrew*. The setting is in front of an alehouse, where there is a confrontation between the proprietor of the alehouse and Christopher Sly, a beggar and mender of pots. Sly is in trouble for breaking glasses in the alehouse, yet he yells back at the proprietor that she should forget about the damage. He argues that she should treat him better, claiming he is a descendent of William the Conqueror, whom he mistakenly calls Richard Conqueror. Drunk and apparently uneducated, Sly uses other words incorrectly as well. Instead of being disturbed when the woman says she will get the authorities, he issues retorts with bravado and promptly falls asleep.

A lord enters with huntsmen and servants. He and one huntsman remark on the abilities of their hunting dogs. They give their opinions as to the best of the dogs, the one that is able to find and keep following even the weakest scent. This could be interpreted as a note to the audience to stay alert and make an effort to follow the meanings in the play. Alternatively, this could be seen as a mirror of what happens in the play, where what appears to be best in one person's view may not be best from another's view.

The lord sees Sly asleep and is repulsed by him, calling him an image of death. He decides he would like to play a trick on Sly and explains to his servants how it will work. Specifically, they will bring Sly into the lord's best room and pretend that Sly himself is a lord. They will have music and fragrance and fancy clothes ready for him and offer to serve him in whatever way he wishes. They will convince Sly that for 15 years he has been mad, mistakenly believing himself a poor tinker. The men carry Sly to the lord's house.

Actors appear and offer their services to the lord. He recognizes one of them, someone whom he saw act the part of a man wooing a woman. The lord praises the actor for the job he did. He tells the actors he would like to have them perform but warns them that one of the observers will be a man who is not used to watching performances. The actors are escorted off to eat, and then the lord speaks with one more servant, explaining yet another part of the trick on Sly. The lord tells the servant that the page must dress up as a woman and pretend to be Sly's wife. The servant must tempt Sly with kisses and cry with joy, supposedly because Sly is now in his right mind. If necessary, the servant can use an onion to bring on the tears. The servant leaves with his orders, and the lord decides he must dress up and play a part in the trick as well; perhaps this will keep the others from laughing during the charade.

All of this extensive preparation creates suspense for the audience members, who wonder how the plan will work out. In scene 2, Sly wakes up and asks for some ale. But he is surrounded by men offering him instead the drinks, foods, and attire of a lord. Sly wants no part of these offers, insists he is not a lord, and describes what he is used to in his own life—for example, shoes with holes where his toes stick out. He gives his lineage, pointing out the lowly life he is used to, and says the fat innkeeper can vouch for him; he even owes her money. The men do not give up on the trick so quickly, however. They tempt him with more offers and give detailed descriptions of all that is available to him; these items are a stark contrast to what he has described as being part of a tinker's life. The contrast between the lowly life and the lord's life is readily apparent in the speech of Sly versus the speech of these men as well.

While the men might have thought Sly would willingly leap at the chance to be a lord, he does not. Here Shakespeare is already commenting on personal identity, the role of wealth, and the use of disguise and trickery. Eventually, though, Sly hears the men describe his wife, and so he gives in to being a lord. The comedy intensifies as the supposed wife enters. "She" gets confused about how to refer to Sly, and Sly himself, not knowing how a nobleman speaks, must rely on his supposed servants to explain what Sly is to call his wife. The trickery continues; when Sly asks her to take off her clothes, she responds that the doctors have told her not to be intimate with Sly just yet because of his condition.

The players enter and Sly finds out that he will be presented with a play. Per his doctor's orders, the play is to make him merry. Sly prepares to watch, as do we the audience.

Act I

In the first scene, Lucentio and his servant enter. We find out that Lucentio has come to Padua to study. His father, the successful merchant Vincentio, has sent him off with a servant, Tranio. Lucentio asks the servant for his advice on how he should proceed, and Tranio references all the areas that are important to study but says that what's most important is that Lucentio not be too stoic and not forget about love. Almost as if on cue, the female characters—who will be the main focus of various wooers in the play—make their appearance. The women, Kate and Bianca, are the daughters of Baptista. With them are Gremio, a foolish old man, and Hortensio, both of whom wish to be suitors to Bianca.

Lucentio and Tranio step aside to see what is going on among these people, watching from the sidelines just as we the audience are.

Baptista informs the two suitors that he has decided that until Kate is married he will keep Bianca from any suitors. Baptista offers Kate to the two men, yet each frankly explains why he would never want her. Kate lashes out at her father for offering her to these men and then lashes out at each of the men who has spoken so poorly of her. She says, for instance, that she would smack Hortensio with a stool and mar his face if he were to woo her. Still unobserved by Baptista and the others, Tranio and Lucentio continue to watch; Tranio finds the action amusing, while Lucentio becomes enraptured with Bianca.

Baptista says it is time for Bianca to go in. Kate calls her the spoiled child, yet Bianca appears obedient at this point and retires. Baptista tells the men that if they know tutors for his daughter, he would be interested. He tells Kate she can stay but that he will go since he has more to discuss with Bianca. Kate is angry that he tells her what to do, and she leaves as well.

Gremio remarks on Kate's horrid temperament. But Hortensio is thinking about how he and Gremio can improve their lot, and he suggests to Gremio that they should find someone to woo Kate. Gremio agrees and the two men leave.

Tranio realizes that Lucentio, seemingly already following Tranio's earlier advice to him, is already in love with Bianca. Lucentio speaks of being in love as not something he was working toward but something that came over him and over which he has no control. Lucentio is so taken with Bianca that he can speak only of her, and he comes back to reality only at Tranio's urging. The two decide that the best thing to do is for Lucentio to pretend to be a tutor for Bianca, so he can be near her. In the meantime, Tranio will take on Lucentio's identity and tell Baptista he wishes to become a suitor to Bianca. The men trade clothes in order to adopt these new identities. Lucentio's other servant, Biondello, appears. Lucentio makes up a story to explain why they have traded clothes, saying that Lucentio has gotten himself in trouble for murdering a man and that Tranio is helping him out so Lucentio will have time to escape.

These men exit, but still left are Sly and two servants from the Induction, who have been watching the action from above. Sly tells them he's enjoying the play and asks if there is more yet to come. The page tells him there is, and while Sly again comments on how good the play is, he adds that he wishes it were over. Indeed, as the lord predicted earlier, the rogue Sly probably does not know what to make of the play. Playgoing is not all merriment, Shakespeare may be saying, but requires more work than the average drunkard may be willing to provide.

Scene 2 takes place in front of Hortensio's house. The scene starts with a farcical routine wherein Petruchio asks Grumio to knock on Hortensio's door, but Grumio is confused about what his master is actually requesting and the two go back and forth with a series of questions and answers. The confusion escalates, and finally Petruchio grabs his servant. Hortensio enters and stops the fight, and Petruchio and Grumio explain what's caused it. This explanation to Hortensio allows the audience more laughs as we relive the comic antics. Hortensio cautions Petruchio to treat his servant fairly, and indeed we find in this play a focus on how servants get treated and how valuable they can really be.

Petruchio explains what has brought him to Padua—his father has died and left him a good deal of money, and he is looking for a wife to make him richer still. At this, Hortensio tells Petruchio he knows a rich woman, but since she is also ill-natured he should hardly wish her on his friend. Petruchio jumps at the mention, though, saying money is what he is after and any problems regarding the woman's nature will not deter him. From here through the rest of this conversation Grumio chimes in with his own advice to Hortensio, reinforcing, for instance, that Petruchio is indeed after money and will not be put off by the worst of women. Throughout Hortensio is honest about just how horrid he believes Kate is, but Petruchio still wants to meet her immediately. Hortensio says he must go with Petruchio, explaining his attraction to Bianca and that he can only woo her if Kate gets married first. He explains his own scheme to Petruchio, a scheme like the one we shortly before heard Lucentio and Tranio devise, and one that will complicate the plot further: Hortentio explains that Petruchio should introduce Hortensio to Baptista as a schoolmaster for Bianca.

Next Gremio enters with Lucentio, who is disguised as a tutor. The others listen from the side before coming forward. We learn that Lucentio has promised Gremio he will advocate on Gremio's behalf when he meets and tutors Bianca. Gremio has fallen for the promise. Then Hortensio, Petruchio, and Grumio approach the two men. Gremio tells Hortensio he has found this tutor for Bianca, and Hortensio tells Gremio that he, also, has found a tutor for her. (Hortensio is alluding to the fact that he plans to dress up as a tutor himself.) Hortensio also explains that Petruchio plans to woo Kate, and Petruchio gives a somewhat lengthy speech about all the trials he's already endured, surmising, therefore, that Kate will prove no difficulty. Hortensio says he told Petruchio that he and Gremio would pay for his wooing, and Gremio agrees, provided the wooing is successful.

Biondello appears with Tranio, who is dressed as Lucentio. The other men learn that this supposed Lucentio plans to be a suitor to Bianca. The other suitors are distressed, yet "Lucentio" explains that even though they are adversaries they still can treat each other as friends. All agree.

Act II

Act II comprises only one scene, which occurs at Baptista's house. It starts with Kate on stage with her sister, whom Kate has tied up. Kate insists that Bianca tell her which suitor, the foolish Gremio or Hortensio, is the one that Bianca really pines for. Bianca believes her sister is jealous of her and tells Kate that she is attracted to neither and that Kate can take either as her suitor. We wonder if Bianca is only saying what she thinks she needs to in order to be untied, and apparently Kate may be wondering the same thing, for she strikes her sister.

Baptista enters and is appalled at what Kate has done to Bianca. He unties Bianca and chastises Kate, who springs forward to harm Bianca again. Baptista tells Bianca to leave, and Kate says that Bianca is really her father's favorite. Kate leaves, upset, and Baptista comments on his sorry state, concerned about himself rather than what he might do to improve his relationship with Kate.

The suitors and supposed tutors enter in a crowd—Gremio; Lucentio, disguised as a tutor; Petruchio; Hortensio, also disguised as a tutor; Tranio, disguised as Lucentio; and Biondello. Petruchio immediately inquires about Kate, whom he describes with many positive adjectives. He explains that he has brought a tutor of music and mathematics, who he calls Litio but who is in fact the disguised Hortensio. Baptista is surprised that anyone wants Kate, but when he finds out who Petruchio's father was, he welcomes Petruchio, saying he has known his father well.

Gremio introduces the disguised Lucentio as Cambio, a tutor who knows many languages. Baptista welcomes Cambio and then asks Tranio (disguised as Lucentio) who he is. The supposed Lucentio explains that he wants to be a suitor to Bianca, and that even though he is from another city, he knows of her wonderful qualities. He also presents Baptista with a lute and Greek and Latin books that Baptista's daughters can use in their education. Baptista asks about "Lucentio's" background and is happy to hear that he is the son of Vincentio. Baptista then tells the tutors to go to his daughters.

Petruchio starts to talk about the money that will be involved when he marries Kate. He says how much he has, asks Baptista what he will contribute, and, satisfied, asks that they draw up papers and sign them. Baptista hesitates, though, concerned that Petruchio may not be able to gain Kate's love. Petruchio is not to be deterred, however, even when Baptista gives him further warning about his daughter. At this point, too, we realize that whereas earlier Petruchio said he was solely concerned about gaining more money through marriage, he did not press Baptista for more money, even though Baptista might very well have agreed to give more. Petruchio apparently is not as driven by money as even he himself previously thought.

Hortensio enters with a head injury. He explains how he now fears Kate and that the injury came about when he was trying to correct Kate in how to play the lute; at that, Kate smashed the instrument over his head. Petruchio says he finds Kate even more appealing now, and instead of going with the others for a walk in the garden he takes Baptista up on his offer to send Kate to Petruchio.

As Petruchio waits for Kate to appear, the audience is held in more suspense. Petruchio explains that he has a plan for wooing Kate. He says he will comment on the negative things she does as if she is doing just the opposite. For instance, when she speaks like a shrew, he will tell her how her voice is as sweet as a nightingale's. In the process, then, he will smother her with compliments. Kate enters, and, after his simple greeting, she finds a way to cut him down, saying people do not call her "Kate." Petruchio immediately launches into a speech about her name and all her good qualities and explains that he is there to woo her. Kate is not so easily flattered, however, and insults him instead. Petruchio twists her words, though, to another meaning, all the while remaining good natured. After every cruel remark from her he responds in this way, at times becoming bawdy with his implications. When he calls himself a gentleman, Kate says she'll put him to the test, and she slaps him. While earlier we saw Petruchio physically attack his servant, here he restrains himself physically. Instead he gives Kate a warning and shortly after returns to his amiable self as he responds to all of her verbal lashings.

When Kate starts to leave, Petruchio restrains her by putting his arm around her. Again he gives her many compliments, and then he remarks that all the others are wrong in what they say about her. When he lets her go, she does not leave. She asks him where he learned to speak the way he does. He answers that all his speech is natural, and, when he asks if he is not wise, she responds that he is. Her negativity has vanished, at least for a bit. Petruchio tells her that her father and he have already agreed to the terms of the marriage and that, no matter what she wants, he will marry her. His meeting her has reinforced his earlier feeling that their personalities are different from the others' and that he and she can go well together.

Baptista, Gremio, and the disguised Tranio all enter to see how the meeting of Petruchio and Kate is progressing. Baptista first asks Petruchio how the encounter has been, and Petruchio answers most positively. When Baptista asks Kate why she is less lively than usual, she quickly lashes out at him for trying to marry her off to a "half lunatic." Petruchio ignores the negative comment and instead says the others are wrong in their descriptions of Kate; he again lists what he says are her positive attributes. He says that, in fact, Kate and he have gotten along so well that they will be married on Sunday. Kate contradicts him, which concerns the two suitors of Bianca, but Petruchio has a quick and apparently convincing comeback, for the men are then satisfied that all is fine. Kate offers no further retort and leaves with Petruchio.

Bianca's suitors then realize that they are free to vie for Bianca's hand, and they immediately begin selling themselves to Baptista. The two suitors argue between themselves about their attributes, until Baptista interrupts and says that whoever can offer the best financial arrangement will have "Bianca's love." While during Shakespeare's time making the best financial arrangement was imperative, here Bianca's father probably also assumes that since Bianca seems so amiable she will go along with his decision, even if that might mean she is to marry the old and foolish Gremio. Gremio gives detailed descriptions of the beautiful items and riches he can offer. In the end, though, the supposed Lucentio offers more. Baptista says "Lucentio" can marry his daughter if "Lucentio" can make assurances of all he's promised, and then the father exits.

Gremio accuses the disguised Tranio of lying about what he can offer, and then Gremio exits. Tranio, on stage by himself now, decides he must do the best he can in this negotiation so that his master, the true Lucentio, will be able to eventually trade places with Tranio and happily marry Bianca. Tranio decides he must find someone who will act like he is Lucentio's father and promise Baptista whatever is necessary.

Act III

The first scene in Act III takes place in Baptista's house. Lucentio and Hortensio, both pretending to be tutors, are arguing with each other. Each is intent on getting Bianca's attention and forcing the other to back away. Bianca interrupts the argument and tells them that she will learn her lessons as she sees fit. She instructs that Hortensio should tune his instrument while she listens to Lucentio's lecture. Then while Lucentio is pretending to teach Bianca, he cleverly explains that he, in fact, is only pretending to be a tutor but that he actually is the son of the well-known Vincentio and has devised this plan to be near her. He tells her that his servant is pretending to be Lucentio and trying to disrupt Gremio in his drive to be Bianca's suitor. Bianca acts as if she is responding to his lesson and tells him she does not trust him but also that he must not despair.

As he tunes his instrument, Hortensio tries to interrupt Lucentio and Bianca. Finally Bianca says she will take some lesson time with Hortensio. He, too, as part of the lesson, gives his own secret message to her, telling her he loves her and wants her to pick him to be her lord. Bianca responds negatively, though, and shortly thereafter a servant calls her to go to her father. Lucentio leaves as well, and Hortensio speaks to himself. He says he is suspicious of Lucentio and that if Bianca will fall for any man who happens to enter her path, he will find another woman to care for.

In scene 2, Baptista, Kate, and others are in front of Baptista's house, waiting for Petruchio to arrive, for it is the wedding day of Petruchio and Kate. Petruchio is so late that Baptista is embarrassed, and Kate says she was forced into this marriage with a madman who has no intention of ever arriving. Tranio (disguised as Lucentio) stands up for Petruchio, saying something must have happened to delay Petruchio. Kate, though, leaves weeping, followed by Bianca and attendants. Biondello arrives and acts rather comically, but finally those waiting realize Petruchio is, according to Biondello, on his way. Biondello also provides a detailed description of the worn-out clothes that Petruchio is wearing, as well as the very sickly horse that he is riding and the valet who accompanies them, poorly and haphazardly dressed as well. Baptista responds that he is still glad that Petruchio is coming, but Biondello causes confusion with a series of comical responses. He provides levity in a scene that has been tense and serious up to this point.

Petruchio arrives with Grumio. Baptista welcomes him, but "Lucentio" remarks that Petruchio should be better dressed. Petruchio is concerned with Kate and asks where she is, but hears that Baptista is unhappy as well about Petruchio's dress. Petruchio says it's not worth it for him to explain why he is late right now, and, even after further urging, he says he will not change his clothes. After all, he says, Kate is marrying him and not his clothes. He goes off to find her, happily anticipating the wedding ceremony, assuming she will be so happy to see him that she will put up with his deplorable appearance.

Baptista, Gremio, and attendants leave, and the supposed Lucentio (Tranio) and the real Lucentio talk together. They discuss the need to find someone who will play the part of Lucentio's father in order to satisfy Baptista. Tranio believes this fake father should promise Baptista even more money than Tranio has already promised. Lucentio is concerned that the plan may not work and believes that it may be best to elope with Bianca and suffer the consequences afterward.

Gremio enters and proceeds to describe the farcical events that occurred at the wedding ceremony. Petruchio's behavior was wild. He responded without the proper decorum when the priest asked if Kate should be Petruchio's wife and also smacked the priest so intensely that he fell. When Petruchio drank the wine, he drank it like a crude sailor. Also, he kissed Kate with such a great intensity as to embarrass all in attendance. Gremio says that Kate was left speechless by the uncouth behavior. In fact, we may begin to realize that Petruchio's behavior is precisely calculated to keep Kate overwhelmed and to prod her to realize that such wild conduct, reminiscent of some of her own horrid behavior, is truly unacceptable. Perhaps, in light of Petruchio's behavior, she will realize that she needs to change her old ways.

The others enter, ready to attend the wedding feast. Petruchio, though, has other plans. He politely thanks all for coming but announces that he must leave immediately. He says if they knew his business they would actually want him to leave. This seems to be a clue that there is a reason for his highly unusual behavior. It seems that even his early departure is carefully calculated to once again keep Kate off balance and keep her from being her earlier shrewish self. Petruchio again rattles off a list of charming adjectives about his wife, and, while many beg him to stay, he insists he cannot. Finally Kate speaks up and says she will stay and she will stay as long as she likes, even if he leaves. Gremio remarks that now Petruchio's scheme is starting to be realized. Kate tells all to enter the dining area; at first Petruchio seems to support her and instructs everyone to follow her orders, but then says he must take his wife with him. He tells Kate to not fight him on this and cleverly acts as if Kate is actually being saved by his taking her away. He tells Grumio to draw his sword, as if they are the heroic knights, protecting his wife, and off they go.

Some of the key remaining characters comment on Petruchio and Kate, believing they really are mad and at the same time quite suited for each other. What the characters do not realize is that Petruchio is not mad but rather acting to get Kate to change. Kate, in turn, has never been truly mad; instead she had assumed a persona, having been slighted by her father and living with a sister who is construed in a more positive light than she deserves. Baptista tells the supposed Lucentio to take Petruchio's place at the table and asks Bianca to take her sister's place. We wonder if the next wedding, between the real Lucentio and Bianca, will take place in a nontraditional way as well.

Act IV

The first scene in Act IV is set at Petruchio's country house. His servant Grumio enters and complains about being beaten, tired, muddied, and thoroughly cold. He calls for Curtis, a servant, to make a fire, and Curtis enters and asks if Petruchio is coming with his new mistress and whether she is as shrewish as people have said. Grumio replies that she used to be shrewish before this frost, and he urges the man to get a fire going. Curtis, though, wants more news; he tells Grumio that the fire and all the servants are ready as they should be. Grumio fools with the man, though, and keeps him in suspense about any news. He also knocks Curtis on the side of the head, reminding us of when Petruchio smacked Grumio much earlier in the play when Petruchio was fooling with him. Grumio also engages in wordplay; he, too, then, is a rather intelligent servant, just as we've seen Tranio to be.

Finally Grumio tells Curtis what happened: that Kate's horse fell and she fell under it, in a quite muddy spot, and that Petruchio beat Grumio because the horse fell, prompting Kate to pull Petruchio away from Grumio to stop the beating. To this, Curtis responds that Petruchio is more of a shrew than Kate, and Grumio warns that there is more to come when Petruchio arrives. Grumio inquires if all is ready for the master's arrival, and Curtis says it is. The other servants are called and all greet Grumio. All are eager to please the master and new mistress.

Petruchio and Kate enter. He immediately complains about the servants, calls them names, and is angry that they haven't rushed to his assistance upon his arrival. Petruchio calls for the servants to bring him his supper; he has another help him take off his boots. Unhappy with the help from this latter servant, Petruchio hits him as well as a servant who enters and spills water. Kate comes to the servant's aid, as she does again when Petruchio becomes inflamed because the supper, he says, is no good, and he throws the food and utensils. Through all of this, though, Petruchio speaks politely to Kate. He tells her, too, she should not be eating such meat. Petruchio, Kate, and Curtis go to the bedroom, and two of the other servants knowingly remark that Petruchio is trying to reform Kate by mimicking her own bad behavior. They exit.

Petruchio comes on stage by himself and tells the audience what he is up to, namely, that he will keep Kate hungry so that he can maintain some control over her. Similarly, he will keep her from sleeping. Yet at every step he will tell his wife that all he does is for her own good.

In scene 2 we return to the subplot. Tranio and Hortensio, both in their disguises, are in front of Baptista's house. Hortensio tells Tranio that he realizes that Bianca doesn't want either one of them but that she wants her other tutor instead. Hortensio takes Tranio aside, where they can observe Bianca and the other tutor (the disguised Lucentio). Bianca and the disguised Lucentio speak of love and walk away. Hortensio then tells Tranio that they should both swear to forget about Bianca. Tranio says he will go along with Hortensio's wishes, and Hortensio also reveals his true identity and tells his plan to marry a widow who has loved him for some time. He would rather have a woman who is kind than one who is beautiful but unkind like Bianca, he says.

Hortensio leaves, and Tranio talks with Bianca and the true Lucentio. He tells them what Hortensio has just told him, and, when Bianca says she wishes Hortensio luck, Tranio says Hortensio will tame the widow. When Bianca asks him about the taming school he mentions, he explains that Petruchio is the master and can "tame a shrew and charm her chattering tongue." Here Tranio clearly sees Petruchio not as a madman as the others do. We also see that he considers other women, not just Kate, as needing taming, whereas Bianca, in contrast, seems to find his thoughts foreign.

Biondello appears and says he has seen a man who might be a good stand-in for Vincentio. Tranio tells the others to leave, so he may set to work on tricking this man into acting as Vincentio. The man enters and Tranio makes up a tale so that the man believes he is in danger and needs to disguise himself. Tranio explains that he can help him by disguising him as Vincentio and keeping him at his home. It seems fair, then, Tranio says, that the man could do him a favor in return, and Tranio begins to explain the promise he needs the man to make to Baptista so that Bianca can be married. The two men walk off in discussion.

Scene 3 returns to Kate, who is in Petruchio's house. She asks Grumio for something to eat and complains about the deplorable treatment she's getting from Petruchio, who, she says, keeps her from eating and sleeping while continually saying he does it for her own good. Grumio says he cannot possibly give her any food but then teases her about what he could bring her, as if he will. The teasing continues, but Kate realizes he will bring her nothing, and so she beats him.

Petruchio enters with Hortensio. He says Kate should be happy since he's brought meat especially for her. When she does not thank him for it, he threatens to take it away, and then she thanks him. Petruchio says they are going to visit Baptista and that they will go dressed in beautiful attire; in fact, a tailor is here who has made a dress for Kate. A haberdasher enters as well. He shows a cap he has made for Kate at Petruchio's request. Petruchio rails against it, enumerating many reasons why it is no good. Kate gives her reasons why the cap *is* good, yet when she is done speaking Petruchio acts as if she has just said it is despicable; the haberdasher then leaves.

The tailor shows what he has made, and again Petruchio cries that the product is no good. This time, though, the tailor brings out written instructions that Grumio gave him regarding how to make the dress. It appears the farce will not continue. Yet with each instruction the tailor reads, Grumio has a sharp comeback, and so the tailor leaves, too. Here, though, we see that Petruchio, in an aside, instructs Hortensio to please make sure the tailor does get paid for his work. It's clear, then, that Petruchio was not really unhappy with the dress but was intent on his goal of making Kate less shrewish.

Petruchio says they can go to Baptista's home anyway, since clothing is really not an indication that one is rich; the mind is. When he comments on the time, he purposefully says the wrong time, and Kate corrects him. Petruchio says, though, that whatever he says, does, or thinks is right, and she must agree with him. He tells her they will not visit Baptista after all. Hortensio gives an aside about Petruchio's powerful abilities. While in the beginning of the scene Hortensio voiced pity for Kate, here and throughout the rest of the scene it appears that he sees what Petruchio is aiming to do regarding Kate.

In scene 4, we return to the Bianca subplot. In front of Baptista's house are Tranio, disguised as Lucentio, and the man who has agreed to pretend to be Vincentio. Biondello arrives and says he has told Baptista that Vincentio has arrived. Baptista enters with the real Lucentio (disguised as a tutor), and the supposed Vincentio explains why he is in this city and that upon hearing of how his son loves Bianca, he has come to promise what is necessary that his son may marry her. The men decide to go to Tranio's house to draw up the agreement, since Gremio and servants are always listening at Baptista's house. In an ironic twist, Baptista sends the real Lucentio off to Bianca to tell her about the plans for her to become the wife of Lucentio (whom Baptista still thinks Tranio is). The supposed Lucentio, the supposed Vincentio, and Baptista leave.

Biondello and the true Lucentio talk by themselves. Biondello explains that an old priest is ready to serve Lucentio. He explains that Lucentio should go to the church with the priest, clerk, and some witnesses, where he can be married to Bianca. Biondello starts to leave but Lucentio doesn't want him to, seemingly unclear about what is to happen. Biondello says he must go, though, since he must be sure all is in place. Again, the servants seem most effective and, in this case, more adept at planning and getting things done. Biondello leaves and Lucentio finally takes pleasure in the thought of marrying Bianca. Under the plan, Baptista will already have agreed for her to be married to Lucentio by the time the secret marriage takes place, although he will believe that a different man is Lucentio.

In scene 5, we revert to Petruchio and Kate, but the subplot seeps into the main plot. Petruchio, Kate, and Hortensio are finally on their way to Baptista's house, when Petruchio remarks on the shining moon. Kate corrects him, saying that the sun is what's shining. Petruchio, though, is incensed and says what's shining is what he says is shining and that unless that is so they must forget going to Baptista's and instead go home. Kate gives in, since they have already traveled far; she tells him the shining object shall be what he says. He says it is the moon; she agrees; then he says it is the sun and she agrees, saying that whatever he calls it, it will be for her as well. Hortensio, in an aside, tells Petruchio he's won his point, and Petruchio says they must continue to Baptista's house.

The real Vincentio enters, and Petruchio greets him and asks who he is. However, in addressing the man, Petruchio calls him a mistress and comments on his lovely beauty—and tells Kate to do the same. Kate goes along with Petruchio, calling the man a beautiful young woman, but then Petruchio turns on her and asks if she's mad since before them is an old man, not the woman she's called him. Kate seamlessly apologizes and refers to the man as an old man, and in a spark of creativity says that the sun, what they have just been arguing about, is what blinded her temporarily from seeing the man clearly.

Petruchio asks Vincentio where he is going and if he would like to travel with them. The group finds out that this is Lucentio's father, and Petruchio explains that they know Lucentio, the man who is to be Bianca's husband. Petruchio says they are happy to meet Vincentio and they will travel together to Baptista's. All leave but Hortensio, who says that he is encouraged to see how Petruchio has changed Kate. He says he will use Petruchio's tricks on the widow if she becomes unruly, and then he exits after the others.

Act V

In the first scene of Act V, we return to the subplot. In front of Lucentio's house, Biondello urges Lucentio to quickly get to the priest with Bianca, and they do so. To the side is Gremio, watching. Next, Petruchio, Kate, Vincentio, and their attendants enter. Petruchio shows Vincentio which is Lucentio's (Vincentio's son's) house, and Vincentio knocks on the door, telling Petruchio to stay and have some refreshment. From a window above, the pedant, who is pretending to be Vincentio, responds rudely to the knock. Petruchio intervenes and tells the pedant to call Lucentio since his father is here. The pedant calls Petruchio a liar and says he is Lucentio's father. Petruchio believes the pedant.

Biondello enters. When Vincentio sees him and calls to him, Biondello denies knowing him and says his master is the pedant. Vincentio attacks Biondello, who leaves, and the pedant goes back inside, calling for help. The pedant, Baptista, Tranio (disguised as Lucentio), and servants appear, and Tranio rails at Vincentio for attacking Biondello, whom he calls his servant. Vincentio sees how Tranio is dressed but still recognizes him as Lucentio's servant. Vincentio assumes that Tranio and Lucentio have been spending his money wildly. When Tranio insists that he is Lucentio, Vincentio then decides that Tranio must have murdered his son. All believe Vincentio is lying, and Tranio calls a police officer. Gremio, who is still watching from the side, intervenes on Vincentio's behalf but then melts into submission when Tranio stands up to him.

Biondello enters with Lucentio and Bianca, and, finally, all gets resolved. Lucentio immediately kneels and asks his father's forgiveness, and Bianca does the same with her father. Biondello, Tranio, and the pedant run off. Lucentio explains why he and Tranio had been disguising themselves and says that he and Bianca are now married. Baptista is not happy about having been tricked, but Vincentio says he will make financial arrangements that will please Baptista. All exit except Petruchio and Kate.

Kate says they should go inside with the others to see what will happen next, curious like the audience is at this point. Petruchio asks for a kiss first, and when Kate asks how can they kiss in the middle of the street, Petruchio reverts to his old methods, saying they will have to go home then. Kate kisses him. She calls him "love," he calls her "sweet Kate," and he asks if this is not better than how they had been treating each other. It is a rhetorical question, for it is clear that the answer is yes and that the two are genuinely happy.

In scene 2, the final scene of the play, all are gathered at Lucentio's house for a feast. Petruchio and Baptista comment on how all is kind in Padua, but Hortensio indicates that he feels differently. Petruchio says Hortensio is unhappy because of the widow he is now married to. The widow quips back. When Petruchio goes further and says that Hortensio is afraid of her, she responds that Petruchio, because he is unhappy with his own shrew, believes Hortensio must be unhappy with his wife as well. Kate confronts the widow, and the husbands egg the women on to fight further. Baptista, Gremio, Bianca, and Vincentio add comments, and we see that Bianca can be shrewish herself. Petruchio encourages her to make more jests, but she is annoyed and leaves, inviting whomever else wishes to go with her to do so, and the widow and Kate do.

Petruchio continues the verbal sparring with the others, and, when Baptista says Petruchio has the "veriest shrew of all," Petruchio disagrees. He says he is ready to prove this and proposes a test wherein each of the three new husbands must call for their wives, so they can see which wife is the most obedient. Lucentio proposes that the bet be 20 crowns, but Petruchio says it should be much more, and so the men agree on 100 crowns instead. The game starts as Lucentio sends Biondello to get his wife, Bianca. Biondello leaves and returns, announcing that Bianca has said she is too busy to come. Next Biondello goes to Hortensio's wife, the widow, and returns with her message that she will not come and that her husband should come to her instead. Petruchio then sends

Grumio to get Kate. Kate arrives, and when she asks Petruchio what he needs, he tells her to get the other two wives.

Kate leaves, and the men, who are so surprised at Kate's behavior, speak with Petruchio. When Hortensio says he wonders what it means that Kate is the only one who came as requested, Petruchio responds, "Marry, peace it bodes, and love, and quiet life." What has occurred is quite a turn of events; the two seemingly mad people, Petruchio and Kate, now seem to have the best marriage, and Petruchio foresees a life of peace. Previously in the play there had been only mayhem with this pair, but now the others are envious of them. Petruchio says he will have Kate show her obedience even further.

Kate returns with the other wives, and Petruchio tells her to take off her cap and step on it. After she does, the other two wives remark on the ridiculousness of this behavior. When Lucentio tells Bianca he has lost 100 crowns because she did not come when he asked for her, she bluntly calls him a fool. The beautiful Bianca is certainly not the sweet woman that all the others had imagined. Petruchio has additional requests for his wife. He tells her to tell the other women how they should behave with their husbands. The widow argues against this, but Kate gives a long speech about how ugly women are when they act negatively toward their husbands. She enumerates all that husbands are required to do for their wives and says that wives, therefore, should act appropriately as well. Petruchio is happy, and all the others are again astounded.

Petruchio and Kate leave. Lucentio has the last line, commenting that it is surprising that Kate has been willing to let herself "be tamed so." The remark leaves us with the view that Petruchio has not forced Kate into submission but that she has in fact decided to behave this way. Petruchio and Kate worked together at the feast; they knew each other well enough that they did not even have to discuss a plan ahead of time. They operate as a couple and are happy because of it, leaving the others disgruntled and envious.

Key Passages in
The Taming of the Shrew

୫ଚ

Induction, ii, 1–23

Sly: For God's sake, a pot of small ale.
Servant 1: Will't please your lordship drink a cup of sack?
Servant 2: Will't please your honor taste of these conserves?
Servant 3: What raiment will your honor wear today?
Sly: I am Christophero Sly, call not me "honor" nor "lordship." I ne'er
drank sack in my life. And if you give me any conserves, give me
conserves of beef. Ne'er ask me what raiment I'll wear, for I have no
more doublets than backs, no more stockings than legs, nor no more
shoes than feet—nay, sometime more feet than shoes, or such shoes as
my toes look through the over-leather.
Lord: Heaven cease this idle humor in your honor!
O that a mighty man of such descent,
Of such possessions, and so high esteem,
Should be infused with so foul a spirit!
Sly: What, would you make me mad? Am not I Christopher Sly, old
Sly's son of Burton-heath, by birth a peddler, by education a card-maker,
by transmutation a bear-herd, and now by present profession a tinker?
Ask Marian Hacket, the fat ale-wife of Wincot, if she know me not.
If she say I am not fourteen pence on the score for sheer ale, score me
up for the lyingest knave in Christendom. What, I am not bestraught.
Here's—

In this passage Christopher Sly awakens from his drunken sleep. He is surrounded by the lord's servants, who are carrying out the lord's plan of trying to
trick Sly into believing he is actually a part of the upper class. Sly's first short
line is what we'd expect from a poor drinker—he asks for a drink of ale. But
rather than getting Sly what he's asked for, each of the three servants offers him
something else, all of these items fit for a man of high stature. Sly responds
directly, first by telling them his name and that they should not address him
with formal titles of "honor" or "lordship." He replies to each of their offers:

19

First, he says he never drinks sack. Second, he does not want their conserves but rather wants conserves of beef. And third, he speaks of clothing, explaining that he has never had a choice of what to wear since he has only the items he's dressed in.

As if that were not a good enough taste of who Sly is, he explains further that sometimes he doesn't even have enough shoes for both feet, since his toes might poke out of the worn leather, his shoes literally being not enough to cover him. At the opening of the Induction, we got a glimpse of who Sly is; now we have more to add to that image. We learn not just who he is but also how he lives. Sly doesn't simply delve into partaking of what the servants offer him. He is insistent on being accepted for who he is. This question of one's real nature is key in the rest of the play.

The disguised lord responds to Sly's explanation as if he is exasperated at Sly's refusal to accept who he is. This time when Sly says his name, he gives some family history as well as a history of his professions. He mentions someone who knows him and who could help clear up the seeming confusion about his identity. Who is she? Fittingly, a woman from an alehouse where he owes money. Even when surrounded by riches, Sly makes no attempt to cover up his lower-class life; to the contrary, it's the life he wants, since it's the life he knows and a part of who he is.

Act I, ii, 98–127

Petruchio: I know her father, though I know not her,
And he knew my deceasèd father well.
I will not sleep Hortensio, till I see her,
And therefore let me be thus bold with you,
To give you over at this first encounter,
Unless you will accompany me thither.
Grumio: (*to Hortensio*) I pray you, sir, let him go while the humor lasts.
O my word, an she knew him as well as I do, she would think scolding would do little good upon him. She may perhaps call him half a score knaves, or so. Why, that's nothing. And he begin once, he'll rail in his rope-tricks. I'll tell you what sir, an she stand him but a little, he will throw a figure in her face, and so disfigure her with it, that she shall have no more eyes to see withal than a cat. You know him not sir.
Hortensio: Tarry Petruchio, I must go with thee,
For in Baptista's keep my treasure is.
He hath the jewel of my life in hold,
His youngest daughter, beautiful Bianca,
And her withholds from me and other more

Suitors to her, and rivals in my love,
Supposing it a thing impossible,
For those defects I have before rehearsed,
That ever Katherina will be wooed.
Therefore this order hath Baptista ta'en,
That none shall have access unto Bianca
Till Katherine the curst have got a husband.
Grumio: Katherine the curst!
A title for a maid of all titles the worst.

Here Petruchio has arrived at his friend Hortensio's house. He has informed Hortensio that he is rich but wants to be richer still by marrying a woman with money. Hortensio tells Petruchio about Kate, giving him an honest description. Despite hearing Kate's terrible traits, Petruchio says he must not only meet her, but he must do so immediately and woo her.

Petruchio's first appearance in the play occurred earlier in this scene, when we saw how harshly he treated his servant. In this conversation at Hortensio's, we make assumptions about Petruchio based not only on what he says and does but also on what his servant says about him. His servant, Grumio, seems to know Petruchio well and does not hesitate to tell Hortensio what he knows. Grumio's lines, in fact, make the scene more lively and funny and help add suspense. We are already wondering what will happen when Petruchio and Kate meet.

Grumio sounds like he knows Petruchio so well that we cannot help but pay attention, even though here Petruchio and Hortensio are the ones having a conversation, while Grumio is just adding to it. From Grumio, first we learn that Petruchio can lose his doggedness—hence Grumio advises that Petruchio should see Kate now, while he's in the spirit. And while Hortensio has provided a rather frightening portrayal of Kate, Grumio says that she still will be no match for his master. Although Grumio was physically assaulted by Petruchio earlier in this scene, when he describes how Petruchio will manage Kate he mentions nothing physical. Instead he speaks of Petruchio's verbal genius, referring, for example, to Petruchio's "rope-tricks"; many have interpreted Grumio as meaning Petruchio's "rhetoric." Grumio goes on to mention that Petruchio will "throw a figure in her face." Indeed this sounds like a physical act, yet Grumio is referring to the fact that Petruchio will use figurative language to get Kate under his control. Of course, at this point Grumio, in making his assumption that Petruchio will have no problem reining in Kate, knows about Kate only from what Hortensio has told him. Kate herself is actually an expert at rhetoric and figurative language, an ample match for Petruchio in the verbal arena.

Grumio says Hortensio really doesn't know Petruchio. Although we know Hortensio and Petruchio are friends, and friends should know each other rather well, this comment refers to an idea that repeatedly comes up in the play—that appearances can be deceiving. We believe Grumio's description of his master, for we've already seen evidence of Petruchio being harsh and controlling with Grumio as well as evidence of Petruchio's skill in using words as part of his weaponry. We've also seen Petruchio cover up his overbearing behavior when Hortensio appears, validating Grumio's remark that Hortensio doesn't really know Petruchio.

It's in Hortensio's best interest for Petruchio to meet Kate quickly, so that Hortensio may more quickly get to woo Bianca. Hortensio gives the typical romanticized description of Bianca, calling her "the jewel of my life" and "my treasure." He explains that Kate must first be married before Baptista will let Bianca's suitors visit. Only at the end of his explanation does he again refer to the evils of Bianca's older sister. He refers to "Katherine the curst" in an almost offhand way, since he and so many others already know this nickname for her. Grumio, though, repeats "Katherine the curst" with emphasis, realizing that this woman may be more to handle than even he imagined. Depending on how the line is delivered, it can be quite funny, and, again, it adds to the suspense over what will actually happen when Petruchio and Kate do meet.

Act II, i, 277–310

Kate: Call you me daughter? Now I promise you
You have showed a tender fatherly regard,
To wish me wed to one half lunatic,
A madcap ruffian, and a swearing Jack,
That thinks with oaths to face the matter out.
Petruchio: Father, 'tis thus, yourself and all the world
That talked of her have talked amiss of her.
If she be curst, it is for policy,
For she's not froward, but modest as the dove,
She is not hot, but temperate as the morn,
For patience she will prove a second Grissel,
And Roman Lucrece for her chastity.
And to conclude, we have 'greed so well together
That upon Sunday is the wedding day.
Kate: I'll see thee hanged on Sunday first.
Gremio: Hark Petruchio, she says she'll see thee hanged first.
Tranio: Is this your speeding? Nay then goodnight our part!
Petruchio: Be patient gentlemen, I choose her for myself,
If she and I be pleased, what's that to you?
'Tis bargained 'twixt us twain being alone,
That she shall still be curst in company.

I tell you 'tis incredible to believe
How much she loves me. O the kindest Kate,
She hung about my neck, and kiss on kiss
She vied so fast, protesting oath on oath,
That in a twink she won me to her love.
O you are novices, 'tis a world to see
How tame, when men and women are alone,
A meacock wretch can make the curstest shrew.
Give my thy hand Kate, I will unto Venice
To buy apparel 'gainst the wedding day.
Provide the feast father, and bid the guests:
I will be sure my Katherine shall be fine.
Baptista: I know not what to say; but give me your hands.
God send you joy, Petruchio, 'tis a match.

This selection starts with Kate seemingly feeling betrayed by her father for setting a madman after her. She says that Petruchio thinks he can get away with things just by making "oaths." Before Baptista, Gremio, or Tranio can react to her words, Petruchio does indeed speak in a most convincing manner. All the bad impressions that others have had of Kate are wrong, he explains, and just as he has done earlier with Kate, he rattles off such a list of compliments about her that it seems hard to believe Petruchio could have purely fabricated them. In addition, he boldly says that since he and Kate have gotten along so well, they've agreed to get married on Sunday. Supposedly the two are not only happy—they are so happy that they do not want to delay the ceremony.

This reasoning might remind us of something that Petruchio's servant Grumio said earlier, namely that Hortensio should take Petruchio to Baptista immediately, in order to take advantage of Petruchio being in a wooing humor before that humor disappears. Now, here, Petruchio realizes that he must marry Kate as quickly as possible in order for the marriage to go through with as few hitches as possible. We see another side of Petruchio's personality as well. While Grumio had warned that Petruchio could be fickle, instead, in all that has occurred so far with Kate, we see Petruchio as not at all fickle but as remaining determined to marry Kate. In the process he has used an array of skills; we see him as smart, witty, excessively patient, tricky, quick, convincing, and never the hot-tempered man who smacked his servant early on in the play.

When Petruchio says he will marry Kate on Sunday, she harshly responds that he will be hanged first. At hearing that, both Gremio and Tranio remark that all is not good. Curiously, Baptista does not chime in and question whether the marriage should take place. Petruchio, of course, will not let anyone remain doubtful that the marriage will occur. Quick on his feet, Petruchio asks the suitors why they should be against the marriage if he and Kate are for it. He comes up with a great excuse that will help him if Kate speaks out against him now or in the future as well; namely, he tells the men that he and Kate have agreed that she will remain shrewish in public. He gives no explanation of why they've agreed to this but quickly starts describing what supposedly happened between him and Kate—she was so infatuated with him that she won him over. This is quite a twist from what the men expected, yet Petruchio is a convincing salesman, apparently.

In the midst of the explanation, Petruchio says, "O you are novices," referring to the fact that these men do not know so much about women and about relationships between men and women. The statement could have another meaning as well, however. It is as if Petruchio is saying that these men are novices when it comes to knowing how Petruchio operates. In other words, as he speaks he sees how relatively easily he can persuade and convince the men of whatever he wants.

Petruchio ends by saying he is off to get clothes for the wedding and that the guests need to get their invitations. There is nothing else to discuss; from his perspective, the wedding preparations are officially under way. Baptista is shocked that all seems to have worked out with his daughter and Petruchio. Notice that he wishes Petruchio, but not Kate, joy. Perhaps he is still afraid to speak directly to Kate. Even so, however, he is willing to set the wedding preparations in motion.

Act III, ii, 105–120

Tranio: See not your bride in these unreverent robes.
Go to my chamber, put on clothes of mine.
Petruchio: Not I, believe me, thus I'll visit her.
Baptista: But thus I trust you will not marry her.
Petruchio: Good sooth even thus, therefore ha' done with words,
To me she's married, not unto my clothes.
Could I repair what she will wear in me,
As I can change these poor accoutrements,
'Twere well for Kate and better for myself.
But what a fool am I to chat with you,
When I should bid good morrow to my bride,
And seal the title with a lovely kiss.
[Exit Petruchio, Grumio, and Biondello]
Tranio: He hath some meaning in his mad attire.
We will persuade him, be it possible,
To put on better ere he go to church.
Baptista: I'll after him and see the event of this.

Just prior to this passage, the wedding guests have been waiting for Petruchio to arrive so he and Kate can be wed. Petruchio is very late. Finally the visitors and family receive word that Petruchio is on his way, but that he is quite inappropriately dressed for a wedding. The audience wonders if the description of Petruchio's clothes is accurate, but, knowing how unconventional Petruchio has been so far, we assume the description is on target and we wonder what will happen next.

When Petruchio arrives he is, in fact, badly dressed, which distresses all the others. Tranio (disguised as Lucentio) and Baptista are the ones who urge Petruchio to change his clothes, but he says he will not. While we expect Baptista to do the urging, we might be surprised that the supposed Lucentio also does so. Apparently, he is already being treated as, and acting as, part of the family, even though Baptista has told him his father must come to give his agreement to the financial arrangements regarding the marriage to Bianca. The supposed Lucentio, in fact, must feel quite secure (or at least thinks it's important to *act* secure) in his position as soon-to-be-son-in-law—for he not only urges, but also orders, Petruchio to change his clothes, stating it as a command, not a request.

What is also interesting about the supposed Lucentio's role in the discussion here is that while he has been arguing for Petruchio to wear clothes deemed appropriate for the situation, he himself has been using clothes in an inappropriate way, using them to pretend to be a suitor while he is actually only a servant. He has been using clothes to trick Baptista, and the fact that the trick has worked shows how much importance people attribute to clothes. Namely, if you wear the clothes of a suitor, people are ready to believe you are a suitor. Obviously, though, Tranio is more intelligent than the average servant, for he has been able to use the language of a suitor and has the know-how and cunning to both hide his true status and win the negotiation for Bianca. (Contrast Tranio's character with Christopher Sly, who, no matter how he might be dressed, would never be able to pass for someone of a higher social status.)

Petruchio's final words to the supposed Lucentio and Baptista are that Kate is marrying him and not his clothes, so therefore the clothes are unimportant. Shakespeare is poking fun at how clothes have acquired such significance in society. Petruchio goes on to say that he wishes it were as easy to "repair" himself as it is to change his clothes. If that were possible, he continues, Kate would benefit and he would benefit even more. The remark shows that Petruchio is truly a complex character. While we have witnessed many aspects of this man, including his bravado and ability to get what he wants, we also see that he has some humility. We realize he is concerned about his wife's desires; he also understands that he has room for improvement but that that improvement takes work. Again, Shakespeare makes us think about changing not our external selves but our internal selves.

Finally, Petruchio walks away from the two men so he can find his wife and the wedding ceremony can take place. Note that Petruchio says he is foolish for staying to talk with them. He politely does not call them fools, which he easily could have. Tranio, the supposed Lucentio, remarks that there is some reason that Petruchio is dressed this way. Again we see that the supposed Lucentio is smart; still, rather than think about that reason for Petruchio's dress, the supposed Lucentio and Baptista are still intent on getting Petruchio to change his clothes.

Act IV, v, 28–49

Petruchio: (to Vincentio) Good morrow, gentle mistress, where away?
Tell me, sweet Kate, and tell me truly too,
Hast thou beheld a fresher gentlewoman?
Such war of white and red within her cheeks!
What stars do spangle heaven with such beauty,
As those two eyes become that heavenly face?
Fair lovely maid, once more good day to thee.
Sweet Kate, embrace her for her beauty's sake.
Hortensio: (aside) 'A will make the man mad, to make the woman of him.
Kate: Young budding virgin, fair and fresh and sweet,
Whither away, or where is thy abode?
Happy the parents of so fair a child,
Happier the man whom favorable stars
Allot thee for his lovely bedfellow.
Petruchio: Why how now, Kate, I hope thou art not mad,
This is a man, old, wrinkled, faded, withered,
And not a maiden, as thou sayest he is.
Kate: Pardon old father my mistaking eyes,
That have been so bedazzled with the sun
That everything I look on seemeth green.
Now I perceive thou art a reverend father.
Pardon I pray thee for my mad mistaking.

Here Petruchio, Hortensio, and Kate are traveling to Baptista's when they come across a fellow traveler, whom they later find out is Vincentio, Lucentio's father. Just prior to this passage, Kate and Petruchio had battled when Petruchio insisted that the moon was out and that his wife must agree—even though, in fact, it was the sun that was out. He had told her that she must go along with everything he says, thinks, and does, or that they would go home again. Kate had given in and called the sun the moon, just as he wanted.

Now Petruchio puts Kate to the test again: He addresses Vincentio as if he were a young woman. Petruchio immediately asks Kate what she thinks of "the gentlewoman" and continues to expound on Vincentio's looks, all the while speaking as if Vincentio were a young lady. As Petruchio draws his description to a close, he again calls to Kate. Shakespeare keeps the audience in suspense just a little longer as to how Kate will respond by inserting an aside from Hortensio. The remark also reminds us how like a madman Petruchio must appear to Vincentio. Especially for people reading the play rather than watching it performed, Hortensio's comment reminds us that Vincentio is standing right before Petruchio and reacting to his outlandish speech.

Kate then chimes in. She addresses Vincentio as if he were a young woman, just as Petruchio did. Just as he did, she remarks on Vincentio's supposedly pretty looks. Petruchio then does a reversal. He asks Kate if she is mad, saying the person before them is not a maiden at all. Petruchio acts as if he himself had not just a moment before repeatedly referred to Vincentio as a woman. Petruchio also shows his lack of regard for good manners by now pointing out that Vincentio is "old, wrinkled, faded, withered." This description undoubtedly will provoke a reaction from Vincentio, but Petruchio is concerned not about that but about Kate's reaction.

Kate goes completely along with Petruchio's whim. She apologizes for not referring to Vincentio as the man that he is. She follows Petruchio's lead, acting as if she were the only one who had mistakenly called Vincentio a woman, as if Petruchio had not done the same. She shows her shrewdness as well by saying that she made her mistake because the sun is shining so brightly. This comment refers to the argument between Petruchio and Kate just prior to meeting up with Vincentio, when Petruchio had insisted the moon was out when in actuality the sun was out; Kate had capitulated and agreed with him, but then Petruchio had changed his mind and said the sun was out. The fact that Kate brings this up again is her way of indirectly reminding her husband of the confrontation and how she had agreed to go along with whatever he said. Recognize, too, that Petruchio, in that argument, had in the end said the sun was out; in short, he had given in to her, too.

<hr/>

Act V, ii, 123–179

Widow: Lord, let me never have a cause to sigh,
Till I be brought to such a silly pass!
Bianca: Fie, what a foolish duty call you this?
Lucentio: I would your duty were as foolish too.

The wisdom of your duty, fair Bianca,
Hath cost me a hundred crowns since supper time.
Bianca: The more fool you for laying on my duty.
Petruchio: Katherine, I charge thee tell these headstrong women
What duty they do owe their lords and husbands.
Widow: Come, come, you're mocking. We will have no telling.
Petruchio: Come on I say, and first begin with her.
Widow: She shall not.
Petruchio: I say she shall, and first begin with her.
Kate: Fie, fie, unknit that threatening unkind brow,
And dart not scornful glances from those eyes,
To wound thy lord, thy king, thy governor.
It blots thy beauty, as frosts do bite the meads,
Confounds thy fame, as whirlwinds shake fair buds,
And in no sense is meet or amiable.
A woman moved is like a fountain troubled,
Muddy, ill-seeming, thick, bereft of beauty,
And while it is so, none so dry or thirsty
Will deign to sip, or touch one drop of it.
Thy husband is thy lord, thy life, thy keeper,
Thy head, thy sovereign—one that cares for thee,
And for thy maintenance commits his body
To painful labor, both by sea and land,
To watch the night in storms, the day in cold,
Whilst thou liest warm at home, secure and safe,
And craves no other tribute at thy hands
But love, fair looks, and true obedience—
Too little payment for so great a debt.
Such duty as the subject owes the prince,
Even such a woman oweth to her husband.
And when she is froward, peevish, sullen, sour,
And not obedient to his honest will,
What is she but a foul contending rebel,
And graceless traitor to her loving lord?
I am ashamed that women are so simple,
To offer war, where they should kneel for peace.
Or seek for rule, supremacy, and sway,
When they are bound to serve, love, and obey.
Why are our bodies soft, and weak, and smooth,
Unapt to toil and trouble in the world,
But that our soft conditions, and our hearts,
Should well agree with our external parts?

Come, come, you froward and unable worms,
My mind hath been as big as one of yours,
My heart as great, my reason haply more,
To bandy word for word, and frown for frown.
But now I see our lances are but straws,
Our strength as weak, our weakness past compare,
That seeming to be most, which we indeed least are.
Then vail your stomachs, for it is no boot,
And place your hands below your husband's foot.
In token of which duty, if he please,
My hand is ready, may it do him ease.

This passage occurs at the end of the play. The widow and Bianca failed to come when their husbands called for them, whereas Kate did. Not only did Kate appear, she brought in the other wives as Petruchio requested and then threw her cap down, again as he requested. The passage shows the wives' reactions; they think this is ridiculous behavior and are quick to bluntly say so. While the audience has already seen the new Kate, who is willing to go along with her husband (in the earlier scene when the two were traveling), this is the first that the other characters in the play have seen this side of Kate. All are amazed.

Kate's behavior stands out because, much earlier in the play, all had seen just how seemingly mad and uncontrollable she was. Her actions stand out even more in contrast to the reactions from the widow and Bianca. Again, there are some surprises here. We did not know much about the widow but had heard earlier that Hortensio had thought she was better than Bianca. In this passage, we see that she speaks her mind and apparently does not believe in blind obedience. In addition to her comments about Kate's behavior, the widow stands up to Petruchio when he says Kate should tell these women how to behave. Even though Petruchio has a very strong personality, the widow does not back down.

Bianca appears even more shrill and unappealing than the widow. Through the early part of the play, so many men (including Baptista) had held Bianca in such high regard that we had believed she deserved this special treatment. Here, though, not only does she exclaim that Kate's obedience is foolish, but when Lucentio tells her that her own lack of obedience cost him a hundred crowns, she does not care and goes so far as to call her new husband a fool. Her heartless nature is completely out in the open now.

When Petruchio tells Kate to tell the other women how to behave, again all are surprised at how she proceeds to do so. Keep in mind that Kate, from the start of the bet, was smart enough to realize that something was going on even though she hadn't heard the men discuss the bet. She saw the servants come—first for one woman, then another, and then herself—and surmised that doing what her husband requested would help him out; show the other women that she was not the wild shrew that they had believed; and make the other women, who had already been antagonistic to her, look bad.

Kate makes a long speech here, addressing the women. She starts by telling them to get rid of their scornful glances. In short, when women are disagreeable, they appear ugly. She reminds them of all that husbands must do for their wives and makes it seem as if, in light of all they do, the least that women can do is be obedient. She compares the situation to that between a prince and his subjects. In light of the fact that Shakespeare wrote this play during Elizabethan times, when the English were happy with their queen and the monarchy, the instruction to be obedient was likely more palatable than it might have been at other times. Kate points out that women's bodies are "soft, and weak, and smooth," indicating that they are not made for "toil and trouble." She reminds the women that she had been like them, but that she realized her weapons were really weak and that, like others, she was "seeming to be most, which we indeed least are."

In the speech, Kate also flatters the women, but slips in a telling comment when she says, "My mind hath been as big as one of yours, / My heart as great, my reason haply more." Notice that she starts with flattery, thus seemingly distracting the women from the insult in her final comment—that she has more reason than they do. This is a subtle comment, suggesting that she can outsmart them (and may be doing so right at this moment). Interestingly, she brings up the idea of portraying one's self one way while actually being someone else. The consequences of such behavior have been an important part of the play. Here, for instance, while all had assumed Kate was an uncontrollable monster, she proves them wrong; similarly, our impressions of Bianca and the widow are also proven wrong. Ultimately, Kate and Petruchio appear to be the ones who will have the happiest marriage. Both have great wit and intelligence, and they understand that when they are working together toward the same goal, their happiness will be great.

List of Characters in
The Taming of the Shrew

A **lord** comes upon Christopher Sly and decides to play a trick on him. The lord is crafty and willing to go far to play a joke.

Christopher Sly is a beggar and tinker. He is poor and uneducated, a contrast to most of the others in the play, but happy to be who he is.

The **hostess** is in charge of the alehouse and insistent that Sly pay the money he owes for destroying some of her property. She, like Sly, gives the audience a taste of what life is like for people in the lower classes.

The **page** is a young male servant who helps in playing the trick on Sly. He pretends to be Sly's wife.

Players (actors) ask the lord if they can entertain him. The lord is happy that these professionals will engage Sly in even further playacting.

The **huntsmen** have been out hunting with the lord. They discuss the importance of following a scent, as the good dogs do, no matter how trying that might be.

The **lord's other servants** also engage in playing the trick on Sly. They treat him just as they would a member of the upper class.

Petruchio is a gentleman of Verona. His father has died and left him money, yet Petruchio says he wants to find a wife who can make him even richer. He is one of the most developed characters in the play—intelligent, witty, clever, good natured, determined, and a nonconformist who sees Kate in a different light.

Grumio is Petruchio's personal servant. He understands his master well; while at times Petruchio is rough with him, Grumio remains loyal. He remarks on

Petruchio's great skill with words, while Grumio himself is skilled in this area as well.

Petruchio's other servants are **Curtis, Nathaniel, Philip, Joseph, Nicholas, and Peter.** They are eager to please, despite being at least temporarily the target of Petruchio's wrath.

Baptista Minola is a rich man of Padua and the father of Kate and Bianca. He favors Bianca and, in the process, helps create a wild Kate. His decision that Kate must be married before Bianca can be wooed sets off a chain of events and subterfuge.

Lucentio is a young man from Pisa who comes to Padua to study but instead falls in love with Bianca and focuses on pursuing her. He disguises himself as the tutor Cambio so he can be near Bianca and woo her, even though Baptista has forbid this until Kate is married.

Vincentio is Lucentio's well-respected father. He has money and values education. He arrives late in the play after much subterfuge has taken place.

Tranio is Lucentio's personal servant. He disguises himself as Lucentio when Lucentio decides he must pretend to be a tutor to Bianca. Disguised as Lucentio, Tranio must completely act the part of someone from the upper class and does a fine job of it. He also plans a scheme so that Lucentio can marry Bianca.

Biondello is another of Lucentio's servants. He is loyal like Tranio and helps Lucentio in the plan to marry Bianca, but he is someone who follows commands, not one smart enough to make them.

Hortensio is Petruchio's friend in Padua who first tells Petruchio about Kate. Hortensio is honest about her and about the fact that Kate must be married before Baptista will let anyone woo Bianca, the woman that Hortensio desires. Hortensio early on sees Bianca for who she is but too quickly decides to marry the widow instead, and thus will suffer.

Gremio is an elderly man in love with Bianca and frequently referred to as a fool. He has money but lacks intelligence. He is one of four men chasing after women in the play and the only one who remains by himself at the end.

The **pedant** is the man that Tranio talks into pretending to be Vincentio. The pedant easily falls for the tale that his life is in danger and readily agrees to disguise himself to save himself. He does not question Tranio's request to trick Baptista.

The **haberdasher** has made a hat for Kate at Petruchio's request. Even though Kate says she likes it and that it's the latest style, Petruchio makes fun of it and says it is unacceptable. The haberdasher is just one of a number of people that Petruchio mistreats in carrying out his plan to change Kate's behavior.

A **tailor** is brought in by Petruchio to tempt Kate with a new dress. The tailor's work is found supposedly unacceptable by Petruchio and Grumio, even though the tailor seems to have followed the instructions Grumio gave him for making the dress.

Other servants are in the play to wait on Baptista and his family.

Kate (Katherina) is Baptista's oldest daughter, who nearly all see as an unbearable shrew. In the beginning she seems to say and do as she pleases regardless of who is harmed. She is smart, creative, adept with words, direct, strong, and eventually admiring of Petruchio.

Bianca is Baptista's younger daughter, whom he spoils. Men are so taken with her beauty that her true personality is not readily apparent to them. She appears the obedient daughter and would seemingly be an obedient wife, but this is not the case.

The **widow,** as Hortensio says, has loved him for a while, and he quickly decides to marry her. He chooses her because he says he would rather have someone who cares about him than Bianca, who would not be loyal. Hortensio is right about Bianca's personality but seems to be wrong about the widow's.

CRITICISM
THROUGH THE AGES

❧

THE TAMING OF THE SHREW IN THE SEVENTEENTH AND EIGHTEENTH CENTURIES

&

As with much early criticism of Shakespeare's works, early criticism of *The Taming of the Shrew* often focused on Shakespeare's sources and background knowledge. The early Shakespearean critic Charles Gildon, for example, cited a speech by Tranio against Stoicism as evidence of Shakespeare's knowledge of Ovid and Aristotle: "The Reader by regarding this whole Speech of Tranio will find that Shakespeare was far from being that Ignoramus in Literature, as some would unaccountably make him." Gildon in general approved of the play, citing one of Grumio's speeches in particular as "very entertaining." He also noted the exemplary wisdom of Kate's "harangue" at the end of the play "on the Duty of Wives to their Husbands."

The great critic Samuel Johnson wrote extensive notes for the edition he published of Shakespeare's plays. He looked not at possible messages of *Shrew* but at the play's structure and overall effect. He saw the play as "very popular and diverting" and enjoyed the "spritely" Kate and Petruchio. In particular, he pointed out Shakespeare's great skill in weaving together the two plots—the wooing of Kate and the wooing of Bianca—though he disliked the arrival of the real Vincentio into the play.

Elizabeth Griffith believed the messages of Shakespeare's plays were of keen importance, so much so that she wrote a book about their morality. She questioned, however, what Shakespeare could offer in this regard in *The Taming of the Shrew*. The advice that the title seems to promise (how to "tame" a shrewish wife) was readily available, she wrote, though it never proved easy to follow. Still, Griffith looked at other types of morals that, in her view, the play presented. For example, early in the play, when Lucentio and Tranio arrive in Padua, Lucentio speaks of being there to study virtue. Tranio, however, advises that studying is only useful when the subject is personally appealing: "No profit grows where is no pleasure taken." This reply "adds a more liberal scope to the uses of travel and study," according to Griffith.

Griffith also examined the scene in which Petruchio has the haberdasher bring in a new cap for Kate but then Petruchio keeps it from her, claiming it is not good enough. Griffith pointed out that it is not only women who can become too attached to items and that such attachments are "ridiculous and unimportant." She agreed with Petruchio's later statement that the mind, not one's garments, make the body rich, but she also remarked that, unfortunately, most people do not seem to understand this. Of Kate's last speech, Griffith, like Gildon, took the words at face value. In Griffith's opinion, Kate goes too far in espousing submission, but she noted that "the most haughty tyrants become the most abject slaves."

1709—Charles Gildon.
From "Remarks on the Plays of Shakespear"

Charles Gildon (1665–1724)—translator, biographer, essayist, playwright, and poet—wrote a series of notes and essays to accompany Nicholas Rowe's edition of Shakespeare, providing the first extensive commentaries of the plays. He counted among his literary enemies Alexander Pope and Jonathan Swift.

A Gentleman of Padua has two Daughters, *Catharine* the Elder, and *Biancha* the Younger. The Elder is so known a Shrew, that no Body wou'd make Love to her in order to Matrimony, while Biancha had many, that address'd to her for that End; But the Father declar'd he wou'd not dispose of the Youngest till the Eldest was marry'd, which making all the Pretenders despair till *Petrucio* of Verona ventur'd upon the Match; Woos her madly, Marries her quickly, and treats her intolerably, till he broke her Stubbornest so that she was the most obedient of the three Wives then there, *viz.* her Sister, who was marry'd to *Lucentio* and a Widow who just marry'd *Hortensio* a Suiter of *Biancha*'s till his Disgust at her listning to *Lucentio*, who appear'd only to be a School-master.

This Play is indeed *Dramatic* for it is all Action, and there is little Room left for Reflections and fine Topics. Tho' it be far from Regular as to Time and Place, yet it is perfectly so in the Action; and some of the Irregularities of Time might easily have been prevented in p. 705 [page numbers refer to Nicholas Rowe's 1709 edition]. In a Matter of twelve Lines there is plainly suppos'd at least twelve if not twenty four Hours to have pass'd; there is scarce indeed a Line for as Hour. The Distick of *Ovid* which Lucentio construes in a pleasant Way is a fresh Proof that *Shakespear* was well acquainted with *Ovid*; and that he had a peculiar Value for that Poet is plain from what *Tranio* says in the first Scene, p. 679.—*Lets be no*

Stoicks nor no Stocks I pray, or so Devote to Aristotle's *Checks, as* Ovid *be an Out-cast quite abjur'd*, &c. The Reader by regarding this whole Speech of *Tranio* will find that Shakespear was far from being that *Ignoramus* in Literature, as some wou'd unaccountably make him.

Grumios's Account of *Petrucio's* Journey with his Bride is very Entertaining, 713.

The Mind not the Habit Valuable.

For 'tis the Mind, that makes the Body rich;
And as the Sun breaks through the darkest Clouds
So Honour peereth in the meanest Habit.
What is the Jay more precious, than the Lark
Because his Feathers are more beautiful?
Or is the Adder better than the Eel
Because the painted Skin contents the Eye, &c. 724.

Catharines Harangue to her Sister and the Widow on the Duty of Wives to their Husbands, if the Ladies wou'd read it with a little Regard, might be of mighty use in this Age. p. 738.

The Story of the Tinker by which this Comedy is introduc'd, may be found in Goulart's *Histoires Admirables*: And *Pontus Heuterus Rerum Burdicarum*. The Comedy it self is his own Invention, as far as we can discover, and so good, that tho' it has been alter'd by Mr. Lacy, yet I do not think it much improv'd; that Comedian committed an odd Blunder in laying the Scene in England; and adding *Sawny* the Scot, and yet retaining all the other Names that were purely Italian. The additional Tryal of Skill on their Return to her Father is well contriv'd.

1765—Samuel Johnson. "Notes on *The Taming of the Shrew*," from *The Plays of William Shakespeare*

Samuel Johnson (1709–1784) is thought by many to be the greatest commentator on Shakespeare. He was a poet, critic, prose writer, lexicographer, editor, and celebrated raconteur. His edition of the works of Shakespeare contained some of his famous thoughts on the plays. The following comments are taken from annotations he supplied to his text of *The Taming of the Shrew*.

Of this play the two plots are so well united, that they can hardly be called two without injury to the art with which they are interwoven. The attention is entertained with all the variety of a double plot, yet is not distracted by unconnected incidents.

The part between Catharine and Petruchio is eminently spritely and diverting. At the marriage of Bianca, the arrival of the real father, perhaps, produces more perplexity than pleasure. The whole play is very popular and diverting.

<hr/>

1775—Elizabeth Griffith. *"The Taming of the Shrew,"* from *The Morality of Shakespeare's Drama*

Elizabeth Griffith was an actress, dramatist, fiction writer, essayist, and translator. She is best known for *A Series of Genuine Letters between Henry and Frances*, a collection of letters published with her husband. She also wrote a critical study of the morality of Shakespeare's plays.

As the business of this Play, declared by the title of it, is, I fear, a work rather of *discipline* than of *precept*, we are to expect but few helps from it toward the enrichment of this collection. There are as many receipts for effecting this purpose, as there are prescriptions for a tooth-ach; and for the same reason, because none of them answer the end, but the getting rid of it; for the old proverb still stands bluff against all such documents, that *Every man can cure, a scold, but he who has her*.

The Introduction.

Scene III.

Among the preparations which are making, in order to deceive the drunken Tinker into the notion of his having been a mad Lord just recovering his senses, some Strollers are introduced to perform a Play for his entertainment; and the Actors meaning to exhibit one of the old religious Farces, stiled the *Mysteries*, upon enumerating the *properties* necessary toward the representation, ask for "a little *vinegar* to make their Devil roar." Upon which passage Dr. Warburton gives the following note:

"When the acting of the *Mysteries* of the Old and New Testament was in vogue, at the representation of the *Mystery* of the *Passion*, Judas and the Devil made a part. And the Devil, wherever he came, was always to suffer some disgrace, to make the people laugh; as here the buffoonery was to apply the *gall* and *vinegar*, to make him roar. And the *Passion* being that, of all the *Mysteries*, which was most frequently represented, *vinegar* became at length the standing implement to torment the Devil, and used for this purpose even after the *Mysteries* ceased, and the *Moralities*[1] came in vogue, where the Devil still continued to bear a considerable part. The mention of it here, was designed to ridicule so absurd a circumstance in these old Farces."

The giving such theatrical representations of Sacred Writ, was rather something more than barely absurd; it was extremely profane: but the device of tormenting the Devil with *gall and vinegar*, had a mystic conceit in it; being certainly intended by the authors of these exhibitions, as an allusion to a circumstance in the *Passion*, mentioned by St. Matthew, where he says, *they gave him vinegar to drink, mingled with gall.* Chap. xxvii. ver. 34. And as the sufferings on the *Cross* were undergone for our *redemption from sin*, the priests, who were the contrivers of this strange and improper species of drama, might have intended this particular to shew the distress of the Devil upon that occasion.

Act I. Scene I.

The proper use and choice of travel and study, of such sort of travel and study as rendered so many men eminent among the Antients, are well treated of here.

Lucentio and Tranio.
Lucentio. Tranio, since for the great desire I had
To see fair Padua, *nursery of arts*,
I am arrived in fruitful Lombardy,
The pleasant garden of great Italy;
And by my father's love and leave, am armed
With his good will, and thy good company
Most trusty servant, well approved in all,
Here let us breathe, and haply institute
A course of learning, and *ingenuous*[2] studies.
Pisa, renowned for grave citizens,
Gave me my being; and my father first,
A merchant of great traffic thro' the world—
Vincentio's come of the Bentivoli,
Lucentio his son, brought up in Florence,
It shall become to serve all hopes conceived,
To deck his fortune with his virtuous deeds—
And therefore, Tranio, for the time I study,
Virtue, and that part of philosophy

Will I apply, that treats of happiness
By virtue specially to be achieved.
Tell me thy mind, for I have Pisa left,
And am to Padua come, as he that leaves
A shallow plash, to plunge him in the deep,
And with satiety seeks to quench his thirst.

The following reply adds a more liberal scope to the uses of study and travel:

> *Tranio. Me pardonato*, gentle master mine,
> I am in all affected as yourself;
> Glad that you thus continue your resolve,
> To sock the sweets of sweet philosophy.
> Only, good master, while we do admire
> This virtue, and this moral discipline,
> Let's be no *Stoics*, nor no *stocks*, I pray,
> Or so devote to Aristotle's checks,
> As Ovid be an outcast quite abjured—
> Talk logic with acquaintance that you have,
> And practise rhetoric in your common talk;
> Music and poetry use to quicken you;
> The mathematics and the metaphysics,
> Fall to them as you find your stomach serves;
> *No profit grows where it is no pleasure ta'en—*
> In brief, Sir, study what you most affect.

Scene III.

A truth is here spoken, which is too frequently evinced by the general practice of the self-interested, or, more properly speaking, avaricious world, where Gremio and Hortensio are conferring together about providing a husband for Catharine, as the younger sister is not to be married till the elder is disposed of.

> *Gremio.* Think'st thou, Hortensio, though her father be very rich, any man is so very a fool to be married to hell?
> *Hortensio.* 'Tush, Gremio; though it pass your patience and mine to endure her loud alarms, why, man, there be *good fellows* in the world, an a man could light on them, *would take her with all her faults, and money enough.*

Scene IV.

Love conceived at first sight, is the subject of most Romances, and the philosophy of these Northern climes looks for it only there; but if we consult the volume of Nature more at large, we shall find that such extempore passions are not infrequent in the more Southern regions of the world: and the clear and warm air of Italy communicates a brisker motion to the heart and spirits, than our natural phlegm can possibly be sensible of.

Tranio, upon perceiving the emotion of Lucentio, on his first view of Bianca, says to him,

> I pray you, Sir, tell me, is it possible
> That love should on a sudden take such hold?
>   *Lucentio*. O, Tranio, till I found it to be true,
> I never thought it possible, or likely.
> But see, while idly I stood looking on,
> I found the effect of *love in idleness*;
> And now in plainness do confess to thee,
> That art to me as secret, and as dear,
> As *Anna* to the queen of *Carthage* was;
> *Tranio*, I burn, I pine; I perish, *Tranio*;
> If I achieve not this young modest girl.
> Counsel me, *Tranio*, for I know thou canst;
> Assist me, *Tranio*, for I know thou wilt.
> Tranio replies, very judiciously,
> Master, it is no time to chide you now;
> Affection is not rated[3] from the heart;
> If love hath *soiled*[4] you, nought remains but so,
> *Redime te captum quam queas minimo.*[5]

Act II. Scene II.

Mildness opposed to violence, with regard to their different effects upon the passions and affections of the mind, is justly illustrated here, by the following simile:

> *Petruchio*. Though little fire grows great with little wind,
> Yet extreme gusts will blow out fire and all.

Act IV. Scene VIII.

Among the various methods that Petruchio makes use of, after his marriage with Catharine; to tame her spirit, the following passage presents us with one, which the satirists of our sex will be apt to say was a severe test of female temper.

> Catharine, Petruchio, Milliner, *and* Mantua-maker.
> *Milliner*. Here is the cap your worship did bespeak.

Petruchio. Why, this was moulded on a porringer,
A velvet dish; fy, fy, 'tis lewd and filthy—
Why, 'tis a cockle, or a walnut-shell,
A knack, a toy, a trick, a baby's cap.
Away with it; come, let me have a bigger,
 Catharine. I'll have no bigger, this doth fit the time[6];
And *gentlewomen* wear such caps as these.
 Petruchio. When you are *gentle*, you shall have one too,
And not till then.
 Catharine. Why, Sir, I trust I may have leave to speak,
And speak I will. I am no child, no babe.
Your betters have endured me say my mind;
And if you cannot, best you stop your ears—
My tongue will tell the anger of my heart,
Or else my heart, concealing it, will break;
And rather than it shall, I will be free,
Even to the utmost, as I please, in words.
 Petruchio. Why, thou say'st true, it is a paltry cap,
A custard coffin, a bauble, a silken pie;
I love thee well in that thou lik'st it not.
 Catharine. Love me, or love me not, I like the cap;
And I will have it, or I will have none.
 Petruchio. The gown—why, ay—Come, taylor, let us see't—
O mercy, Heaven, what masking stuff is here?
What? this a sleeve? 'tis like a demi-cannon—
What ups and downs, carved like an apple-tart?
Here's snip, and snip, and stish, and slash,
Like to a center in a barber's shop—
Why, what, a devil's name, taylor, call'st thou this?
 Mantua-maker. You bid me make it orderly and well.
According to the fashion of the time.
 Catharine. I never saw a better fashioned gown.
More quaint, more pleasing, nor more commendable—
Belike you mean to make a puppet of me.

Upon this passage, Doctor Warburton has passed the following stricture:

"Shakespeare has here copied Nature with great skill. Petruchio, by frightening, starving, and over-watching his wife, had tamed her into gentleness and submission; and the audience expects to hear no more of the shrew; when, on her being, crossed in the article of fashion and

finery, the most inveterate folly of the sex, she flies out again, though
for the last time, into all the intemperate rage of her character."

This is being severe on our sex at a very cheap rate, indeed; foibles, passions,
and inconsiderable attachments, are equally common to all mankind, without
distinction of gender; and the difference of objects gives no sort of advantage to
men, over us; as all eager pursuits, except those of virtue, are alike ridiculous and
unimportant, in the candid and impartial estimation of reason and philosophy:

"Another Florio doating on a flower." YOUNG.

Petruchio having gained a conquest in this material point, proceeds to dress
her and himself in poor attire, and proposes that they should go pay a visit to her
family in such mean garments; upon which occasion he expresses a sentiment
to just in itself, that it betrays a sad corruption in the morals of mankind, that
experience cannot support it.

> *Petruchio.* Well, come, my Kate, we will unto your father's,
> Even in these honest mean habiliments;
> Our purses shall be proud, our garments poor;
> *For 'tis the mind that makes the body rich;*
> *And, as the fun breaks through the darkest clouds,*
> *So honour peereth in the meanest habit.*
> What! is the jay more precious than the lark,
> Because his feathers are more beautiful?
> Or is the adder better than the eel,
> Because his painted skin contents the eye?
> Oh, no, good Kate; neither art thou the worse
> For this poor furniture, and mean array.

Act V. Scene V.

After Catharine has been thoroughly reclaimed, she takes an occasion, from
a circumstance in the Play, of reproving another married woman, in an admirable
speech; wherein the description of a wayward wife, with the duty and submission
which ought to be shewn to a husband, are finely set forth.

> Fy! fy! unknit that threatening unkind brow,
> And dart not scornful glances from those eyes,
> To wound thy lord, thy king, thy governor.
> It blots thy beauty, as frosts bite the meads;
> Confounds thy fame, as whirlwinds make fair buds,

And in no sense is meet or amiable.
A woman moved is like a fountain troubled,
Muddy, ill-seeming, thick, bereft of beauty;
And while it is so, none to dry or thirsty
Will deign to sip, or touch one drop of it.
Thy husband is thy lord, thy life, thy keeper,
Thy head, thy sovereign; one that cares for thee,
And for thy maintenance commits his body
To painful labour, both by sea and land;
To watch the night in storms, the day in cold,
While thou lyest warm at home, secure and safe;
And craves no other tribute at thy hands,
But love, fair looks, and true obedience;
Too little payment for so great a debt.
Such duty as the subject owes the prince,
Even such a woman oweth to her husband;
And when she's froward, peevish, sullen, sour,
And not obedient to his honest will,
What is she but a foul contending rebel,
And graceless traitor, to her loving lord?
I am ashamed that women are so simple,
To offer war, where they should kneel for peace;
Or seek, for rule, supremacy, and sway,
When they are bound to serve, love, and obey.
Why are our bodies soft, and weak, and smooth,
Unapt to toil and trouble in the world,
But that our soft conditions and our hearts
Should well agree with our external parts?
Come, come, you froward and unable worms,
My mind has been as big as one of yours,
My heart as great, my reason haply more,
To bandy word for word, and frown for frown;
But now I see our lances are but straws,
Our strength as weak, our weakness past compare;
That seeming to be most, which we indeed least are.

I have stopped short here, as thinking that the following lines might have marred the whole beauty of the speech; the doctrine of *passive obedience and non-resistance* in the state of marriage, being there carried, perhaps, rather a little too far. But I shall quote them here, as they afford me an opportunity of remarking on the nature of too prompt reformees, who are apt to run into the very contrary extreme, at once; betraying more of the *time-server*, than the *convert*.

But, in general, indeed, it has been observed, that the most haughty tyrants become, on a reverse of fortune, the most abject slaves; and this from a like principle, in both cases; that they are apt to impute the same spirit of despotism to the conqueror, they were before imprest with themselves; and consequently, are brought to tremble at the apprehension of their own vice.

The lines I allude to, are these:

Then vail[7] your stomachs, for it is no boot,
And place your hands beneath your husband's foot;
In token of which duty, if he please,
My hand is ready, may it do him safe.

NOTES

1. Certain allegorical pieces, where the Virtues and Vices were personified, which succeeded to the stage, upon the prohibition of the former.

2. Instead of *ingenious*. Doctor Johnson. The context of the speech vouches the propriety of the alteration.

3. *Rated*, to be chid or counselled away.

4. *Toiled, ensnared*, instead of touched. Warburton.

5. Get out of the *net* as well at you can. Terence.

6. *Is fashionable*.

7. To vail is to submit, to be awed by authority.

THE TAMING OF THE SHREW IN THE NINETEENTH CENTURY

⊱⊰

In the 1800s criticism about the play focused more on the characters and the meaning of the work. William Hazlitt, who wrote extensively on Shakespeare's characters, marveled at Shakespeare's invention of Petruchio. Hazlitt pointed out that although Petruchio speaks hardly a word of truth, he is, in fact, very honest. Petruchio simply assumes a fictional persona to bring out the real Kate, acting with "the most fantastical extravagance," while always steadfast in his purpose and continually good-natured and energetic. Hazlitt also found the character Sly to be especially appealing, comparing him to Sancho Panza in Cervantes's *Don Quixote*.

Later in the century, Edward Dowden agreed with Hazlitt's assessment of Petruchio. According to Dowden, Petruchio skillfully manages Kate and, while acting mad, is completely mindful of what he is doing. At the same time, Kate, despite her wild behavior, is in no way evil. Writing a few years earlier, Frederick James Furnivall pointed out that Petruchio makes himself appear worse than he truly is by saying he is interested in finding a rich woman to marry. Actually, according to Furnivall, Petruchio would not just marry for money; he is attracted to Kate because she is so strong. Kate herself is confounded by the fact that Petruchio never loses his composure; she "must admire him" for not cowering from her and is pleased that he appreciates her beauty.

The German critic August Wilhelm Schlegel saw Kate as lacking in the usual elements that make women attractive. The playwright George Bernard Shaw, however, felt pity for her. While Shaw acknowledged the positive traits in Petruchio that other critics had pointed out, he wrote that the only thing that makes Petruchio's taming of Kate "bearable" is that Petruchio is not a cruel man. Shaw saw the last scene (where Petruchio bets that his wife will be obedient and Kate not only obeys but also gives a long speech on the topic) as "altogether distasteful to modern sensibility." Many other critics, less in tune with modern sensibilities, such as Hermann Ulrici and Furnivall, saw Petruchio and Kate as an excellent match and so approved of the play's ending. Hazlitt, too, believed that Shakespeare had done quite a fine job of showing how a strong will can only be tamed by a stronger one.

In terms of the play's structure and theme, Hazlitt found it almost the only one of Shakespeare's plays that had a "regular" plot as well as a clear moral. Ulrici wrote that a key idea of the play is that people must be true to the roles that nature has assigned them. To take a few examples: Kate does not act as a woman should, in Ulrici's view, and so lives an unbearable life until Petruchio appears; Vincentio and Baptista do not act as strongly as fathers should, and so Lucentio and Kate act uncontrollably; Lucentio and Horensio do not act as husbands should and so lose the bet with Petruchio; Gremio, as an old man, shouldn't be chasing a young woman and so is rightly a laughingstock. Schlegel also praised the play's Induction, or "prelude," in which Sly the tinker is transferred to a palace.

Commentators in the nineteenth century, as in the eighteenth, also examined the question of Shakespeare's source for the play. One puzzle for critics, then as now, is the existence of another play with a similar title—*The Taming of a Shrew* (1594)—written at about the same time. According to the poet and critic Algernon Charles Swinburne, Shakespeare ingeniously recast his play from this earlier and much clumsier play, which is sometimes thought to be by Christopher Marlowe. In Swinburne's view, this earlier playwright was unskilled in writing comedy, so Shakespeare's contributions to the play are clear. Swinburne cited in particular the example of the original play's character Ferando, whose temperament is "at once refined and invigorated through its transmutation into the hearty and humorous manliness of Petruchio's." Dowden, however, saw the play's authorship differently. He believed the original play, *The Taming of a Shrew*, was expanded by yet another author, and that Shakespeare then enlarged the play from there into his *The Taming of the Shrew*. Dowden admitted that this was only a theory but felt that it could be supported by the various styles of the different parts of the play.

Samuel Hickson took a markedly different view of the play's authorship. He believed that it was unfair to say that Shakespeare had taken from Marlowe's work; instead, it was more likely that Shakespeare wrote an early version of *The Taming of the Shrew* and that Marlowe imitated that in his *The Taming of a Shrew*.

1817—William Hazlitt. "*The Taming of the Shrew*," from *Characters of Shakespear's Plays*

William Hazlitt (1778-1830) was an English essayist and and one of the finest Shakespeare critics of the nineteenth century. He also examined the work of poets, dramatists, essayists, and novelists of his own and earlier times. His essays appeared in such volumes as *English Poets*, *English Comic Writers*, and *A View of the English Stage*.

THE TAMING OF THE SHREW is almost the only one of Shakespear's comedies that has a regular plot, and downright moral. It is full of bustle, animation, and rapidity of action. It shews admirably how self-will is only to be got the better of by stronger will, and how one degree of ridiculous perversity is only to be driven out by another still greater. Petruchio is a madman in his senses; a very honest fellow, who hardly speaks a word of truth, and succeeds in all his tricks and impostures. He acts his assumed character to the life, with the most fantastical extravagance, with complete presence of mind, with untired animal spirits, and without a particle of ill humour from beginning to end.—The situation of poor Katherine, worn out by his incessant persecutions, becomes at last almost as pitiable as it is ludicrous, and it is difficult to say which to admire most, the unaccountableness of his actions, or the unalterableness of his resolutions. It is a character which most husbands ought to study, unless perhaps the very audacity of Petruchio's attempt might alarm them more than his success would encourage them. What a sound must the following speech carry to some married ears!

'Think you a little din can daunt my ears?
Have I not in my time heard lions roar?
Have I not heard the sea, puff'd up with winds,
Rage like an angry boar, chafed with sweat?
Have I not heard great ordnance in the field?
And heav'n's artillery thunder in the skies?
Have I not in a pitched battle heard
Loud larums, neighing steeds, and trumpets clang?
And do you tell me of a woman's tongue,
That gives not half so great a blow to hear,
As will a chesnut in a farmer's fire?'

Not all Petruchio's rhetoric would persuade more than 'some dozen followers' to be of this heretical way of thinking. He unfolds his scheme for the *Taming of the Shrew*, on a principle of contradiction, thus:—

'I'll woo her with some spirit when she comes.
Say that she rail, why then I'll tell her plain
She sings as sweetly as a nightingale;
Say that she frown, I'll say she looks as clear
As morning roses newly wash'd with dew;
Say she be mute, and will not speak a word,
Then I'll commend her volubility,
And say she uttereth piercing eloquence:
If she do bid me pack, I'll give her thanks,
As though she bid me stay by her a week;

If she deny to wed, I'll crave the day,
When I shall ask the banns, and when be married?'

He accordingly gains her consent to the match, by telling her father that he
has got it; disappoints her by not returning at the time he has promised to
wed her, and when he returns, creates no small consternation by the oddity of
his dress and equipage. This, however, is nothing to the astonishment excited
by his mad-brained behaviour at the marriage. Here is the account of it by an
eye-witness:—

'*Gremio.* Tut, she's a lamb, a dove, a fool to him:
I'll tell you, Sir Lucentio; when the priest
Should ask if Katherine should be his wife?
Ay, by gogs woons, quoth he; and swore so loud,
That, all amaz'd the priest let fall the book;
And as he stooped again to take it up,
This mad-brain'd bridegroom took him such a cuff,
That down fell priest and book, and book and priest.
Now take them up, quoth he, if any list.
    Tranio. What said the wench when he rose up again?
    Gremio. Trembled and shook; for why, he stamp'd and swore,
As if the vicar meant to cozen him.
But after many ceremonies done,
He calls for wine; a health, quoth he; as if
He'ad been abroad carousing with his mates
After a storm; quaft off the muscadel,
And threw the sops all in the sexton's face;
Having no other cause but that his beard
Grew thin and hungerly, and seem'd to ask
His sops as he was drinking. This done, he took
The bride about the neck, and kiss'd her lips
With such a clamourous smack, that at their parting
All the church echoed: and I seeing this,
Came thence for very shame; and after me,
I know, the rout is coming;—
Such a mad marriage never was before.'

The most striking and at the same time laughable feature in the character of
Petruchio throughout, is the studied approximation to the intractable character
of real madness, his apparent insensibility to all external considerations, and
utter indifference to every thing but the wild and extravagant freaks of his own
self-will. There is no contending with a person on whom nothing makes any

impression but his own purposes, and who is bent on his own whims just in proportion as they seem to want common sense. With him a thing's being plain and reasonable is a reason against it. The airs he gives himself are infinite, and his caprices as sudden as they are groundless. The whole of his treatment of his wife at home is in the same spirit of ironical attention and inverted gallantry. Every thing flies before his will, like a conjuror's wand, and he only metamorphoses his wife's temper by metamorphosing her senses and all the objects she sees, at a word's speaking. Such are his insisting that it is the moon and not the sun which they see, &c. This extravagance reaches its most pleasant and poetical height in the scene where, on their return to her father's, they meet old Vincentio, whom Petruchio immediately addresses as a young lady:—

> '*Petruchio.* Good morrow, gentle mistress, where away?
> Tell me, sweet Kate, and tell me truly too,
> Hast thou beheld a fresher gentlewoman?
> Such war of white and red within her cheeks;
> What stars do spangle heaven with such beauty,
> As those two eyes become that heav'nly face?
> Fair lovely maid, once more good day to thee:
> Sweet Kate, embrace her for her beauty's sake.
>   *Hortensio.* He'll make the man mad to make a woman of him.
>   *Katherine.* Young budding virgin, fair and fresh and sweet,
> Whither away, or where is thy abode?
> Happy the parents of so fair a child;
> Happier the man whom favourable stars
> Allot thee for his lovely bed-fellow.
>   *Petruchio.* Why, how now, Kate, I hope thou art not mad:
> This is a man, old, wrinkled, faded, wither'd,
> And not a maiden, as thou say'st he is.
>   *Katherine.* Pardon, old father, my mistaken eyes
> That have been so bedazed with the sun
> That every thing I look on seemeth green.
> Now I perceive thou art a reverend father.'

The whole is carried off with equal spirit, as if the poet's comic Muse had wings of fire. It is strange how one man could be so many things; but so it is. The concluding scene, in which trial is made of the obedience of the new-married wives (so triumphantly for Petruchio) is a very happy one.—In some parts of this play there is a little too much about music-masters and masters of philosophy. They were things of greater rarity in those days than they are now. Nothing however can be better than the advice which Tranio gives his master for the prosecution of his studies:—

'The mathematics, and the metaphysics,
Fall to them as you find your stomach serves you:
No profit grows, where is no pleasure ta'en:
In brief, sir, study what you most affect.'

We have heard the *Honey-Moon* called 'an elegant Katherine and Petruchio.' We suspect we do not understand this word *elegant* in the sense that many people do. But in our sense of the word, we should call Lucentio's description of his mistress elegant.

'Tranio, I saw her coral lips to move,
And with her breath she did perfume the air:
Sacred and sweet was all I saw in her.'

When Biondello tells the same Lucentio for his encouragement, 'I knew a wench married in an afternoon as she went to the garden for parsley to stuff a rabbit, and so may you, sir'—there is nothing elegant in this, and yet we hardly know which of the two passages is the best.

The Taming of the Shrew is a play within a play. It is supposed to be a play acted for the benefit of Sly the tinker, who is made to believe himself a lord, when he wakes after a drunken brawl. The character of Sly and the remarks with which he accompanies the play are as good as the play itself. His answer when he is asked how he likes it, 'Indifferent well; 'tis a good piece of work, would twere done,' is in good keeping, as if he were thinking of his Saturday night's job. Sly does not change his tastes with his new situation, but in the midst of splendour and luxury still calls out lustily and repeatedly 'for a pot o' the smallest ale.' He is very slow in giving up his personal identity in his sudden advancement.—'I am Christophero Sly, call not me honour nor lordship. I ne'er drank sack in my life: and if you give me any conserves, give me conserves of beef: ne'er ask me what raiment I'll wear, for I have no more doublets than backs, no more stockings than legs, nor no more shoes than feet, nay, sometimes more feet than shoes, or such shoes as my toes look through the over-leather.—What, would you make me mad? Am not I Christophero Sly, old Sly's son of Burton-heath, by birth a pedlar, by education a card-maker, by transmutation a bear-herd, and now by present profession a tinker? Ask Marion Hacket, the fat alewife of Wincot, if she know me not; if she say I am not fourteen-pence on the score for sheer ale, score me up for the lying'st knave in Christendom.'

This is honest. 'The Slies are no rogues,' as he says of himself. We have a great predilection for this representative of the family; and what makes us like him the better is, that we take him to be of kin (not many degrees removed) to Sancho Panza.

1846—August Wilhelm Schlegel.
"Criticisms on Shakspeare's Comedies," from
Lectures on Dramatic Art and Literature

August Wilhelm Schlegel (1767–1845) was a scholar, critic, poet, and professor at the University of Bonn. He translated a number of Shakespeare's plays into the German language and was one of the most influential disseminators of the ideas of the German Romantic movement.

The Taming of the Shrew has the air of an Italian comedy; and indeed the love intrigue, which constitutes the main part of it, is derived mediately or immediately from a piece of Ariosto. The characters and passions are lightly sketched; the intrigue is introduced without much preparation, and in its rapid progress impeded by no sort of difficulties; while, in the manner in which Petruchio, though previously cautioned as to Katherine, still encounters the risks in marrying her, and contrives to tame her—in all this the character and peculiar humour of the English are distinctly visible. The colours are laid on somewhat coarsely, but the ground is good. That the obstinacy of a young and untamed girl, possessed of none of the attractions of her sex, and neither supported by bodily nor mental strength, must soon yield to the still rougher and more capricious but assumed self-will of a man: such a lesson can only be taught on the stage with all the perspicuity of a proverb.

The prelude is still more remarkable than the play itself: a drunken tinker, removed in his sleep to a palace, where he is deceived into the belief of being a nobleman. The invention, however, is not Shakspeare's. Holberg has handled the same subject in a masterly manner, and with inimitable truth; but he has spun it out to five acts, for which such material is hardly sufficient. He probably did not borrow from the English dramatist, but like him took the hint from a popular story. There are several comic motives of this description, which go back to a very remote age, without ever becoming antiquated. Here, as well as everywhere else, Shakspeare has proved himself a great poet: the whole is merely a slight sketch, but in elegance and delicate propriety it will hardly ever be excelled. Neither has he overlooked the irony which the subject naturally suggested: the great lord, who is driven by idleness and ennui to deceive a poor drunkard, can make no better use of his situation than the latter, who every moment relapses into his vulgar habits. The last half of this prelude, that in which the tinker, in his new state, again drinks himself out of his senses, and is transformed in his sleep into his former condition, is, from some accident or other, lost. It ought to have followed at the end of the larger piece. The occasional remarks of the tinker, during the course of the representation of the comedy, might have been improvisatory; but it is hardly credible that Shakspeare should have trusted to the momentary suggestions of the players, whom he did not hold in high estimation, the conclusion, however short, of a work which he had so carefully commenced. Moreover, the only circumstance which connects the play with the prelude is, that it belongs to the new life of the supposed nobleman to have plays acted in his castle by strolling actors. This invention of introducing spectators on the stage, who contribute to the entertainment, has been very wittily used by later English poets.

⸺⸺ ⸺⸺ ⸺⸺

1850—Samuel Hickson.
"*The Taming of the Shrew,*" from *Notes and Queries*

Samuel Hickson examined the questions of sources and dates regarding various plays of Shakespeare.

In two former communications on a subject incidental to that to which I now beg leave to call your attention, I hinted at a result far more important than the discovery of the author of the *Taming of a Shrew*. That result I lay before your readers, in stating that I think I can show grounds for the assertion that the *Taming of the Shrew*, by Shakspeare, is the *original* play; and that the *Taming of a Shrew*, by Marlowe or what other writer soever, is a *later* work, and an *imitation*. I must first, however, state, that having seen Mr. Dyce's edition of Marlowe, I find that this writer's claim to the latter work had already been advanced by an American gentleman, in a work so obvious for reference as Knight's *Library Edition of Shakspeare*. I was pretty well acquainted with the contents of Mr. Knight's *first* edition; and knowing that the subsequent work of Mr. Collier contained nothing bearing upon the point, I did not think of referring to an edition published, as I understood, rather for the variation of form than on account of the accumulation of new matter. Mr. Dyce appears to consider the passages cited as instances of imitation, and not proofs of the identity of the writer. His opinion is certainly entitled to great respect: yet it may, nevertheless, be remarked, first that the instance given, supposing Marlowe not to be the author, would be cases of theft rather than imitation, and which, done on so large a scale, would scarcely be confined to the works of one writer; and, secondly, that in original passages there are instances of an independence and vigour of thought equal to the best things that Marlowe ever wrote—a circumstance not to be reconciled with the former supposition. The following passage exhibits a freedom of thought more characteristic of this writer's reputation than are most of his known works:—

"And custom-free, you marchants shall commerce
And interchange the profits of your land,
Sending you gold for brasse, silver for lead,
Casses of silke for packes of wol and cloth,
To bind this friendship and confirme this league."
Six Old Plays, p. 204

A short account of the process by which I came to a conclusion which, if established, must overthrow so many ingenious theories, will not, I trust, be uninteresting to your readers. In the relationship between these two plays there always seemed to be something which needed explanation. It was the only instance among the works of Shakspeare in which a direct copy, even to matters of detail, appeared to have been made; and, in spite of all attempts to gloss over and palliate, it was impossible to deny that an unblushing act of mere piracy seemed to have been committed, of which I never could bring myself to believe that Shakspeare had been guilty. The readiness to impute this act to him was to me but an instance of the unworthy manner in which he had almost universally been treated; and, without at the time having any suspicion of what I now take to be the fact, I determined, if possible, to find it out. The first question I put to myself was, Had Shakspeare himself any concern in the older play? A second glance at the work sufficed for an answer in the negative. I next asked myself on what authority we called it an "older" play. The answer I found myself obliged to give was, greatly to my own surprise, On no authority whatever! But there was still a difficulty in conceiving how, with Shakspeare's work before him, so unscrupulous an imitator should have made so poor an imitation. I should not have felt this difficulty had I then recollected that the play in question was not published; but, as the case stood, I carefully examined the two plays together, especially those passages which were identical, or nearly so, in both, and noted, in these cases, the minutest variations. The result was, that I satisfied myself that the original conception was invariably to be found in Shakspeare's play. I have confirmed this result in a variety of ways, which your space will not allow me to enter upon; therefore, reserving such circumstances for the present as require to be enforced by argument, I will content myself with pointing out certain passages that bear out my view. I must first, however, remind your readers that while some plays, from their worthlessness, were never printed, some were withheld from the press on account of their very value; and of this latter class were the works of Shakspeare. The late publication of his works created the impression, not yet quite worn out, of his being a later writer than many of his contemporaries, solely because their printed works are dated earlier by twenty or thirty years. But for the obstinate effects of this impression, it is difficult to conceive how any one could miss the original invention of Shakspeare in the induction, and such scenes as that between Grumio and the tailor; the humour of which shines, even in the feeble reflection of the imitation, in striking contrast with those comic (?) scenes which are the undisputed invention of the author of the *Taming of a Shrew*.

The first passage I take is from Act IV. Sc. 3.

> "*Grumio:* Thou hast fac'd many *things*?
> "*Tailor:* I have.
> "*Grumio:* Face not me: thou hast brav'd many men; brave not me. I will neither be fac'd nor brav'd."

In this passage there is a play upon the terms "fac'd" and "brav'd." In the tailor's sense, "things" may be "fac'd" and "men" may be "brav'd;" and, by means of this play, the tailor is entrapped into an answer. The imitator, having probably seen the play represented, has carried away the words, but by transposing them, and with the change of one expression—"men" for "things"—has lost the spirit: there is a pun no longer. He might have played upon "brav'd," but there he does not wait for the tailor's answer; and "fac'd," as he has it, can be understood but in one sense, and the tailor's admission becomes meaningless. The passage is as follows:—

> "*Saudre:* Dost thou hear, tailor? thou hast brav'd many men; brave not me. Th'ast fac'd many men.
> "*Tailor:* Well, Sir?
> "*Saudre:* Face not me; I'll neither be fac'd nor brav'd at thy hands, I can tell thee."—p. 198.

A little before, in the same scene, Grumio says, "Master, if ever I said loose-bodied gown, sew me in the skirts of it, and beat me to death with a bottom of brown thread." I am almost tempted to ask if passages such as this be not evidence sufficient. In the *Taming of a Shrew*, with the variation of "sew me in a *seam*" for "sew me in *the skirts of it*," the passage is also to be found; but who can doubt the whole of this scene to be by Shakspeare, rather than by the author of such scenes, intended to be comic, as one referred to in my last communication (No. 15. p. 227., numbered 7.), and shown to be identical with one in *Doctor Faustus*? I will just remark, too, that the best appreciation of the spirit of the passage, which, one would think, should point out the author, is shown in the expression, "sew me in the *skirts of it*," which has meaning, whereas the variation has none. A little earlier, still in the same scene, the following bit of dialogue occurs:—

> "*Kath:* I'll have no bigger; this doth fit the time,
> And gentlewomen wear such caps as these.

"*Pet:* When you are gentle, you shall have one too,
and not till then."

Katharine's use of the term "gentlewomen" suggests here Petruchio's "gentle." In the other play the reply is evidently imitated, but with the absence of the suggestive cue:—

"For I will home again unto my father's house.
"*Ferando:* I, when y'are meeke and gentle, but not before."—p. 194.
Petruchio, having dispatched the tailor and haberbasher, proceeds—
"Well, come my Kate: we will unto your father's,
Even in these honest mean habiliments;
Our purses shall be proud, our garments poor;"—p. 198.

throughout continuing to urge the vanity of outward appearance, in reference to the "ruffs and cuffs, and farthingales and things," which he had promised her, and with which the phrase "honest mean habiliments" is used in contrast. The sufficiency *to the mind* of these,

"For 'tis the mind that makes the body rich,"

is the very pith and purpose of the speech. Commencing in nearly the same words, the imitator entirely mistakes this, in stating the object of clothing to be to "shrowd us from the winter's rage;" which is, nevertheless, true enough, though completely beside the purpose. In Act II. Sc. 1., Petruchio says,—

"Say that she frown; I'll say she looks as clear
As morning roses newly wash'd with dew."

Here is perfect consistency: the clearness of the "morning *roses*," arising from their being "wash'd with dew;" at all events, the quality being heightened by the circumstance. In a passage of the so-called "older" play, the duke is addressed by Kate as "fair, lovely lady," &c.

"As glorious as the morning wash'd with dew."—p. 203

As the morning does not derive its glory from the circumstance of its being "wash'd with dew," and as it is not a peculiarly apposite comparison, I conclude that here, too, as in other instances, the sound alone has caught the ear of the imitator.

In Act V. Sc. 2., Katharine says,—

"Then vail your stomachs; for it is no boot;
And place your hand below your husband's foot;
In token of which duty, if he please,
My hand is ready: may it do him ease."

Though Shakspeare was, in general, a most correct and careful writer, that he sometimes wrote hastily it would be vain to deny. In the third line of the foregoing extract, the meaning clearly is, "as which token of duty;" and it is the performance of this "token of duty" which Katharine hopes may "do him ease." The imitator, as usual, has caught something of the words of the original which he has laboured to reproduce at a most unusual sacrifice of grammar and sense; the following passage appearing to represent that the wives, by laying their hands under their husbands' feet—no reference being made to the act as a token of duty—in some unexplained manner, "might procure them ease."

"Laying our hands under their feet to tread,
If that by that we might procure their ease,
And, for a precedent, I'll first begin
And lay my hand under my husband's feet."—p. 213.

One more instance, and I have done. Shakspeare has imparted a dashing humorous character to this play, exemplified, among other peculiarities, by such rhyming of following words as—

"Haply to *wive* and *thrive* as least I may."
"We will have *rings* and *things* and fine array."
"With *ruffs*, and *cuffs*, and farthingales and things."

I quote these to show that the habit was Shakspeare's. In Act I. Sc. 1. occurs the passage—"that would thoroughly woo her, wed her, and bed her, and rid the house of her." The sequence here is perfectly natural: but observe the change: in Ferando's first interview with Kate, he says,—

"My mind, sweet Kate, doth say I am the man
Must wed and bed *and marrie* bonnie Kate."—p. 172.

In the last scene, Petruchio says,—

"Come, Kate, we'll to bed:
We three are married, but you two are sped."

Ferando has it thus:—

> "'Tis Kate and I am wed, and you are sped:
> And so, farewell, for we will to our bed."—p. 214.

Is it not evident that Shakespeare chose the word "sped" as a rhyme to "bed," and that the imitator, in endeavouring to recollect the jingle, has not only spoiled the rhyme, but missed the fact that all "three" were "married," notwithstanding that "two" were "sped"?

It is not in the nature of such things that instances should be either numerous or very glaring; but it will be perceived that in all of the foregoing, the purpose, and sometimes even the meaning, is intelligible only in the form in which we find it in Shakespeare. I have not urged all that I might, even in this branch of the question; but respect for your space makes me pause. In conclusion, I will merely state, that I have no doubt myself of the author of the *Taming of a Shrew* having been Marlowe; and that, if in some scenes it appear to fall short of what we might have expected from such a writer, such inferiority arises from the fact of its being an imitation, and probably required at a short notice. At the same time, though I do not believe Shakspeare's play to contain a line of any other writer, I think it extremely probable that we have it only in a revised form, and that, consequently, the play which Marlow imitated might not necessarily have been that fund of life and humour that we find it now.

<hr/>

1876—Hermann Ulrici. *"Taming of the Shrew,"* from *Shakspeare's Dramatic Art*

Hermann Ulrici (1806–1884) was a German scholar, professor of philosophy at the University of Halle, and author of works on Greek poetry and Shakespeare. He wrote books that severely criticized Hegel's ideas and later explored the relationship of philosophy to science.

I connect 'Much Ado About Nothing' with another comedy of intrigue apparently very different in character, because, in my opinion, notwithstanding all the dissimilarities, it is internally related to it, both in spirit and character, and may be regarded as a kind of forerunner to 'Much Ado About Nothing.'

The 'Taming of the Shrew,' according to Tieck, was not written before 1606 or 1607; he thinks that Shakspeare, in the Induction, speaks in commendation of an actor (called Sincklo in the folio edition) and of the part he played (that of

Soto, a jovial young farmer) in a comedy of Fletcher's; also, that Fletcher made his first appearance as a poet in 1604 or 1605 at the earliest, that accordingly, the comedy entitled 'Women Pleas'd,'—the one here referred to—although one of his later works, was probably not written till 1605 or 1606. Collier[1] was, at first, of the same opinion, but for a different reason. He believed that act i., 1, contained an allusion to Th. Heywood's 'Woman Killed with Kindness,' which did not appear till after 1602. But we have already, in the case of 'Twelfth Night,' had sufficient proof of how deceptive are such solitary indications and allusions. Collier[2] was afterwards of the opinion that it appeared in the beginning of 1602 (after 'Hamlet,' which he assigns to the year 1601) inasmuch as Shakspeare there makes a wrong use of the name Baptista, by applying it to a woman, whereas he has here employed it correctly as the name of Catherine's father. However, style and character, language and versification in the 'Taming of the Shrew,' more especially the many passages entirely in rhyme, the frequent rhyming-couplets, the doggerel lines, the sketchy delineation of several of the characters, the loose connection of the action—more particularly between the intriguing play of Bianca's suitors and Petruchio's undertakings (as Tieck and Collier also admit)—speak decidedly in favour of an earlier origin, except that some passages as clearly give indications of later corrections; such, however, may be presupposed in the case of every one of Shakspeare's works. This would, accordingly, not only explain the above allusions, but also the poet's better knowledge of the Italian language, to which Brown[3] has directed attention, and which certainly is very striking compared with his earlier pieces (as in 'The Two Gentlemen of Verona' and others). The first appearance of the play, as I think, falls to about the same date as 'All's Well that Ends Well,' that is, to about the year 1593. The fact of Meres not mentioning it, might have arisen from his not unjustly considering it a mere remodelling of the older 'Taming of a Shrew' (a piece printed in 1594, but doubtless some years older)[4] which not only furnished Shakspeare with his subject-matter, but forms the basis of his remodelling inasmuch as it refers and points back to it.

The drama, as we now have it, has the peculiarity of appearing to be both complete and incomplete. If we confine our attention to the principal part, to the play within the play which gives its name to the piece, it appears quite complete and finished. But the induction—in which a common drunkard is accidentally met by a noble lord, and transported to the latter's castle while in a state of drunken unconsciousness, and on awakening is treated by the nobleman and his attendants as if he were a rich and powerful lord, merely labouring under the fixed delusion of being a common tinker, to amuse and distract whom strolling players are then called in to exhibit the actual play—looks like a mere prelude, like a beginning without either development or end. For the merry introductory device is very soon set aside, and the piece concludes with the play within the play. In so far, therefore, the drama is incomplete. It may be that Shakspeare intentionally refrained from working out the double plot introduced, because he found that the play would thereby become too long, and thus lose its suitability for the stage; it may also be that it has, by some accident, come down to us in an actually imperfect form, or that a portion of it has been lost; this is far from being impossible, as the drama was not printed till 1623, and several of the later prints of Shakspeare's plays were collected from the scrolls of the actors. It is probable, however, that Shakspeare did not add the termination of the prelude because it was sufficiently well known, not merely from the older 'Taming of a Shrew,' but also from other old pieces; for the same prelude is met with in several old English dramas of the Elizabethan period and seems to have been very popular with the theatrical public of the day. Criticism, however, has to regard the whole as a whole, and, accordingly, must here also endeavour to supply what is wanting. There exist two plays which, taken together, will furnish a safe point to start from. In the first place Holberg's *Jeppe vom Berge* which is constructed upon an exactly similar plan. We here have a peasant-lord who uses his power in so uncouth and intolerable a manner, who is so wholly ignorant of how to use his unaccustomed authority, and whose domineering spirit degenerates so completely into caprice and violence that a sleeping potion has speedily to be brought to him, in order that he may be cast back upon the dunghill to which he belongs. On awakening he looks upon all that has happened as a dream or a visit to paradise. A similar turn—and one that is poetically true—is taken by the older 'Taming of a Shrew' in the ending which it gives to the prelude. Even though this piece was certainly not—as Tieck thought—one of Shakspeare's youthful compositions, still it cannot be denied that it contains much that is good, and therefore, I think, it cannot seem surprising that Shakspeare in his play not only followed the course of the action step by step (it is only the intrigues of Bianca's lovers against one another that are his own invention), but that he has not unfrequently admitted into his test the same imagery and modes of expression, occasionally even whole lines of the old play; in short, that he has not actually composed a new drama, but remodelled the older one in his own fashion. In accordance with this supposition we may obviously assume that Shakspeare, although retaining, and essentially improving the old and favourite 'induction,' nevertheless did not care to repeat the well-known conclusion, either because he supposed that he might be allowed to leave the end to the imagination of the spectators, or (what seems to be more likely) because he considered the short ending to the old play good enough as it was, and therefore did not introduce it into his manuscript, but left it to the actors to reproduce it more or less freely. This hypothesis would also explain the change of the natural title of 'Taming of a Shrew' into the unnatural one of 'Taming of the Shrew,' inasmuch as Shakspeare meant thereby to refer to the older play and to say, Taming of *the* Shrew, *well known from the older play*; and it, at the same time, throws light upon the circumstance (very remarkable when we bear in mind Shakspeare's usual care in remodelling and revising his plays) of his having left this play without a conclusion—a conclusion without which the groundlings would scarcely have been content, considering their doubtless great pleasure in the character and doings of Sly. But, in accordance with this, we shall also have to assume that Shakspeare's remodelling appeared at a time when the older play was still upon the stage. I therefore believe that the 'Tamynge of a Shrowe' which, according to Henslowe[5] was performed at the theatre in Newington, was not the older piece, but Shakspeare's play. This supposition is supported by the circumstance that in 1594 Shakspeare's company, together with the Lord Admiral's players, were then under Henslowe's direction, and played in Newington, and that the older 'Taming of a Shrew' belonged to neither of these two companies—as the title of the print intimates—but to the company of the Earl of Pembroke, and, accordingly, could not well have been given by Henslowe.

But the principal argument for my conjecture lies in the drama itself. It would unquestionably fall into two halves, in a very inartistic manner, were the connection between the 'induction' and conclusion only external and arbitrary, and not also internally and organically related to the centre, that is, to the play within the play. An artistic, organic connection is, however, not possible in this case, except by means of the unity in the fundamental idea of both. If the latter agrees with the unknown termination of the prelude then, at all events, the missing part has been correctly supplied, even though the poet himself should have conceived it otherwise. If, therefore, we assume that the end of the joke played upon the drunken tinker was similar to that in Holberg's comedy, then the prelude and the conclusion clearly express the not very deep maxim which we find in Holberg: that he who is born a peasant makes a bad lord and master. The same thought is at least intimated in the older 'Taming of a Shrew,' inasmuch as Sly, there, repeatedly interrupts the play that is being acted before him and, in his domineering mood, raises objections to the commands given by the Duke in the play, and besides this, drinks so much wine that he falls into a drunken sleep, and in this condition is carried by the lord's servants to the same spot whence they had brought him. If, however, we examine further into the leading and fundamental motive of the 'induction' and conclusion, we find there that conception of human life which is very well adapted for comic treatment, and which views it from the side of that almost unconquerable power which man's natural circumstances and inherent relations exercise upon him. The tinker-lord shows us, in a few, but life-like features, on the one hand, the folly and perversity into which man readily falls, when the path assigned to him by nature is torn from its proper track—whether it be with his consent or not—on the other hand, man's incapacity of maintaining himself in a sphere which lies beyond that allotted to him by nature. Sly, at the end of the older 'Taming of a Shrew,' considers his life as a lord to have been a mere dream, and all that happened to him there he has forgotten; his first words on awakening are 'more wine.' The only thing he remembers is, how to tame a shrew, his own wife being one; in other words, Sly is and remains a tinker, whether he drinks wine and sleeps in a feather bed, like a lord, or gets drunk on small beer and takes his night's rest on the naked earth, like a tinker.

The same meaning, however, evidently applies to the play within the play; we have the same fundamental idea, the same view of life, except that it is here more clearly developed, and more fully worked out. As, in the first case, Sly, in spite of his imaginary splendour, always remains the tinker, falling asleep over the more refined enjoyments that are prepared for him, and makes no further use of his dignity as lord, than to get drunk, so in the principal play, Katharina, the haughty shrew who despises the natural vocation of woman, has stepped out of the sphere which nature had assigned to her, and hence, in her obstinacy, arrogance and love of dominion, commits acts of foolishness that are excusable only in a spoilt child. As, in the first case, the tinker's state of lordship terminates in the nothingness of a mere joke, and he, in the end, becomes what he really is, even though against his own will, so we find that the Shrew can, as little, maintain her assumed high position as uncontrolled mistress of the household; she, in the end, is cured by a device on the part of her husband, who, by displaying a much greater amount of the same perversity, holds up before her a reflex of her own distorted image; thus put to shame, she returns to her own, proper sphere. The folly and perversity— the whole weight of which falls back upon her—naturally neutralise each other: the assumed perversity of Katharina's husband becomes the means of curing the actual disease of her mind. The play, at the same time, is based upon profound psychological observations: it is the trial of the homoeopathic treatment in the domain of ethics, which, when properly carried out, is generally successful.

The subordinate parts of the play—the intrigues of Bianca's suitors against one another, the love affairs of Gremio, of Hortensio and the widow, of Lucentio and Bianca—are, as already remarked, but very loosely interwoven with the main action, and thus stand opposed to it in the form of a second, independent half. This is a defect which Shakspeare could, indeed, not very well have avoided unless he meant entirely to change the old play. And yet upon a closer examination there are nevertheless indications which point to the fundamental motive of the whole, and thus connect the subordinate portions with the principal part. A character like Katharina can be accounted for only by her having received an entirely wrong education, and a false mode of treatment; the father of such a daughter must have wholly misunderstood his position as a father, and, in place of ruling his house with paternal strictness and manly authority, must have abandoned himself to effeminacy and weakness. And this is precisely what good old Baptista appears to have done, for although he makes no secret of his daughter's faults he does not even attempt to correct them. Vincentio also, to judge from the little we see of the development of his character, must have suffered from a similar weakness, otherwise Lucentio, his light-headed son, would not have so entirely forgotten all filial duty and respect towards him as to venture to pass off a ridiculous pedant as his own father, merely to promote his own interests; and Vincentio himself would not have permitted his son to be accompanied by servants equally inconsiderate of their position as servants. Gremio, the old suitor, is very rightly outwitted and made laughing-stock for forgetting his years and becoming the rival of a spirited youth for the love of a pretty girl. Lastly, Lucentio and Hortensio lose their wager against Petruchio, and are deservedly put to shame for perpetually playing the part of devoted and obsequious lovers, and thus losing sight of the seriousness of their position as men, and their dignity as husbands, accordingly, for having likewise placed themselves in a false and unbecoming position. Petruchio seems to be the only rational character in the whole piece; but the perversity of the others obliges him also to play the fool and to make himself ridiculous, although, finally, the laughing is completely on his side. All the other personages, except Petruchio and Katharina, are sketched with but a few touches, lightly and superficially; this is a defect that must ever remain a defect, even though the plan of the piece scarcely permitted of a more detailed and deeper delineation of character, and although the few touches are correct and to the point, and made by a skilful hand. There is but one trait in Katharina's character that might seem to be wrongly drawn, namely, that the self-willed, violent, refractory girl should so quickly and readily consent to marry Petruchio, and that she obeys him almost without resistance, with, indeed, a nay on her lips, but a yea in her heart. However, upon a closer examination we shall again have to admit this to be a proof of the poet's thorough knowledge of human nature. It would unquestionably have been an easy matter to have given more obvious motives for Katharina's consent, but the best motive here was the very surprise, the irresistible impression made upon her by an energetic and thoroughly manly spirit. In Petruchio she probably, for the first time in her life, met with a man worthy the name of a man; hitherto she had been surrounded only by women in male attire. A genuine man she could not but esteem, nay even love, and accordingly obey. This, in fact, is the result of woman's nature in general, and the psychological result of the pride and unusual energy of her character. Petruchio and Katharina, therefore, are excellently suited to one another, and as the closing scene intimates, their marriage will prove a happy one. And herein again we find an indication of the fundamental idea of the whole: that only that which is natural, and in accordance with the nature of mankind and things, is enduring, and a guarantee of happiness and contentment.

NOTES

1. *History of English Dramatic Poetry*, iii. 77.

2. His *Shakespeare*, iii. 104.

3. *Shakspeare's Autobiographical Poems*, p. 104 f.

4. Reprinted in the *Six old Plays*, etc., vol. ii.—It contains a number of passages taken word for word from Marlowe's *Tamburlaine* and *Dr. Faustus*, and others

which are indeed not word for word the same, but give Marlowe's similes, imagery and phrases with but slight modifications (Knight, *Shaksp. Studies*, p. 141 f.). Probably, therefore, if the piece was not one of Marlowe's own, it must have been written by one of his admirers and disciples, and, accordingly, have been written at a time when Marlowe was still the hero of the day, that is, somewhere about 1591–92. This conjecture is also shared by Dyce and Delius (See his *Einleitung* to Shakspeare's *Taming of the Shrew*, p. xiv.). The subject is probably derived from an anecdote related of Philip the Good of Burgundy, and reported by Heuterus *de rebus Burgundicis*, lib. iv., and occupies a place in the old English collection of amusing tales by Richard Edwards, which was printed in 1570. And yet a very similar story is told even of Chalif Harun al Raschid in the *Arabian Nights*. See also, G. H. Norton in the *Shakspeare Society's Papers*, ii. 2 f.; also Simrock, *l.c.* iii., 225 ff.

    5. *Diary*, p. 36.

1877—Frederick James Furnivall. "Introduction to the Play," from *The Leopold Shakspere*

F. J. Furnivall, a philologist and editor, was one of the originators of the *Oxford English Dictionary*. He also founded a number of learned societies about English literature, including the New Shakspere Society, and was a founder of and teacher at the London Working Men's College.

. . . It is the only play with an Induction; and Sly is carelessly left on the stage, and not taken off it, as in the old play. The double plot of the winning of the two sisters is admirably worked, and the stage situations are first-rate. We must recollect the position of women in early times in England. We start in the eighth century—

> "A king shall with bargain buy a queen. . . . A damsel it
> beseems to be at her board [table]. . . . A rambling woman
> scatters words. She is often charged with faults, a man thinks of
> her with contempt, oft smites her cheek."
> —*Exeter Book*, pp. 338, 367.

Every reader of Chaucer remembers the Merchant's wife, "the worste that may be," who'd overmatch the devil if he were coupled to her; the host's cruel wife, too; and the *Boke of Mayd Emlyn's* opinion of wives—

> "For of theyr properte,
> Shrewes all they be,
> And styll can they prate."

Before 1575 (it is mentioned by Laneham) is "A Merry Geste of a Shrewd and Curst Wife lapped in Morrelles Skin," a popular poem, in which a man with a shrewish wife thrashes her till she bleeds, and then wraps her in the salted hide of his old horse Morrell. So the subject of taming shrews was a familiar one to the Elizabethan mind, and no one then would have been offended by Petruchio's likening of the training of a wife to that of a falcon, in iv. 1. We must look on Petruchio as a man wanting a hunting mare now, a goer, never mind her temper. He looks at her in the stable: she kicks and bites; he quietly rakes her straw and hay out; lets her stand all night; gallops her next day till she can't stand; tames her, and is then in the first flight ever after. Accept this view, and then look at the play. Kate is a spoiled child, strong-willed, spoiled by her father's weakness and her sister's gentleness. She has a genuine grievance, that she, the strong, the mistress-mind, is not to have a husband, while her weak sister is to have one. As she says, ii. 1—

"*She* is your treasure, *she* must have a husband;
I must dance barefoot on her wedding-day,
And, for your love to her, lead apes in hell."

Kate, like all reasonable girls, wants to get married, and though she is not the cooey, turtle-dovey girl that her sister is, who so attracts men, she knows she has that in her which is worthy of a man. She is soured by neglect, and she bullies her sister from envy; old Gremio calls her a devil, and hell. Petruchio comes. She sees he means business, though she snaps at him. She sees that he admires her beauty; she is flattered, and minds his opinion when she walks to show him she doesn't limp. She must admire him as the first man who stands up to her and overrules her. She is bewildered by his coolness and assurance too. She had forfeited by her childish bad temper a woman's right to chivalrous courtesy, and she feels that she has no right to complain of her lover's roughness. As a woman, too, she likes the promise of finery, and she makes up her mind to marry him. Nay, she actually cries when he comes too late. She who has scoffed at every one cannot bear the thought that—

"Now must the world point at poor Katherine,
And say, Lo, there is mad Petruchio's wife,
If it would please him come and marry her."

To avoid this, Petruchio in any clothes is welcome; and she takes him at once, notwithstanding his outrageous and slovenly dress. She trembles and shakes at his hitting the priest (if he'd do that to God's representative, what wouldn't he do to her?). Having got him, she is to be balked of the wedding-feast (cruellest of all blows to a bride). Under the influence of the wedding she is tender at first. "Let me entreat you now; if you love me, stay" (iii. 2). And we almost wish that Petruchio had taken advantage of this tenderness, and tried taming by love. But then we should have lost the best scenes of the play. However, her entreaties are rejected, and she stands up really for the first time for her rights. Now or never: it is her best time, with all her friends around her. Now or never she will struggle for what women most desire, rule over their husbands.[1] And the result is not now. Petruchio's drawing his sword and hustling her away, with the further taming on the journey and on reaching home, are most admirably handled, while the first signs of weakness, the humbling of herself to Grumio, the fresh fight again over her clothes (if a woman mayn't choose her clothes, what on earth may she do?), bring the conviction to her that resistance will not pay. The dispute over the sun and moon she evidently treats as fun, and enters into the joke. She has given in once for all, has learned her lesson. She is convinced of her past folly, and goes through with her task as far on the good side as on the bad before. Why rebel and be tamed again? No sense in that. "Peace it bodes and quiet life," etc. She is a new daughter to Baptista. It is the best result for her time, though Tennyson shows us a better for our Victorian era in his *Princess*.

Petruchio is like Faulconbridge in making himself out worse than he really is. Though he declares his object is only to wive wealthily, and Grumio says he'd marry any foul old hag with money, yet this is plain exaggeration. He's one of those men who like a bit of devil in the girl he marries and the mare he rides. "None of your namby-pamby ones for me." He knows he can tame her: if she is sharp-tempered, he is sharper. It's a word and a blow with him, as Grumio has experienced. When he hears of Kate, he won't sleep till he sees her; when she comes, he takes the lead and keeps it. He means to have it and her. He ridicules her in such a pleasant, madcap fashion, that one can't help liking him. He understands women, and flatters her. Note the limping touch. He praises her beauty; promises her finery; keeps her waiting; makes her put up with his dress, and tremble at church; outs with his sword and makes her go with him; declares his wife's his chattel; leaves her horse on her when she falls during the journey, and makes her beg for Grumio; will give no choleric food to choleric folk; in fact he "kills her in her own humour;" tames her by pretended love; starves her till she thanks him for meat he's dressed; and then when her food has made her saucy, and she rebels again about her dress (which was indeed enough to make the most angelic woman's temper rise), he beats her in the old way by pretending to sympathize with her. Then he stops her going home, because she won't say two is seven. When she gives in, he no doubt tries her too hardly, but then she has tried him before, and the result is that they two alone are married, while the other two, Hortensio and Lucentio, are only "sped." ("Let us hope though," says Miss Constance O'Brien, "that Petruchio gave up choosing Kate's dresses and caps.") If Petruchio is not a *gentleman*, and Kate not a lady, their day differed from ours:

they were a happy couple, we may be sure. Kate would obey him with a will, for her husband had fairly beaten her at her own game, and won her respect.

The farce and rich humour of the character, the delightful exaggeration of sliding down his body, after a run down his head and neck, the dry humour of his account of the accident, his scene with the tailor (enlarged from the old play), his entering into the humour of his master's taming Kate, make Grumio the finest character in comedy that we have yet had from Shakspere's hand. We must pass over Bianca—the sweet and gentle, whose breath perfumed the air, who yet had a will of her own, and that ever-Italian love of intrigue—only noting, as in private duty bound, that literature and language beat music, and win the girl. In Baptista we note his weakness, his being an old Italian fox, yet taken in for all his cleverness; his base willingness to sell his daughter for money. Lucentio loves at first sight, like Romeo does Juliet, and he cuts out the two older lovers and wins. Though Hortensio finds Petruchio to marry Kate, he yet loses Bianca. He is a straightforward fellow about love, and cannot stand her flirting. In the Induction, we notice Sly with his humour, standing between Bottom and Grumio, and with his Warwickshire allusions of Burton Heath and the fat ale-wife of Wincot; while the lord reproduces Shakspere's love of hounds which we saw in Theseus in the *Mid-summer-Night's Dream*. . . . The comical sham translation of the Latin lesson may have been suggested by a like bit in *The 3 Lords and 3 Ladies of London*, A.D. 1588, pr. 1590 (Hazlitt's *Dodsley*, vi. 500), "*O, singulariter nominativo*, wise Lord Pleasure; *genitivo*, bind him to the post; *dativo*, give me my torch; *accusativo*, for I say he's a cosener; *vocativo*, O, give me room to run at him; *ablativo*, take and blind me."

NOTE

1. See Chaucer's *Wife of Bath's Tale*; and the marriage of Sir Gawaine, in the *Percy Ballads* (i. 112); and the bequest in the *Wyll of the Deuyll*, "Item, I geue to all women souereygntee, which they most desyre."

—————

1879—Algernon Charles Swinburne. "Second Period: Comic and Historic," from *A Study of Shakespeare*

Algernon Charles Swinburne, most famous for his lyric poetry, was also an astute critic.

—————

. . . The refined instinct, artistic judgment, and consummate taste of Shakespeare were perhaps never so wonderfully shown as in his recast of another man's work—a man of real if rough genius for comedy—which we get in the *Taming of The Shrew*. Only the collation of scene with scene, then of speech with speech, then of line with line, will show how much may be borrowed from a stranger's material and how much may be added to it by the same stroke of a single hand. All the force and humour alike of character and situation belong to Shakespeare's eclipsed and forlorn precursor; he has added nothing; he has tempered and enriched everything. That the luckless author of the first sketch is like to remain a man as nameless as the deed of the witches in *Macbeth*, unless some chance or caprice of accident should suddenly flash favouring light on his now impersonal and indiscoverable individuality, seems clear enough when we take into account the double and final disproof of his imaginary identity with Marlowe, which Mr. Dyce has put forward with such unanswerable certitude. He is a clumsy and coarse-fingered plagiarist from that poet, and his stolen jewels of expression look so grossly out of place in the homely setting of his usual style that they seem transmuted from real to sham. On the other hand, he is of all the Pre-Shakespeareans known to us incomparably the truest, the richest, the most powerful and original humourist; one indeed without a second on that ground, for "the rest are nowhere." Now Marlowe, it need scarcely be once again reiterated, was as certainly one of the least and worst among jesters as he was one of the best and greatest among poets. There can therefore be no serious question of his partnership in a play wherein the comic achievement is excellent and the poetic attempts are execrable throughout.

The recast of it in which a greater than Berni has deigned to play the part of that poet towards a lesser than Bojardo shows tact and delicacy perhaps without a parallel in literature. No chance of improvement is missed, while nothing of value is dropped or thrown away.[1] There is just now and then a momentary return perceptible to the skipping metre and fantastic manner of the first period, which may have been unconsciously suggested by the nature of the task in hand—a task of itself implying or suggesting some new study of old models; but the main style of the play in all its weightier parts is as distinctly proper to the second period, as clear an evidence of inner and spiritual affinity (with actual tabulation of dates, were such a thing as feasible as it is impossible, I must repeat that the argument would here be—what it is now—in no wise concerned), as is the handling of character throughout; but most especially the subtle force, the impeccable and careful instinct, the masculine delicacy of touch, by which the somewhat ruffianly temperament of the original Ferando is at once refined and invigorated through its transmutation into the hearty and humorous manliness of Petruchio's. . .

NOTE

1. Possibly some readers may agree with my second thoughts, in thinking that one exception may here be made and some surprise be here expressed at

Shakespeare's rejection of Sly's memorable query—"When will the fool come again, Sim?" It is true that he could well afford to spare it, as what could he not well afford to spare? but I will confess that it seems to me worthy of a place among his own Sly's most admirable and notable sallies of humour.

—⁓— —⁓— —⁓—

1883— Edward Dowden.
"The Taming of the Shrew," from *Shakspere*

Edward Dowden was a critic, a poet, and a literature professor at the University of Oxford and Trinity College, Cambridge. He wrote a number of books on Shakespeare as well as a biography of Shelley.

The Taming of the Shrew is first found in the folio, 1623, but it is in some way closely connected with a play published in 1594, and bearing the almost identical title, *The Taming of a Shrew*. We cannot accept Pope's opinion that both plays are by Shakspere, nor agree with another critic who ingeniously maintained that the earlier printed play was the later written, being suggested by Shakspere's comedy of *the* Shrew. The play in the folio is certainly an enlargement and alteration of *The Taming of a Shrew*, and it only remains to ask, was Shakspere the sole reviser and adapter, or did his task consist of adding and altering certain scenes, so as to render yet more amusing and successful an enlarged version of the play of 1594, already made by some unknown hand? This last seems upon the whole the opinion best supported by the internal evidence. In *The Taming of the Shrew* we may distinguish three parts: (1) The humorous Induction, in which Sly, the drunken tinker, is the chief person; (2) A comedy of character, the Shrew and her tamer, Petruchio, being the hero and heroine; (3) A comedy of intrigue—the story of Bianca and her rival lovers. Now the old play of *A Shrew* contains, in a rude form, the scenes of the Induction, and the chief scenes in which Petruchio and Katharina (named by the original writer Ferando and Kate) appear; but nothing in this old play corresponds with the intrigues of Bianca's disguised lovers. It is, however, in the scenes concerned with these intrigues that Shakspere's hand is least apparent. It may be said that Shakspere's genius goes in and out with the person of Katharina. We would therefore conjecturally assign the intrigue-comedy,—which is founded upon Gascoigne's *Supposes*, a translation of Ariosto's *Gli Suepositi*—to the adapter of the old play, reserving for Shakspere a title to those scenes—in the main enlarged from the play of *A Shrew*—in which Katharina, Petruchio, and Grumio are speakers. Turning this statement into figures, we find that Shakspere's part of *The Taming of the Shrew* is comprised in the following portions: Induction; Act II. Sc. i. L. 169–326; Act III. Sc. ii. L. 1–125, and 151–241; Act IV. Sc. i.; Act IV. Sc iii.; Act IV. Sc. v.; Act V. Sc. ii. L. 1–180. Such a division, it must be borne in mind, is no more than a conjecture, but it seems to be suggested and fairly indicated by the style of the several parts of the comedy.

However this may be, it is clear that Shakspere cared little for the other characters in comparison with Sly, Katharina, and Petruchio. Sly is of the family of Sancho Panza, gross and materialistic in his tastes and habits, but withal so good-humoured and self-contented that we would fain leave him unvexed by higher ideas or aspirations; all the pains taken to delude him into the notion that he is a lord will not make him essentially other than "old Sly's son, of Burton Heath," who has run up so long a score with the fat ale-wife of Wincot. The Katharina and Petruchio scenes border upon the farcical, but Shakspere's interest in the characters of the Shrew and her tamer keep these scenes from passing into downright farce. Katharina with all her indulged wilfulness and violence of temper has no evil in her; in her home-enclosure she seems a formidable creature; but when caught away by the tempest of Petruchio's masculine force, the comparative weakness of her sex shows itself; she, who has strength of her own, and has ascertained its limits, can recognise superior strength, and once subdued she is the least rebellious of subjects. Petruchio acts his assumed part "with complete presence of mind, with untired animal spirits, and without a particle of ill-humour from beginning to end." The play is full of energy and bustling movement.

Widely separated dates have been assigned for *The Taming of the Shrew*, from 1594 to 1606. The best portions are in the manner of Shakspere's comedies of the second period; and attributing the Bianca intrigue-comedy to a writer intermediate between the author of the play of *A Shrew* and Shakspere, there is no difficulty in supposing that the Shakspere scenes were written about 1597. The same spirit in which *The Merry Wives of Windsor* was created was here employed by Shakspere to furnish his theatrical company with this enlarged version of a popular comedy.

It should be noted that the comedy of *The Shrew* is a play within a play, and there is no provision, such as is found in the older *Shrew*, for disposing of Sly at the end of the fifth act. The jest of bewildering a poor man into the idea that he is rich and great is found in the Arabian Nights; such a jest is attributed to Philip the Good of Burgundy, and the story is given in a collection of *Tales* compiled by R. Edwards, and printed in 1570. Fletcher wrote a humorous continuation of Shakspere's play, entitled *The Woman's Prise, or the Tamer Tamed*, in which Petruchio reappears.

1897—George Bernard Shaw.
"Chin, Chon, Chino," from *The Saturday Review*

George Bernard Shaw, one of the great dramatists of his time, was also known for his sometimes idiosyncratic criticism. His views of Shakespeare were often less than favorable. Among his most famous plays are *Saint Joan*, *Pygmalion* (later adapted into the musical and film *My Fair Lady*), *Man and Superman*, and *Caesar and Cleopatra*.

…Up to a late hour on Monday night I persuaded myself that I would hasten from the Globe to Her Majesty's, and do my stern duty by "Katharine and Petruchio." But when it came to the point I sacrificed duty to personal considerations. "The Taming of the Shrew" is a remarkable example of Shakspear's repeated attempts to make the public accept realistic comedy. Petruchio is worth fifty Orlandos as a human study. The preliminary scenes in which he shows his character by pricking up his ears at the news that there is a fortune to be got by any man who will take an ugly and ill-tempered woman off her father's hands, and hurrying off to strike the bargain before somebody else picks it up, are not romantic; but they give an honest and masterly picture of a real man, whose like we have all met. The actual taming of the woman by the methods used in taming wild beasts belongs to his determination to make himself rich and comfortable, and his perfect freedom from all delicacy in using his strength and opportunities for that purpose. The process is quite bearable, because the selfishness of the man is healthily good-humoured and untainted by wanton cruelty; and it is good for the shrew to encounter a force like that and be brought to her senses. Unfortunately, Shakspear's own immaturity, as well as the immaturity of the art he was experimenting in, made it impossible for him to keep the play on the realistic plane to the end; and the last scene is altogether disgusting to modern sensibility. No man with any decency of feeling can sit it out in the company of a woman without feeling extremely ashamed of the lord-of-creation moral implied in the wager and the speech put into the woman's own mouth. Therefore the play, though still worthy of a complete and efficient representation, would need, even at that, some apology. But the Garrick version of it, as a farcical afterpiece!—thank you: no.

THE TAMING OF THE SHREW
IN THE TWENTIETH CENTURY

❧

In the twentieth century, changing attitudes toward the role of women in society naturally led to critical reassessments of *The Taming of the Shrew*. Some critics, however, continued to explore traditional questions of structure and form. Early in the century, the critic Richard G. Moulton focused on Shakespeare's use of intrigue and irony, especially in the play's secondary plot. In contrast, Moulton saw the main plot, the wooing of Kate, as full of paradox, which in his view is slightly different from irony. In the main plot, Petruchio fights to win an unwanted woman and, in doing so, "sets himself to reverse everything expected of the conventional wooer."

Later in the century, Bertrand Evans also viewed the treatment of the two plots as quite distinct. The subplot, from his perspective, is where characters are duped to various degrees, leaving them with "discrepancies in awareness." In the main plot concerning Kate and Petruchio, however, there are none of these gaps in awareness; in fact, characters ensure that Petruchio has a clear understanding of what they think Kate is like, making this aspect of the play "curiously un-Shakespearian."

The critic Edmund K. Chambers declared that the play should be designated as a farce, a popular form in English drama of the early sixteenth century and up to Shakespeare's time. Chambers pointed out that farce differs from traditional comedy in that it presents a brutal or cynical outlook and an "extravagant or burlesque perversion of life." While farce in general is not concerned with ethics, Chambers nonetheless viewed Kate as an example of the wrongs done to women.

Many other commentators throughout the century examined the character of Kate and her taming, especially through the emerging critical lens of feminism. Some found Kate to be more psychologically complex than commonly assumed. Ruth Nevo, for example, saw Kate as being full of defenses and in need of assurance, completely envious and suspicious. Petruchio, through his outrageous behavior, forces her to see herself, appeals to her intelligence, and draws out "the self she would like to be."

William Empson explored Kate's psychology as well. Empson argued that Kate is not as brutalized as some believe; for example, her "tamer" does not beat her (though this would have been "normal practice" in Shakespeare's day) and her father is doing his best to get her married. Empson believed that previous critics had ignored Kate's strength. As he put it, "The lady is bullied not because she is weak but because she is strong."

Another important critic, Harold C. Goddard, also wrote of the psychology exhibited in the play. His view was that Shakespeare wrote the play knowing that its meaning would be misconstrued by the multitude. Kate is not the tamed but the tamer, though she lets her husband believe he is in charge. Her "shrewishness" is merely superficial and caused by her father, who favors Bianca, leaving Kate "starved for love." Goddard pointed out that Shakespeare in his comedies always empowers his heroines, and this play is no exception. The key to the true meaning of *The Taming of the Shrew,* he felt, could be found in the play's Induction.

The earlier commentator William Winter held quite a different perspective. He found Kate "disagreeable" and declared that her father's "partiality for her younger sister . . . does not justify her in her perverse and quarrelsome proceedings." Both Kate and Petruchio are "more animal than mental, and somewhat common." Like Goddard, Winter believed Petruchio appealed to the "coarser audience of the time," but unlike Goddard he did not see that Petruchio could also be viewed in an entirely different light.

Toward the end of the century, an increasing number of critics examined the social and political implications of the play. Camille Wells Slights saw it as a commentary on the overwhelming strictness of society. The Induction, then, dramatizes the common dream of being able to bend society as one wishes. In Slights's view, the town of Padua is overly concerned with money and possessions, and Petruchio upsets its customary ways. He liberates not only Kate but indirectly Bianca as well, who, like Kate, is rebelling against social constraints and is "determined to have her own way in spite of social coercion."

Not every critic agreed that the play was important or even especially interesting. The poet Alice Meynell, in an introduction to the play written in 1907, wrote that it was clearly Shakespearean but "almost Shakespeare's worst"— with the exception of the Induction, which she considered a true achievement.

1903—Richard G. Moulton. From "Personality and Its Dramatic Expression in Intrigue and Irony," in *The Moral System of Shakespeare*

Richard G. Moulton was a professor of English at the University of Chicago. He wrote *The Moral System of Shakespeare* and *The Literary Study of the Bible,* among other titles.

. . . It is obvious enough that intrigue and irony naturally go together in the moral system of a dramatic literature: as intrigue is specially consecrated to the dramatic expression of individual will, so irony has the function of conveying the clash of individual wills with one another or with circumstances.

In connection with this part of our subject no play of Shakespeare is more brilliant than *The Taming of the Shrew*.[1] It has a primary and a secondary plot: the first is occupied with the wooing of Katherine, the shrew; the second with the wooing of her sister Bianca, a natural and winsome girl. Three suitors are seeking the hand of this Bianca; their suits are made intrigues by the circumstance that her widower father, burdened with the task of finding husbands for his two children, has hit upon the ingenious plan of announcing to his world that he will receive no overture for Bianca until her shrewish elder sister is married; this forces Bianca's lovers to use secrecy and contrivance. It might seem as if this secondary plot, with a triple intrigue and all its possibilities of irony, would overbalance the primary plot. But what this last lacks in quantity it makes up for in quality; the wooing of Katherine is saturated through and through, not exactly with irony, but with a dramatic quality akin to irony—the interest of paradox.

We naturally woo that which is attractive; Petruchio paradoxically undertakes to win what is repellent.

> *Gremio.* But will you woo this wild-cat?
> *Petruchio.* Will I live? . . .
> Why came I hither but to that intent?
> Think you a little din can daunt mine ears?
> Have I not in my time heard lions roar?
> Have I not heard the sea puff'd up with winds
> Rage like an angry boar chafed with sweat?
> Have I not heard great ordnance in the field,
> And heaven's artillery thunder in the skies?
> Have I not in a pitched battle heard
> Loud 'larums, neighing steeds, and trumpets' clang?
> And do you tell me of a woman's tongue,
> That gives not hall so great a blow to hear
> As will a chestnut in a farmer's fire?

The method of the wooing is even more paradoxical than the purpose to woo. Petruchio may be described as a social 'hustler': he has all the hustler's accentuated egoism, and understands the force of mere social momentum. He sets himself to reverse everything expected of the conventional wooer; in the bewilderment that ensues he will sweep resistance off its feet by the resolute pace of his movements. While Katherine's shrewishness is the common talk of the city, Petruchio announces himself to the father as a suitor attracted by—

> Her affability and bashful modesty,
> Her wondrous qualities, and mild behaviour.

The delighted Baptista must nevertheless adjourn the interview, as other guests are present, but the hustler cannot wait.

> Signior Baptism, my business asketh haste,
> And every day I cannot come to woo.

Katherine is sent for; in a parenthesis of soliloquy Petruchio unfolds his system of paradox.

> Say that she rail; why then I'll tell her plain
> She sings as sweetly as a nightingale:
> Say that she frown; I'll say she looks as clear
> As morning roses newly wash'd with dew;
> Say she be mute and will not speak a word;
> Then I'll commend her volubility,
> And say she uttereth piercing eloquence:
> If she do bid me pack, I'll give her thanks,
> As though she bid me stay by her a week;
> If she deny to wed, I'll crave the day
> When I shall ask the banns, and when be married.

A stormy scene ensues, but Petruchio will see nothing stormy.

> I find you passing gentle,
> 'Twas told me you were rough and coy and sullen,
> And now I find report a very liar;
> For thou art pleasant, gamesome, passing courteous,
> But slow in speech, yet sweet as spring-time flowers.

The shrew lets off her rage against this wooer to the assembling company, but Petruchio is unmoved.

> *Petru.* If she be curst, it is for policy,
> For she's not froward, but modest as the dove ...
> And to conclude, we have greed so well together,
> That upon Sunday is the wedding-day.

Kath. I'll see thee hang'd on Sunday first.
Gremio. Hark, Petruchio; she says she'll see thee hang'd first.
Tranio. Is this your speeding? nay, then, good night our part!
Petru. Be patient, gentlemen; I choose her for myself:
If she and I be pleased, what's that to you?
'Tis bargain'd twixt us twain, being alone,
That she shall still be curst in company.

Whirled at this pace to a wedding-day, the shrew, with no distinct plan of resistance, can only find a fresh grievance in her proposed bridegroom keeping her waiting, after a while this is lost in a tour-de-force of paradox.

> Petruchio is coming in a new hat and an old jerkin, a pair of old breeches thrice turned, a pair of boots that have been candle-cases, one buckled, another laced, an old rusty sword ta'en out of the town-armoury, with a broken hilt, and chapeless; with two broken points; his horse hipped with an old mothy saddle and stirrups of no kindred; besides, possessed with the glanders and like to mose in the chine; troubled with the lampass, infected with the fashions, full of windgalls, sped with spavins, rayed with the yellows, past cure of the fives, stark spoiled with the staggers, begnawn with the bots, swayed in the back and shoulder-shotten; near-legged before and with a half-checked bit and a head-stall of sheep's leather which, being restrained to keep him from stumbling, hath been often burst and now repaired with knots; one girth six times pieced and a woman's crupper of velure, which hath two letters for her name fairly set down in studs, and here and there pieced with pack-thread.

Even the anxious father has to remonstrate, but Petruchio will not explain.

> To me she's married, not unto my clothes.

How the momentum of Petruchio's wildness gets the parties into the church we can only conjecture, for that part of the story goes on behind the scenes; but the proceedings in the church are related by Gremio: how the mad bridegroom swears his 'ay' so loud that the priest drops the book, and is cuffed as he picks it up again; how he ends by drinking a health, and throws the sops in the sexton's face. Katherine at last wakes up her resistance when the newly wedded man will go away on unexplained business before the wedding feast; Petruchio sweeps away the resisting bride as in a fervour of delivering gallantry.

> Grumio,
> Draw forth thy weapon, we are beset with thieves;

Rescue thy mistress, if thou be a man.
Fear not, sweet wench, they shall not touch thee, Kate;
I'll buckler thee against a million.

The paradoxical taming is continued at home.

> *Katherine.* I, who never knew how to entreat,
> Nor never needed that I should entreat,
> Am starved for meat, giddy for lack of sleep;
> With oaths kept waking, and with brawling fed;
> And that which spites me more than all these wants,
> He does it under name of perfect love;
> As who should say, if I should sleep or eat,
> 'Twere deadly sickness or else present death.[2]

The paradoxical conclusion of this primary plot is that the tamed shrew reads to the mild Bianca and other normal wives a long lecture on wifely submissiveness.

What the interest of paradox is to the primary, the interest of irony is to the secondary plot. As we have seen, three lovers make conflicting suits for the hand of the pretty Bianca. Hortensio is a neighbour: Gremio has the common combination of age with wealth; Lucentio is a newcomer to Padua, and with him it is a case of love at first sight.[3] All three lovers have to make their approach indirectly. Hortensio, in return for introducing his friend Petruchio as a suitor for Katherine, arranges that his friend shall introduce himself disguised as a teacher of music for Bianca. Gremio on his part will have an agent for his interests among Bianca's teachers. But Lucentio, in scholar's disguise, applies for this agency; already we get our first flash of irony as Gremio unconsciously introduces into the circle of Bianca's instructors his dangerous rival. As the story progresses, a situation of prolonged irony appears: the disguised rivals have to carry on their wooing in the presence of one another.[4] The fair pupil has some trouble to keep the peace between her masters; she sets the musician to getting his difficult instrument in order, while the teacher of poetry has his chance.

> *Lucentio.* '*Hic ibat Simois; hic est Sigeia tellus;*
> *Hic steterat Priami regia celsa senis.*'

> 'Hic ibat,' as I told you before,— 'Simois,' I am Lucentio,—'hic est,'
> son unto Vincentio of Pisa,—'Sigeia tellus,' disguised thus to get your
> love;—'Hic steterat,' and that Lucentio that comes a-wooing,—Priami,
> is my man Tranio,—regia, bearing my port,—celsa senis, that we might
> beguile the old pantaloon.

Bianca tries if she has learned her lesson.

> 'Hic ibat Simois,' I know you not,—'hic est Sigeia tellus,' I trust you
> not,—'Hic steterat Priami,' take heed he hear us not,—'regia,' presume
> not,—'celsa senis' despair not.

The music-teacher in his turn begs Bianca to read a new gamut, newer than
anything taught in his trade before—the gamut of Hortensio.

> *Bianca (reads)* "'Gamut' I am, the ground of all accord,
> 'A re,' to plead Hortensio's passion;
> 'B mi,' Bianca, take him for thy lord,
> 'C fa ut,' that loves with all affection:
> 'D sol re,' one clef, two notes have I:
> 'E la mi,' show pity, or I die."
> Call you this gamut? tut, I like it not:
> Old fashions please me best; I am not so nice,
> To change true rules for old inventions.

But the finesse of intrigue in the secondary plot goes far beyond this. Lucentio has
come to Padua with a certain amount of state; he has servants, and a family name
to support. One of his servants is Tranio, in whom we recognise a modernisation
of a type familiar to Roman Comedy, the scheming slave or professional sharper.
When, therefore, Lucentio assumes his disguise, he makes this Tranio take his
master's name and position; more than this, the pseudo-Lucentio is to go in
state to Baptista's house, and be in name one more suitor for the hand of Bianca;
he will thus be always at hand to second his master's secret play.[5] Tranio acts
the gentleman to perfection, and makes a social impression for the name of
'Lucentio.'[6] Thus the real Lucentio carries on a double campaign, wooing the
lady in his own (disguised) person, and through his servant heading off his rivals.
Two more strokes of irony are due to the machinations of Tranio, soi-disant
Lucentio. When one of the rivals, Hortensio, is getting discouraged—since
the teacher of poetry steadily gains upon the teacher of music—the supposed
Lucentio with easy magnanimity moves Hortensio to mutual renunciation of
their claims.[7]

> *Hortensio.* Quick proceeders, marry! Now, tell me, I pray,
> You that durst swear that your mistress Bianca
> Loved none in the world so well as Lucentio.
> *Tranio.* O despiteful love! unconstant womankind!
> I tell thee, Licio, this is wonderful.
> *Hortensio.* Mistake no more: I am not Licio,
> Nor a musician, as I seem to be;

But one that scorn to live in this disguise. . . .
Know, sir, that I am call'd Hortensio.
   Tranio. Signior Hortensio, I have often heard
Of your entire affection to Bianca;
And since mine eyes are witness of her lightness,
I will with you, if you be so contented,
Forswear Bianca and her love for ever.
   Hortensio. See, how they kiss and court! Signior Lucentio,
Here is my hand, and here I firmly vow
Never to woo her more, but do forswear her,
As one unworthy all the former favours
That I have fondly flatter'd her withal.
   Tranio. And here I take the like unfeigned oath,
Never to marry with her though she would entreat.

Not less ironical is the situation when the assumed Lucentio makes his play against the other rival.[8] Gremio has no attractions of youth; his time comes when the question is of settlements. But even Gremio's wealth is made to look small by one who can draw upon the bank of imagination.

   Baptista. Say, Signior Gremio, what can you assure her?
   Gremio. First, as you know, my house within the city
Is richly furnished with plate and gold;
Basins and ewers to lave her dainty hands;
My hangings all of Tyrian tapestry;
In ivory coffers I have stuff'd my crowns;
In cypress chests my arras counterpoints,
Costly apparel, tents, and canopies,
Fine linen, Turkey cushions boss'd with pearl,
Valance of Venice gold in needlework,
Pewter and brass and all things that belong
To house or housekeeping: then, at my farm
I have a hundred milch-kine to the pail,
Sixscore fat oxen standing in my stalls,
And all things answerable to this portion.
Myself am struck in years, I must confess;
And if I die to-morrow, this is hers,
If whilst I live she will be only mine.
   Tranio. That 'only' came well in. Sir, list to me:
I am my father's heir and only son:
If I may have your daughter to my wife,
I'll leave her houses three or four as good,

Within rich Pisa walls, as any one
Old Signior Gremio has in Padua;
Besides two thousand ducats by the year
Of fruitful land, all which shall be her jointure.
What, have I pinch'd you, Signior Gremio?
   Gremio. Two thousand ducats by the year of land!
My land amounts not to so much in all;
That she shall have; besides an argosy
That now is lying in Marseilles' road.
What, have I choked you with an argosy?
   Tranio. Gremio, 'tis known my father hath no less
Than three great argosies; besides two galliases,
And twelve tight galleys: these I will assure her,
And twice as much, whate'er thou offer'st next.
   Gremio. Nay, I have offer'd all, I have no more;
And she can have no more than all I have.

Four fine situations of irony have thus sprung from the clash of intrigues in the secondary plot. A fifth is added as at last the secondary plot is made to clash with the primary. Tranio, playing the rôle of his master, has had it all his own way so far; but he is now, naturally enough, called upon to make good his promises by a pledge from Lucentio's father.[9] Without a blush he undertakes this.

'Tis in my head to do my master good;
I see no reason, but supposed Lucentio
Must get a father, call'd 'supposed Vincentio';
And that's a wonder: fathers commonly
Do get their children; but in this case of wooing,
A child shall get a sire, if I fail not of my cunning.

The plan is a simple one: the strangers entering the city are scanned, until a suitable figure is found in a certain Pedant.[10]

   Tranio. What countryman, I pray?
   Pedant. Of Mantua.
   Tranio. Of Mantua, sir? marry, God forbid!
And come to Padua, careless of your life?
   Pedant. My life, sir! how, I pray? for that goes hard.
   Tranio. 'Tis death for any one in Mantua
To come to Padua. Know you not the cause?

Your ships are stay'd at Venice, and the duke,
For private quarrel twixt your duke and him,
Hath publish'd and proclaim'd it openly:
'Tis marvel, but that you are but newly come,
You might have heard it else proclaim'd about.
    Pedant. Alas, sir, it is worse for me than so!
For I have bills for money by exchange
From Florence and must here deliver them.

Tranio obligingly proposes that the stranger shall assume the personality of one Sir Vincentio of Pisa, shortly expected to arrange a matter of dowry for his son on his marriage to Signior Baptista's daughter; the Pedant is only too glad to save his life on these easy terms. So far the intrigue of Tranio is triumphant; but meanwhile the train of events which makes the primary plot of the play is preparing for it a collision. Petruchio and his Katherine journeying to Padua fall in by the way with a reverend senior travelling in the same direction;[11] when the name of Vincentio of Pisa is mentioned, Petruchio hails him as a prospective marriage connection, and escorts him to the house where his son will be found to have made a wealthy and influential match. As they knock at the door[12] the real and the assumed Vincentio clash.

    Pedant (*looking out at the window*). What's he that knocks as he would beat down the gate?
    Vincentio. Is Signior Lucentio within, sir?
    Pedant. He's within, sir, but not to be spoken withal.
    Vincentio. What if a man bring him a hundred pound or two, to make merry withal.
    Pedant. Keep your hundred pounds to yourself: he shall need none, so long as I live.
    Petruchio. Nay, I told you your son was well beloved in Padua. Do you hear, sir? To leave frivolous circumstances, I pray you, tell Signior Lucentio, that his father is come from Pisa, and is here at the door to speak with him.
    Pedant. Thou liest: his father is come from Padua, and here looking out at the window.
    Vincentio. Art thou his father?
    Pedant. Ay, sir; so his mother says, if I may believe her.
    Petruchio (*to Vincentio*). Why, how now, gentleman! why, this is flat knavery, to take upon you another man's name.
    Pedant. Lay hands on the villain: I believe a' means to cozen somebody in this city under my countenance.

The ironical situation is prolonged as Lucentio's servants come on the scene, and hasten to take part against their master's own father; stormy passages ensue, until Lucentio comes in person, but comes with his bride on his arm fresh from the church. There is explanation and confession: but the essential of the marriage has been secured, and the irate father can only make the best of the circumstances: irony gives place to the usual happy ending.

For Shakespeare's treatment of intrigue and irony it seems natural to mention first this play of *The Taming of the Shrew*; no other drama is richer in ironic situations, while the personal will, of which intrigue is the embodiment, seems to find its climax in a sustained paradox. . .

NOTES

1. Compare the scheme of the play in the Appendix below, page 344.
2. *Taming of Shrew* IV. iii. 8.
3. *Taming of Shrew* I. i. 152, and whole scene.
4. III. i.
5. I. i, from 203.
6. II. i, from 87; I. ii, from 219.
7. IV. ii.
8. II. i, from 343.
9. I. i, from 389.
10. IV. ii, from 59.
11. IV. v, from 26.
12. V. i.

1904—Charlotte Carmichael Stopes.
"*The Taming of the Shrew*," from *The Atheneum*

Charlotte Carmichael Stopes was the author of a number of books on Shakespeare, including *Burbage and Shakespeare's Stage* and *Shakespeare's Warwickshire Contemporaries*.

[June 11, 1904]

There are several peculiarities in this play which make it difficult to classify among Shakspeare's works. Others are comedies; this, called a history, is nearly a farce. Others have a Prologue or Chorus to introduce the action, or an Epilogue to sum it up; but this is the only one that has an Induction, which seems totally unconnected with the main action, and does not in any way illustrate its meaning. If, for a moment, we treat the Induction as the play in itself, we may find some parallels in *Hamlet*. By the flourish of trumpets the players announce their approach in both cases, as distinguished travellers would—

> Belike some noble gentleman that means,
> Travelling some journey, to repose him here.
>   (Ind. Sc. i.)

The travelling players come to offer their services in a fortunate hour. In *Hamlet* "the tragedians of the city" are forced to take the less reputable exercises of their calling in the provinces, because the "aery of children," "little eyases," are now the fashion in the metropolis (a curious incongruity, seeing Hamlet was *in the city*, and *at the Court*). In both plays they are cordially received. They have acted well before. The Lord and Hamlet each discuss some well-known parts, to prepare them to decide which play should be performed. The Lord has some sport in hand, and wants a comedy; Hamlet has a terrible secret, and wants a tragedy. The Lord tells them, "Your cunning can assist me much"; Hamlet talks indefinitely to the players while others are present, recalling one play by its mentioning "savoury sallets," and straining his memory to fix the lines about Pyrrhus and Hecuba to confuse Polonius. As soon as the Chamberlain goes, Hamlet bids the chief player fix *The Murder of Gonzago* for the next night, adding, "You could, for a need, study a speech of some dozen or sixteen lines, which I would set down and insert in it, could you not?" Then he meditates—

> The play's the thing
> Wherein I'll catch the conscience of the King!

The Lord tells his servants, "Let them want nothing that my house affords"; Hamlet says to Polonius, "Good my lord, will you see the players well bestowed?...Do you hear? Let them be well used." Polonius did not care much for players, and equivocates, "My lord, I will use them according to their deserts." To which Hamlet replies, "God's bodkin, man, much better!" Hamlet's play within the play is introduced by a dumb show, an induction to the performance, whereby the King's conscience is awakened before he has heard all. The Lord is not so particular, and he lets the players choose; but it is to be supposed that before a liberal patron they would perform their newest and their best.

The Induction is a humorous fragment rather than a play, but it is worth all the comedy it nominally initiates. The story was based on an incident in the life of Philip the Good, Duke of Burgundy, who carried into his house an artisan whom he had found lying drunk in the streets. He offered his visitor many more amusements than were laid before Sly, "after which they played a pleasant comedy," the name of which is not given, and the conclusion to the waking dreamer is the same.

The Taming of the Shrew is a play complete in itself, and would only suffer in length by being separated from the Induction. The question naturally rises, Why were they so connected? As far as regards Shakspeare, it may be only because they are combined in the old play which suggested his. On June 11th, 1594, Henslowe notes receipts at performance, by "my Lord Admirell and my Lord Chamberlen men," *of The Taming of a Shrew*, which, curiously enough, immediately follows a similar entry on their playing *Hamlet*, which must have been the old version. In that same year was published "A pleasant conceited historic called *The Taming of a Shrew*, as it hath been lately performed by the Earl of Pembroke's servants." This was a rival company. Could it be the same play? Mr. Charles Knight suggests that the two sets of performers might have separate renderings from some older source now lost, probably, from the style, a play written by Greene. The scene of the printed version—*i.e.*, that of Pembroke's servants—is laid in Athens. In Shakspeare's (which may have been that of the Chamberlain's men in 1594) all the names are changed except that of Kate, and the language is modified to such an extent that the editors of the First Folio saw fit to include it among his works, though it does not appear in the lists of those copies entered to them or to any other publisher, neither does Meres mention it.

Had he thought it necessary, Shakspeare might have changed the situations fundamentally. As he accepted them, we may discuss the play as his own. While he changed the scene, with much advantage, from Athens to Padua, it must not be forgotten that he also changed the scene of the Induction from *anywhere* to *somewhere*. The old Induction, though using the name of Sly (the name also of one of the company), might have represented London or anywhere else. The new Induction belongs clearly to Warwickshire. Christopher was son of the Sly of Barton-on-the-Heath, the home of Shakspeare's uncle and cousin Lambert, who foreclosed the mortgage on his maternal inheritance. There was a Stephen sly, labourer, working at Welcombe at that very time. The Hackets were well known in the district, and some of the family did keep an inn. It is quite possible that there was a personal dig at some hostess who "did bring stone jugs and no sealed quarts," who deserved to be presented at the Leet. "The Lord" is nameless now, but it is not at all certain that he was not recognizable then by his characteristics. Shakspeare changes the tapster of the old Induction into a hostess. She has evidently had within the house a hot discussion, not yet concluded when she gets him out of doors. His first words seem to be a repetition of what she has just said to him. To make her meaning clear, she adds, "A pair of stocks, you rogue!" The acceptance of this question-begging epithet would put him at once in danger of statutes concerning "rogues and vagabonds," and he was sober enough to claim immunity because he was a man of ancient family. The substitution of "Richard" for William was probably a bit of byplay, complimentary to Burbage. Why the drunken tinker should be made to use a Spanish phrase to a country alewife is not clear, unless it was intended to suggest that during his pedlar experience, his cardmaker education, or his transmutation into a bearherd, he had been to London and picked it up at the bear-baiting or bull-baiting there. The same remark applies to "denier" and "Jeronymy." This is generally read as "Go by," a phrase from the old part of Hieronomo. But it is quite certain that Sly at the time felt like swearing, and that he would have a special oath of his own, though as hazily founded as his "Richard Conqueror." I read it that he was ordering the hostess back to her house: "Go! by S. Jeronymy, go! to thy cold bed and warm thee!"[1] The hostess retorts that she must rather "go fetch the thirdborough!" or constable. Sly, confident that he could answer *him* in law, disdained to fly at the threat, and lay down where he could be at hand. There he was found, not by the thirdborough, but by the Lord, who must have lived near, as he thought of carrying the drunken man home, rather than bestowing him in the inn. The Lord paints a rough sketch of him: "O monstrous beast, how like a swine he lies." He seems in his condition "foul and loathsome." Sly took a good deal of persuading to believe that he was a lord, and only accepted his position with Prince Henry's reservation in regard to his love for a pot of small ale. The season seems to have been December, not only from allusions to the cold, but because he asks if the *commonty* is to be "a Christmas gambol or a tumbling trick." The page describes it as more pleasing stuff, a kind of history. Sly had said to his hostess, "Let the world slide." Now again he says to his dream-wife, as he settles down by her side to watch the play, provided with cates and surrounded by lords and gentlemen, "Let the world slip." For this strangely consorted audience, and not for us, as the play in *Hamlet* is not for us, but for the King, *the history* that they had selected is performed by the travelling actors.

If it had been selected for the clown, it is hard to say why the scene should have been laid at a university town in Italy, among gentlemen and scholars. Did Shakspeare, or his players, aim at the Lord? Was there anything personal or satirical in it?

The underplot is essentially Italian. Lucentio comes to the University of Padua to study, as he states, chiefly the higher philosophy of Epicurus, but before he ever matriculates, Romeo-like, he falls in love, and becomes not a student, but a tutor in the *art of love*, wins Bianca, in spite of his rivals, and secures her by a stolen marriage. The character of Kate is only possible to English comedy. Her unlady like violence of temper is, however, accounted for in the first scene. A motherless girl of high spirit, she had always taken her own way with her foolish father and her younger sister. Capable among incapables, she had expressed her mind freely among her equals, and domineered over her inferiors, even to the using of her fists. She had hitherto thought of nothing but the mood of the moment. Now a crisis had arrived in her life. Her father had made her heart bitter by a pronounced preference for her sister. Two men had come a-wooing to the house. She had not thought of a husband until then, but the idea was naturally suggested, just as she discovered that *both* of the men desired her sister. The awkwardness might have passed over; she might have consoled herself on the sour-grape theory that Gremio was too old and Hortensio too weak for her, that she would have no rival at home were but her sister married; but her unwise father, not content with having discoursed openly of her vile temper, repeats before her and others his desire to get rid of her, and offers her to either of her sister's suitors, without consulting her taste or theirs. Their insolent refusal shows them to be no gentlemen, and prevents her regretting their loss, while it shows her they reckon her influence in the house as naught, seeing she was not worth conciliating with a show of courtesy. When her father secludes her sister, ostensibly to give *her* a chance, he apologizes—

Good Bianca,
For I will love thee ne'er the less, my girl!

He bids Kate stay back, as he wished to commune with her sister; but the embittered girl follows in a passion. The two suitors see it their policy to find her a husband to get rid of her, as her father desires to do.

Here "the Presenters above speak." Sly had said to the hostess "paucas pallabris." He has found the "commonty" *nothing but words;* he finds it dull, and wishes it were done. Did Shakspeare allow him then to sink into his second sleep, or did he merely leave the part to Kemp's inspiration? We cannot help wishing that we had more of him. Akin to Grumio, to Sancho Panza, and Autolycus, he was a fit follower for Sir John Falstaff.

Scene ii. introduces Petruchio's violent temper and his severity to Grumio. He has come to Padua not to study, but "to wive and thrive." He cares not whether his bride be ugly, old, diseased, be curst or shrew,

As wealth is the burden of my wooing dance.

Hortensio tells him of Kate, young, rich, beauteous, cultured, but curst. Petruchio cares not, money covers all. The other gentlemen speak roughly of the girl; Tranio is the only one who treats the question like a gentleman, and recognizes Baptista's

Firm resolve
In the preferment of his elder daughter.

The painful scene in which Kate has bound her sister, and then strikes her through envy and jealousy, comes to a climax when her father intervenes to protect Bianca:—

> She is your treasure, she must have a husband.
> I must dance barefoot on her wedding-day,
> And, for your love to her, *lead apes in hell.*

Many illustrations might be given of this curious phrase, commonly used of those who died old maids. But the only reference I know to the converse is from a fragment of Capt. Cox's *Old Book of Fortune:*—

> Thou a stale bachelor wilt die,
> And not a maiden for thee cry,
> For apes that maids in hell do lead
> Are men that die and will not wed.

Kate goes off to weep violently, and think of revenge, just before Petruchio comes in to ask Baptista for her hand.

The mock-tutors are sent to their pupils, Baptista invites the others to the orchard. Petruchio detains him. His suit is pressing—"Every day I cannot come to woo." His haste awakes Baptista too late to his duty, or a pretence of it—

> When the special thing is well obtained,
> That is, her love, for that is all in all.

Petruchio, secure of all that *he* wanted, exclaims, "That is nothing." He felt sure he could win any woman's love, if so he chose, and cure any woman's temper. He knew that he had a disposition, called politely among men "peremptory," among women impolitely "shrewish." It is only the amount of friction or opposition which determines the degree of noise made. Hortensio comes in with his head broken. Lucentio had secured Bianca with his books; Kate, in her wrathful mood, had discovered either stupidity or *sham* in the music-master. Possibly she recognized him, and had a part of her "revenge" thus. Petruchio is delighted. She had done just what he would have liked to do himself. A genuine feeling of admiration is awakened, and a desire of mastering her high spirit. Henceforth the action must be read, as Justice Madden points out in *The Diary of Master William Silence,* through the light of the language of falconry. Petruchio meant to "man a haggard" for himself rather than teach an "eyas." He has the advantage over her in being prepared. Baptista asks him whether he would come within to be introduced formally as a suitor, or whether he would like Kate sent to him—a most unfatherly suggestion. One wonders how the excited Baptista worded the message to Kate that at last a suitor had come for her, and whether he stirred her anger, pride, or joy. She had at least curiosity enough to come, doubtless slowly and with dignity, and a fierce modesty covering her heart-hunger to hear words of love. He does not even introduce himself, but with cool effrontery says, as if she had been a milkmaid, "Good morrow, Kate, for that's your name, I hear." Her temper blazed, but she controlled it courteously as she checked him justly. He rudely said she "lied," broke into nonsensical exclamations, and wound up by saying he wooed her for his wife.

Thereafter a dialogue of sharp repartee, until Kate strikes him. Then, apparently, he caught her by the wrists, and let her feel his strength: "I chafe you, if I tarry: let me go!" After mock praise of her gentleness, he cunningly suggests: "Why does the world report mat Kate doth limp?" She could not walk away, as if to answer this, and therefore bids him begone. More praise, and then to business. She had not been consulted—was not to be consulted. Her father had already consented, everything was arranged: "and will you, nill you, I will marry you."

Baptista did not come alone, as he ought to have done, to inquire how matters had gone, but with a total stranger on one side, and the old Gremio, who had so scornfully refused her, on the other. Petruchio had at least not insulted her in this manner. She might have been advised, but her father's words rubbed her the wrong way, and she broke forth into reproaches for his desire to see her wed a man half lunatic. Petruchio out-talked her, and belied her words, skilfully interwove suggestions about finery and a feast next Sunday, and his audacity and lies, his praise, and perhaps his appearance, restore her maidenly pride. Here was a chance of taking the higher social level of a bride, and of leaving forever the little daily irritations of her present life. Doubtless she was thinking deeply when she let her last chance pass of protesting, and she found herself betrothed, with due witnesses, before she knew what she was about, and Petruchio had gone to prepare for the wedding on Sunday.

Having thus got rid of his tiresome daughter to the first man who would have her, Baptista is free to sell the daughter he loves to the highest bidder. She is settling affairs for herself. Meek as she had seemed beside Kate, there is a spice of the same self-will in her (shown in Act V. sc. ii. 1. 130)—

I'll not be tied to hours nor 'pointed times,
But learn my lessons as I please myself.

She had been tired of Hortensio before she offered him to her sister. She prefers literature to music, associated as it was with a new face. She bids Lucentio "presume not, but despair not."

After the whirl of preparations for the ceremony on Sunday, the "taming of the haggard" began in earnest. The bridegroom did not arrive in time, and, enforced to wait, on poor Kate there dawns a fear that she was about to be mocked in a more galling way than her father or Hortensio or Gremio had ever done. She had "been forced to give her hand without her heart," and now her betrothed did not trouble himself to come for her. Passionate tears flowed, and for the first time her father showed a kindly sympathy with her. Then the expected Petruchio comes without the garb even of a gentleman, without the manners of a gentleman, irreverent not only to his bride, her father, and their friends, but to Holy Church and its officiating minister. Well might Kate be daunted, who had never known fear before. She soon learnt the folly and ridiculousness of violence through her husband's explosions. She came to long for ordinary world-like ways and peace at any price. Her family resemblance to Bianca began to appear. She had not exercised her violent temper without a purpose. She had used it as means to an end. She wanted her own way, and, like other spoiled children, she had hitherto found that noise secured it. Now, amid her husband's storms, she found she must try another method: she must spoil him, as she had been spoiled, by humouring him. That was not sufficient. She must do that through hypocrisy and falsehood, alien to her direct nature. Petruchio made her a time-server. She had to agree that black was white, the sun the moon, old age fair youth, and then two was seven, and they started homewards. She wanted home, and thus she had her way.

Then came the famous wager, and Kate's more famous speech. The old "Kate" based her argument for women's submission on the popular derivation of "woman," for by her came woe to man in the creation. The change in Kate's argument is curious, or rather in her two arguments: one because a man is stronger than a woman, and the other because he toiled for her that "she might lie warm at home secure and safe." Kate's clear brain knew that *strength* was a variable quantity, and that the argument could not therefore *universally* apply, and in regard to the second argument, in her own case at least, that she was talking as arrant nonsense as when she praised old Vincentio as a young maiden. For she knew that Petruchio had not married her in order to toil for her, but to save him from toiling for himself; that if any were *breadwinner* it was her father, who had given sufficient to supply all her needs, without any self-sacrifice on Petruchio's part. If this argument had any force, if the *bread-provider* was to rule, *she* was more entitled to pre-eminence than he. But she outdid patient Griselda in her speech, though any critical listener might have thought, "The lady protests too much, methinks" (*Hamlet,* III. ii.). There is no real thought of such submission in Kate any more than in the young tree, that bends till the blast be past and strengthens itself meanwhile to withstand future ones.

A touch from the old play is missed in Shakspeare's. Sly said at first, "I hardly think that he can tame her"; and again, "For when he has done, she will do what she list," a suggestion caught up by John Fletcher, who was probably "the second hand" in this play, and elaborated in his *Woman's Prize; or, the Tamer Tamed.* The old Sly felt happy in the experiences he had gained. He knew now how to tame a shrew, and he named his wife one when she reproached him for his evil ways. But Sly had vanished from Shakspeare's action; the moral of the play, if moral there was, seems to have been a lesson to, or a satire for, the Lord. Did he represent some real gentleman of Warwickshire, known to the audience who heard the play performed there? It might have suggested Ludovic Greville, of Milcote, had not his violent life been closed by a tragic end in 1589. There might have been some other. But I have often thought that *this,* and not Justice Shallow, was intended as a dig at Sir Thomas Lucy. His marriage had been so long ago that few would remember the circumstances, but there might have been some amplified tradition of the action of the country-bred bridegroom of fourteen who sought his bride of twelve, as Petruchio did his, for her wealth. He might have thought it necessary betimes to assert his marital supremacy in a way which seemed only to himself to succeed.

But two *facts* are certain—that the Lady Joyce Lucy was declared, on the testimony of her son-in-law,[2] Sir Edward Aston, of Tixhall, to be *a veritable vixen,* and that when she died on February 10th, 1595/6, her laudatory epitaph reads as an apology and defence against charges known to have been made "by the envious." If it were so, the play must have been completed by 1595 at least.

It is curious that Meres does not mention it, and that there is no contemporary praise of the comedy. But there is a reference to the Induction, which shows that it was popular, in Sir Aston Cokaine's *Poems,* published 1658. Addressing his friend Mr. Clement Fisher, of Wincot, he says:—

Shakespeare your Wincot ale hath much renowned
That foxed a beggar so (by chance was founde
Sleeping) that there needed not many a word,
To make him to believe he was a Lord.
But you affirm (and in it seem most eager)
'Twill make a Lord as drunk as any beggar.
Bid Norton brew such ale as Shakespeare fancies
Did put Kit Sly into such lordly trances,
And let us meet there (for a fit of gladness)
And drink ourselves merry in sober sadness.

The play *of The Taming of the Shrew* differs entirely from Shakspeare's usual treatment of character and argument, in the basis for the providence of the *denotement.* It distinctly suggests some *sous-entendu* meaning, some satire, understood rather than to be explained.

Therefore it is hardly surprising that it is the only one of Shakspeare's plays which had what may be termed "a counterblast" written against it by a contemporary hand. I have noted my belief that John Fletcher was associated with the play as it appears in the First Folio, and his hand was therefore the most fit to point out the errors of the "morale" of the play. In his *Woman's Prize; or, the Tamer Tamed,* he shows that Petruchio had never really tamed Kate— that her temper remained the same—because he had never tamed *himself and* had remained a violent tyrant all his married life. He had worried Kate into her grave, and he seeks a new wife, Maria, who had always been meek and modest, and wins her from her father, for now *he* is rich. But the second wife, sympathetic with the wrongs of the first one, and warned by her fate, rebels at once in defence of her freedom. Bianca backs her up in her schemes; and the women of the town rise *en masse* to support her. Petruchio reproaches himself for marrying again:—

> Was I not well warned…
> And beaten to repentance in the days
> Of my first doting?

When, as a ruse, he feigns to be dead, Maria pretends to weep, not for his loss, but

> To think what this man was, to think how simple,
> How far below a man, how far from reason,
> From common understanding, and all gentry,
> While he was living here, he walked among us.

The Epilogue tells men that

> In their lives
> They should not reign as tyrants o'er their wives…
> it being aptly meant
> To teach both sexes due equality,
> And, as they stand bound, to love mutually.

Fletcher died in 1625, so this was written about the date of the First Folio. It was performed before the King and Queen on November 28th, 1633, as an old play, revised by Sir Henry Herbert, and "very well likt."

NOTES

1. Cp. *King Lear*, III. iv. 49.

2. He had married, as his second wife, Anne, only daughter of Sir Thomas Lucy. But the partial testimony of sons-in-law is not always to be accepted.

1907—Alice Meynell. "Introduction,"
from *The Complete Works of William Shakespeare*

Alice Meynell was a respected poet and essayist, known particularly for her religious poetry. Her books of essays include *The Rhythm of Life* and *The Second Person Singular*.

There are two plays within plays wherein Shakespeare commits extravagance: the "Hamlet" interlude and "The Taming of the Shrew." Needless to say, the inter-relation of the four plays is different; the inner play being a brief incident in the tragedy, and the outer play a mere incident in the comedy. But the inner play is in each case removed, set further than ordinary drama from the conditions of actual life,—the life of the audience seated at this table of double entertainment. Now, it seems evident that when he thus took two conventions, erected one proscenium within another, added fiction to fiction, lapped a play with a play, and proclaimed a second make-believe, Shakespeare took full advantage of this circumstance of art. He who knew the separation of drama from life knew the added separation of a drama within a drama from life, and gave himself a fantastic permission to exceed, and not only to exceed but to ignore, to *glisser*, to evade, to refuse us the right to look as deep as we may look into single, ordinary and primary drama. Into the comedy of "The Taming of the Shrew" we may not look, we look *upon* it. Nor do we, if we are wise, ask for leave to do more. "*N'appuyons pas.*" If we wish to pause, let it be on the slight play which is the first and the immediate drama,—that is, the "Induction," the comedy of Christopher Sly. Here is something to linger over, here are a very few things, but rich ones; here is something human, something richly alive, and responsible to Nature. Through one proscenium, through one convention, we look upon that life once removed from reality which is drama. The "Induction" is a very small play, but a play full of slightly scenic nature; "The Taming of the Shrew" itself is a long play, but a play vacant of nature. The Elizabethan dramatist took his ease in that inn of the stage, and took it the more whimsically in that stage-alcove, the inner scene whereon the Player King and the Player Queen, Petruchio and Katharine, act their parts. Fantastic, wilful, arbitrary, defiant, unchallengeable is "The Taming of the Shrew." Whatever pleasure we can take in this comedy is manifestly to be taken at a glance. To the Elizabethan audience the pleasure was not small; to us to-day it is not great. Such as it is, it must be taken with gaiety, without insistence, without exaction, and in haste. We must certainly not be either tender or stern; we must not incline to the pathos of mortal things. Not long ago an essayist found out pathos in Christopher Sly. Having looked close and sadly, and with a modern mind, to the tinker, he erected himself again, as it were, turned round, and told us it was this that he had discovered,—namely, pathos. It seems an undramatic quest and an importunate suggestion; a lapse of tact, and under the guise of more than common imagination, an utter defect of phantasy,—this fond curiosity and this soft heart of the modern writer. Yet if he must be moved; and if he must compel Shakespeare to serve him in his emotions; and if he will not keep them for his living brothers, but must spend them on the comic drama, why then at least let him have his way with Christopher Sly and the "Induction" only; let him stop there. Let him not intrude upon the inner play, and find the pathos of life in that gay interior where the light heart of drama takes sanctuary; let him not attribute pathos to Katharine, or study Petruchio, or make a symbol of the Pedant.

Nevertheless, this, or nearly this, is what he has in fact done—or rather she; for a woman, once well and honourably known for her Shakespearean studies, and in particular for a Concordance, did point the moral of Katharine and Bianca, making a story of the earlier girlhood of each, setting forth that once before had this shrew been tamed by a strong-handed boy,—Petruchio's precursor; that this generous nature of woman did but wait for love and a master; and so forth. The thing is just worthy of mention because it may stand as a perfect example of the kind of attention, the kind of sympathy, the seriousness, of which "The Taming of the Shrew" ought not to be the subject. Nay, it might be worth while to pretend to take such a commentary seriously for a while, in order to show the kind writer to what she would commit herself. Granting her, then, that the heroine of a tender story, a sentimental shrew honestly in need of love and a respectable master, is appropriately to be tamed by famine, cold, ignominy, insolence, and violence, to what end are these rigours practised in the play? To what end but to make of her a hypocrite—her husband the while happy to have her so? For a woman who feigns, under menace, to see a young maid where an old man: stands, or a sun where the moon shines, is no other. Katharine does this for fear of the repetition of outrage—more famine, more cold, more contempt, at the hands of the strong man: the strong man of her girlish dreams, quotha! See to what a pass an earnest view of this play will bring us. But no need to confound the sentimentalist further with the monstrous morality—the merry drama. No, these sweet ways of feeling are out of place in the audience at the playing of "The Taming of the Shrew"; and as the audience, so must the readers be. The comedy is drama, and only by concomitance and only insomuch as all composed language is literary, is it literature. And yet literature stands between it and life—nearer than life. Therefore neither to Katharine's past nor to her future have we to look, neither to her spirit nor to anything that can be called a woman's womanhood are we led by Shakespeare. She is not a woman of this world, she is a shrew of the inner stage. Let us look on her drama, not into it, and not through it. And in fact Shakespeare may have taken the convention of his comedy all the more easily because the Katharine played before him was not a woman. The squeaking Katharine who "boy'd her greatness" surely helped him to his irresponsibility. He had before him a romping youth, not a raging woman. In so far as this Katharine was a woman she was a grotesque and intolerable creature, to be overcome and broken by grotesque and intolerable means. This doubtless was the shrew of that society. She has vanished from ours. A shrew may scold, in our day, in the alleys of a town, but not in "Petruchio's house in the country"; not in the person of a beautiful, young, and well-taught woman. In Goldoni's comedies, of a century and a half later than Shakespeare's, there are still shrews. For a defect of dress, for a dowry, for a dispute with a mother-in-law, *rabbia* is the name of the lesser and earlier stages of a woman's anger, and *tutte le furie* of the greater and later. The men of those Venetian households, occupied with the choice of paste for the soup, and going in and out in the course of a long day on little affairs and bargainings, have for their principal preoccupation this tendency to *rabbia* and *tutte le furie* amongst the women—the ladies; let us give them the name that both Shakespeare and Goldoni give. It is to be noted that the Goldoni husband has no hope or expectation of a remedy; like Petruchio, he has no thought of appealing to the reason or the conscience of the woman; unlike Petruchio, he has no mind to quell her by force. Like Petruchio, again, he does her not so much honour as lies in a reproach; to responsible humanity belong reproof, rebuke, remonstrance, or even dislike, even forgiveness, but not to a woman married into a family of Venice. The husband in Goldoni's comedies neither hates nor pardons the furies—he does no more than evade them. If the noise will but spend itself and the daughter-in-law and the mother-in-law return to their own apartments, pacified by promises, all is well for the time. The master-mind was never more tolerant or unmoved than in this master of a tempestuous household. He makes no comment, and generalises not at all. *Il ne fait que constater.* Sufficient for the day is the storm. After a reading of Goldoni, it might be worth while—for the love of Shakespeare, but hardly for the love of this play of his—to disentangle what is Italian from what is English. We have plenty of evidence of the currency of a popular play, "Taming of a Shrew," in England in the time of Shakespeare. Other parts of Shakespeare's play are derived remotely from the Italian of Ariosto, and, moreover, the author of the comedy of which

Petruchio is hero had a small piece of Italian knowledge of which the author of the tragedy that has Hamlet for hero was ignorant,—the gender, that is, of the Italian name Baptista, or, as the English plays have it, Baptists. Its final vowel gave it a feminine sound, and it is a woman's name in "Hamlet," but a man's, as it should be, in "The Taming of the Shrew." This disparity has of course been remarked by those who have not thought the play last named to be the work of Shakespeare; but the incident is too slight to bear any such significance. Obviously, Shakespeare might forget his scholarship on the point of Italian Christian names, if, as seems to be the case, we must not suppose that he corrected it, because "Hamlet" was the later work. Whatever may be the conflict of expert opinion as to the entire authorship, on the external ground, the testimony of the play itself is surely that, although Shakespeare the manager borrowed his plot, the scenes are the writing of Shakespeare the dramatist. "The Taming of the Shrew" is authentically Shakespeare's to the reader. Circumstantial evidence apart, the Shakespearean who is in every man and woman of letters, English and American, will not hesitate to pronounce it veritably Shakespeare's, almost Shakespeare's worst (the "Induction" apart), but as certainly his as "Lear" itself; yet will be willing to accept any well-accredited origin for the dramatic story—Italian lendings, or popular current English horse-play, or any other. The note of the time is no more manifest than the tone of the man of the time. Shakespeare's tone, even when it is hardly significant enough to be called Shakespeare's style, is assuredly to be recognised like a voice. The note is Elizabethan; and the dramatists, the lyrists, the sonneteers sing it alike; but who would doubt the tone of the driest couplet in one of Shakespeare's sonnets? Hardly more can one doubt whose voice in literature it is that speaks a slight speech for Bianca or for Tranio. Tranio, by the way, is very Italian. That manner of man, who survived so buoyantly in the comedy of Molière, is evidently the Arlecchino, or Harlequin, of the primitive stage of Italy: the tricksy and shifty spirit, the trusty rogue, the wonder-worker, the man in disguise, the Mercurial one. He is many times modified, and is exquisitely altered by the loss of his customary good luck, in Shakespeare's "Romeo and Juliet." For when Mercutio falls, there falls with him the gay but inhuman figure—falls, for English literature, perhaps finally. It lives, it takes a mortal wound at Tybalt's sword-point, it bleeds and dies. The primitive Italian tradition is, moreover, touched in another place, where Lucentio speaks to the smooth Bianca of her father, behind his back, as "the old Pantaloon." Baptista is very little of a Pantaleone; except insomuch as he suffers deception, he is a person of sufficient dignity. And that he is subject to this deception is a token both of the Italian and of the Shakespearean humour. Of the two—the typical Italian primitive and the single Shakespeare—it may be suspected that it was Shakespeare who best loved a mystification; the word is not a good one in

English, but we may quote it from the French, to describe precisely the kind of jest. That Shakespeare took some Puckish pleasure in that jest we know. "The Comedy of Errors" bears witness to this, so does "Twelfth Night," so does "All's Well that Ends Well." Nay, a brief mystification comes to pass in the course of a tragedy; it hampers the urgency of some passage of passionate feeling; the moment, stretched with apprehension and dismay, is made to include a misunderstanding, such as that of Juliet and her nurse after the death of Tybalt. What Shakespeare manifestly loved was the error, but he loved it best in the form of mystification. The beguiling of Baptists by his daughter Bianca, the denying of Vincentio by his men, and the presentation of the Pedant in his place are perfect examples of that unjust pleasantry the sufferer whereof has no defence, for no wit nor wisdom nor wariness could avail him—he is entirely in the hands of a tormentor who has all the knowledge and all the advantage, and uses them for sport with delight, and without sparing, against the aged, the reverend, or the noble. It is true that the hero—son and lover—does not follow the jest to the utmost; that is left for Arlecchino, the merry rogue without a conscience. Whoever was Shakespeare's coadjutor—if he had one, and in some scenes in the part of Bianca it seems probable—Shakespeare in person took a sharp interest in this "coney-catching." To the greater number of modern spirits it is of so little interest, and so little to be loved, as to stand somewhat between them and their dramatist,—a difference involving the very substructure of humour. There is nothing for it but a reconciliation in the most humorous "Induction." And what is this but a mystification also? Although it is not perhaps the delusion of the tinker that so takes us, but his nature under all fortunes. We have Christopher Sly in common with Shakespeare, let his lord use him as he may. Careless Shakespeare, having carried his inner play to a jolly end, with a preposterous grave moral, sweeps the persons off their little sanctuary stage, and forgets to close up the outer comedy at all; so that we know no more of the tinker, nor of his restoration to the ale-house on the heath and to his quarrel with the ale-wife. Or the conclusion is lost. But, as it stands, the inner play carries off the victory, and the "Induction" is forgotten. The tinker ceases in the illusion of the lord's house. He ceases and vanishes, and the dramatist does not stay to have the laugh finally against him. No one waits to see Christopher Sly himself again, or to hear him attempt an indignant Marian Hacket with the recital of his adventure. So that the last we hear from him is the restless sigh offered by the clown to the fancy of drama and mirth:—Comes there any more of it? . . . 'Tis a very excellent piece of work, madam lady; would't were done."

A scientific inquiry into the evidence touching the authorship of the play in all its parts is not within the province of this short essay. But it does belong to the appreciation of the comedy, and it is in the competence of a student

of verse, to dwell for a moment upon the metrical testimony to the identity
of the author of "Love's Labour's Lost" and the author of "The Taming of
the Shrew." Anapæsts (I speak of course of anapæsts as one may adapt the
word to the use of English prosody) are rare in English literature before the
eighteenth century made them its lighter favourites, and peculiarly its own, the
expression of its dapper and commonplace gaiety and frolic, whether in the
age of Anne or when Mrs. Thrale was rendering epigrams from the French.
The sixteenth and seventeenth centuries meddled little with this kind of verse.
The iambic movement, the noble gait of English poetry, rarely interrupted by a
brief shifting to the springing foot of the trochee, is, in all its composure and
simplicity, the very pace of these two great centuries. Lyrical poetry goes by in
procession, from the stanza of Surrey to the ode of Dryden, to that measure.
The dramatist in this matter keeps step and time with the lyrist; the numbers
are different, the foot is the same. And Shakespeare's rhymes in the plays are,
habitually, iambic—heroic couplets. In "Love's Labour's Lost," however, occurs,
among the varied short iambic rhymed verses, the altered rhythm of a rough
and imperfect anapæstic verse:—

> "My lips are no common, though several they be."
> "Belonging to whom?" "To my fortunes and me."

And in "The Taming of the Shrew" is this, with—in various places—two or three
more couplets like it:—

> "Twas I won the wager, though you hit the white;
> And being the winner, God give you good night."

Nothing sounds stranger than such a movement in Shakespeare's verse, but
the strangeness is common—with a quite evident identity of lax and careless
rhythm—to the two plays.

    After all, the value of this comedy is in the "Induction," and the value of the
"Induction" is not only in its excellent humour, but in the external incidents—
the direct allusion made here by Shakespeare to the daily landscape, the house,
the householder of the Warwickshire village known to him. Only in "The
Merry Wives of Windsor" and in the "Second Part of Henry IV" do we come
thus near to the roads that Shakespeare walked, the heath he looked upon, the
man and woman he watched brawling. "The Taming of the Shrew," if it be of
earlier date than the two plays just named, has the first passages of this homely
external intimacy, and Sit Sly brings us and the Past acquainted. We let the
Shrew go by—the excuse for her story is that it passes; but not so the Tinker.

1915—William Winter.
"Characters of Katharine and Petruchio,"
from *Shakespeare on the Stage*

William Winter was a poet and the drama critic for the *New York Tribune*. His book *Shakespeare on the Stage* includes information on the origin and date of Shakespeare's plays as well as discussions of various performances and actors.

The major characters in Shakespeare's plays, while not obscure,—his style being perfectly distinct and simple,—are complex, in the sense that they are compounded of many and various attributes, for which reason they are profoundly interesting subjects for close study and analysis. His minor characters, among which *Katharine* and *Petruchio* seem rightly placed, are, as a rule, instantly perspicuous. The *Shrew* and her *Tamer* are specially so. Both are young (*Petruchio's* age is thirty-two), sturdy, healthful, handsome, more animal than mental, and somewhat common. *Katharine*, intrinsically, is the better-natured, the finer, and the more interesting person. Commonness and hardness, in her, have resulted from lack of proper discipline; in *Petruchio* they are constitutional. Some enthusiasts of Shakespeare have, however, discovered in this character a virtue and a charm which common-sense is unable to discern. Thus, Hazlitt wrote of him:

> "*Petruchio* is a madman in his senses; a very honest fellow, who hardly speaks a word of truth and succeeds in all his tricks and impostures. He acts his assumed character to the life, with the most fantastical extravagance, with complete presence of mind, with untired animal spirits, and without a particle of ill-humor from beginning to end."

Petruchio does, now and then, play a part, pretending to be more fractious, boisterous, belligerent, and violent than he really is, but mostly he is himself, and he does according to his nature. Clever actors can gloss the character, and make it advantageous to themselves, in representation,—as some of them have done: but *Petruchio*, as he stands in Shakespeare's play, is coarse, turbulent, contentious, domineering; tyrannical, and mercenary. His first act is to beat his servant, for not understanding an order. His first explanatory statement about himself, to his old friend *Hortensio*, is that he has inherited money, and that his object is to obtain more by marrying a woman who is wealthy:

> "If you know
> One *rich enough* to be Petruchio's wife
> (As wealth is burthen of my wedding dance)

Be she as foul as was Florentius' love,
As old as Sybil, and as *curst and shrewd*
As Socrates' Xantippe, or *a worse,*
She moves me not, or not removes, at least,
Affection's edge in me. . . .
I come to wive it wealthily in Padua;
If *wealthily,* then happily in Padua."

On being told about *Katharine,* that she is rich, young, and handsome, but an intolerable shrew, he instantly declares that he "will not sleep" till he has seen her and bespoken her in marriage, and that he "will board her, though she chide as loud as thunder." His immediate resolve is to marry the *Shrew* for her money, and then to tame her by violence,—to "kill her in her own humor." No such resolve is formed by a gentleman, and no such conduct is possible to one. The character of *Petruchio* was drawn in a period of rude manners and for the coarser audience of the time. It typifies an old and obnoxious principle of English law whereby a wife's person, estate, goods, and earnings become the property of the husband. *Petruchio,* indeed, specifically proclaims that principle, vociferating, after the wedding, "I will be *master* of what is *mine own.* She is my goods, my house, my household stuff, my field, my barn, my horse, my ox, my ass, my *anything,*" etc. His position was strictly legal; for, as old Theophilus Parsons used to say, when lecturing at the Harvard Law School, in my student days, according to the English Common Law, "The husband and the wife are one, and *the husband is that one.*" The spirit thus indicated was supreme in Shakespeare's time, and, notwithstanding the advance of civilization, it is still existent; and I believe that a considerable public sympathy with it underlies, to some extent, the enduring success of "The Taming of the Shrew."

The character of *Katharine,*—which also can be, and has been, glossed in representation and provided with various charms which are only faintly, if at all, indicated in Shakespeare's page,—is, nevertheless, more agreeable than that of *Petruchio.* She believes, as is not unnatural with elder sisters, that the elder sister should be married before the younger is, but it does not appear that she is either self-seeking or mercenary. She is, undoubtedly, a vixen. Her temper is red-hot; her conduct pugnacious and unruly. She binds and beats her sister; she threatens *Hortensio* with a noodle combed with a three-leggèd stool, and, later, when he is in his disguise as a *Music-Master* and endeavoring to teach her, she breaks his head with a lute; she strikes *Petruchio,* at their first meeting, and she openly flouts her father, in the presence of their wedding-guests. "A couple of quiet ones" in very truth—she and her "Mad-cap ruffian" of a husband! *Katharine's* meekness and her gentle speeches, after she has been married, and has been bullied into submission, are, perhaps, warrant for the belief that, all the while, she has been, inwardly, a sweet and lovely woman, but physically disordered,—though that seems an extreme theory, more fanciful than sensible. Her disposition is clearly shown to be imperious and her conduct almost ferocious. One valid ground of discontent she must be allowed, namely, her father's partiality for her younger sister: but that does not justify her in her perverse and quarrelsome proceedings. Such an unbridled young "devil" as the comedy surely implies might well deserve to be curbed in *Petruchio's* harsh way, and would not be amenable to any other discipline. This subject of feminine shrewishness, the disorder being in fact a malady, cannot be deemed agreeable, and it would be offensive on the stage, if seriously treated. Daly was judicious, therefore, when he caused the play to be acted as a farcical comedy, and cast *Katharine* to an actress as lovely in her nature as in her person, and well aware that the essence of farcical acting is absolute gravity, and sometimes the semblance of passionate ardor, in comically preposterous situations.

1926—Edmund K. Chambers.
"*The Taming of the Shrew*," from *Shakespeare: A Survey*

Edmund K. Chambers was a historian, editor, and literary scholar. He wrote a number of books on Shakespeare and English literature, including *William Shakespeare: A Study of Facts and Problems* and *The Elizabethan Stage*.

An age which flatters itself, so far at least as its formal professions of faith are concerned, that it has rounded Cape Turk, must needs make it a point of honour to take offence at the theme and temper of *The Taming of the Shrew*. The Odyssey of the fair lady of Padua is certainly conceived in a spirit which suggests the author of *The First Blast of the Trumpet against the Monstrous Regiment of Women* rather than the author of *The Subjection of Women*. And if you have wept for the hunted Diana, you can hardly refuse to shed a tear for the humiliation of Katherina, for the impetuous haggard tamed to wear the hood and jesses of the secular tyranny of man. Wedded against her will to her 'mad-brain rudesby,' bemoiled with the mire of her bridal journey, railed at from bed and board, her gown rejected for an apple-tart and her cap bemocked for a porringer, compelled at last to show herself ridiculous in the public road and obsequious at home, she, no less than her nineteenth-century sister, stands for all time as a type of the wrongs done to her much-enduring sex. You do not need her final sermon, with the symbolical placing of her head beneath the foot of the genial ruffian who has subdued her, to point the obsolete and degrading moral:

> Such duty as the subject owes the prince,
> Even such a woman oweth to her husband.

It is perhaps the duty of the critic to explain how all this can be true, as no doubt it is true, beyond all possibility of cavil, and how the play can still remain, as it clearly does remain, a well of hearty and not unwholesome laughter. It is not, I think, sufficient to say that the paradox affords an example of Shakespeare's immortal humour triumphant in the handling of an unsympathetic plot for which Shakespeare is not himself responsible. The attempt to brand as non-Shakespearean everything, which in style or ethics fails to come up to a preconceived and wholly sentimental ideal of the national dramatist of England, is one which is responsible for the introduction of a good deal of confusion into English literary criticism. It is plain enough that *The Taming of the Shrew* is of the nature of a revision of an earlier play, which was published in 1594, probably about the time at which the revision was done, under the title of *The Taming of a Shrew*; and further that, while the revised play only occasionally reproduces the actual wording of the original, it throughout follows it very closely in its structure and the ordering of its incidents. It is therefore the author of *The Taming of a Shrew* rather than the author of *The Taming of the Shrew* who is primarily responsible for fixing those relations between Petruchio and Katherina to which exception is taken. But it is by no means so clear that Shakespeare is thereby cleared even of primary responsibility. It is, in fact, one of the most difficult outstanding problems of Shakespearean scholarship to determine on the one hand how much Shakespeare wrote of *The Taming of the Shrew*, and on the other how little, if any, he wrote of *The Taming of a Shrew*. It is closely cognate to that other problem of *Henry the Sixth*. The rest of the earlier play may be neglected, but the Ferando and Kate scenes in it read like a first draft of the Petruchio and Katherina scenes of its successor, just in the same way in which the Jack Cade scenes in *The Contention of York and Lancaster* read like a first draft of the similar scenes in *Henry the Sixth*. Both *The Taming of a Shrew* and *The Contention of York and Lancaster* appear to have originally belonged to a company of actors passing under the protection of the Earl of Pembroke; and one is almost forced to the alternative, that either Lord Pembroke's men had the advantage of a forgotten writer who possessed considerable comic power and to whom Shakespeare was content to owe no little debt, or that Shakespeare himself began his dramatic career by contributing to plays for these men, and that, when he made use of the Ferando and Kate and the Jack Cade scenes at a later date, he was doing no more than reclaim his own. I do not pretend to decide between these hypotheses. Nor, for my present purpose, is it necessary to do so. For if Shakespeare did not conceive the relations of the shrew and her tamer, he at least adopted them, and bent all the resources of his invention to give them laughable expression; and thereby I fear he must be held to have assumed responsibility, and laid himself open to any ethical criticism which they may entail.

It is a further question, how far the ethical critic has really a *locus standi*. There is more than one way of meeting him. Obviously, one may appeal to the historic sense, and say that it is absurd to bring Shakespeare to the bar of a sentiment which has in the main been evolved since his day. This is, no doubt, true, so far as it goes. The doctrine of the equality of the sexes, as an ethical principle, would not have meant very much to an Elizabethan. And the saying that Shakespeare 'was not of an age, but for all time' is about as true as many another mortuary phrase. Like every other vital writer, he is instinct with the spirit of his age, and vital largely because he is instinct with it; and, without the historic sense, his ethical standpoint is in many respects incomprehensible to those who come after him. His attitude towards Shylock in *The Merchant of Venice* is, of course, a crucial instance. But I do not know that the appreciation of this takes one very far, critically, in understanding *The Taming of the Shrew*. For, as a matter of fact, *The Merchant of Venice* and *The Taming of the Shrew*, although Heminges and Condell classed them both as comedies, belong to wholly different dramatic types. The moral ideas of *The Merchant of Venice* are essential to its structure. It is a drama of emotions, a tragicomedy; and it is precisely out of its moral ideas, out of the conflict of Love and Hate which it sets forth, that its emotions arise. *The Taming of the Shrew*, on the other hand, is not a drama of the emotions at all. It is a comedy, or more strictly a farce, in the true sense. It approaches its theme, the eternal theme of the duel of sex, neither from the ethical standpoint of the Elizabethan pulpiter nor from that of the Pioneer Club. It does not approach it from an ethical standpoint at all, but merely from that of humorous and dispassionate observation, which is at least one of the permitted attitudes of Thalia towards all the facts of human life. The humour of strange bedfellows; that is its burden. Petruchio of Verona is as peremptory as Katherina Minola is proud-minded. Let us see how these two curst characters hit it off in the rough-and-tumble of matrimony. The clash of temperaments and the inevitable domination in the long run of the stronger furnish forth a situation and a process, which surely bear regarding in their laughable aspect without any evocation of ethical theories as to the heaven-determined position of the husband in the domestic hierarchy. Art is entitled to make such abstractions from the totality of things. That the point is not a sociological one is shown by the fact that it would be in no way lost if the positions were inverted, and the dominating will given to the wife instead of the husband; as indeed was done by John Fletcher, whose *The Tamer Tamed* presents Petruchio *en secondes noces*, the butt of a verier shrew than either Katherina or himself. Such an inversion would naturally be unthinkable if an ethical judgment, feminist or anti-feminist, were involved. Perhaps Shakespeare has left some handle to the misunderstanding in giving prominence to Katherina's sermon, as if it were the key-note of the whole play and expressed the dramatist's moral summing-up of the conflict he has depicted. Katherina speaks it; but she is Petruchio's mouthpiece, not Shakespeare's; and she should recite her lesson on the boards with a wry face which shall make it clear that it is but the last triumph of Petruchio's famous medicine for a curst wife. Petruchio meanwhile must applaud and clink his glass, in appreciative glee at his own astonishing masterfulness.

It must be admitted that the treatment of the central theme in *The Taming of the Shrew* has a brutality about it. Brutality, especially in sexual matters, is quite in the tradition of farce, and one of the notes which serve to differentiate it from other sub-varieties of comedy. For farce, properly regarded, is not a thing disparate from comedy, but rather a mode of it, comedy as it appeals to intellects which are far from being tickle of the sere and need a compelling stimulus to clap them into horse-laughter. Of course it is necessary to distinguish. The Early Victorian writers for the stage have led us to look upon farce as a type of drama whose humour is wholly external, due to absurdities of situation arising by logical development from some impossibility assumed as a starting-point. We have forgotten to expect from it that outlook upon real life which is very properly recognized as suitable to true comedy. *The Comedy of Errors*, in which the complete facial identity of the two pairs of brothers affords the initial impossibility, is perhaps the only play of Shakespeare's that really answers to the formula of farce so defined. Yet it would be difficult to class either *The Taming of the Shrew* or *The Merry Wives of Windsor*, to say nothing of the underplots in many of the tragicomedies, as anything but farces. And if one goes back a little further than the Early Victorian order of ideas, one finds that the farce of complicated situation has neither the sole nor the original right to claim the title. Farce, as it may be traced from the very dawn of the history of drama, was primarily not a drama of incident and intrigue, but a drama of the outlook upon life, just as much as comedy itself. You may call it *bourgeois* comedy, or comedy of the market-place, if you will. It differs from typical comedy in two ways; firstly, not by the absence of outlook upon life, but by an outlook upon life definitely brutal or cynical, instead of sympathetic or at most ironical; and, secondly, in that it proceeds at a greater distance from the normal facts of life, of which it presents an extravagant or burlesque perversion, instead of merely a humorous or whimsical arrangement. It is also more universal. Fine comedy has emerged but here and there in the literary history of the civilized peoples of Europe. It demands a special organization of humanity, a quick-witted urban folk, trained in the arena of the *salon* to applaud the give-and-take of dialogue and to discern nice shades in the surface of things. Meredith has analysed it:

> There are plain reasons why the Comic poet is not a frequent apparition; and why the great Comic poet remains without a fellow. A society of cultivated men and women is required, wherein ideas are current and the perceptions quick, that he may be supplied with matter and an audience. The semi-barbarism of merely giddy communities, and feverish emotional periods, repel him; and also a state of marked social inequality of the sexes; nor can he whose business is to address the mind be understood where there is not a moderate degree of intellectual activity.

But the broad leer of farce is everywhere, and scholars and courtiers have never disdained to be clapped from time to time on the back with the same jests that have tickled the ribs of boors and citizens. Farce, crude and obscene, was the stock-in-trade of the innumerable army of mimes who drove tragedy and comedy from stage after stage of the Roman Empire. The politer modes of literature were whelmed in the night of the dark ages; but farce, one may shrewdly suspect, survived, to burst forth in extraordinary exuberance during the fourteenth century, together with that *fabliau* to which, in actual subject-matter as well as in spirit, it is so closely related. In the earlier English drama of the sixteenth century, farce comes only second to didactic allegory in popularity. And so the tradition is handed on to the immediate predecessors of Shakespeare himself. Throughout its history the themes of farce have not varied essentially. Certain topics have proved inexhaustible; the tricks of ill-reputed trades, such as that of the miller; the warfare of the townsman and the clerk; the greed and hypocrisy of priests and friars; the ingenious wiles of miching rogues, a Pathelin, an Autolycus. And above all it has made its merriment of the duel of sex, in that marital form in which the common consent of all peoples has agreed to find the duel of sex most amusing. The beaten wife and the hen-pecked husband, the cuckold and the shrew, are among the oldest of its conventions; and in painting the battles and the reconciliation of Petruchio and Katherina, Shakespeare was merely, one may be sure, reproducing for the thousandth time a situation at which many a mediaeval green or castle hall, no less than many a theatre of Antioch or Byzantium, had often laughed its fill.

1951—Harold C. Goddard. *"The Taming of the Shrew,"* from *The Meaning of Shakespeare*

Harold C. Goddard (1878-1950) was head of the English Department at Swarthmore College. One of the most important twentieth-century books on Shakespeare is his *The Meaning of Shakespeare*, published after his death.

I

Richard III proves that *double-entendre* was a passion of the youthful Shakespeare, and both *The Two Gentlemen of Verona* and *Love's Labour's Lost* illustrate the fact that he was fond of under- and overmeanings he could not have expected his audience as a whole to get. But it is *The Taming of the Shrew* that is possibly the most striking example among his early works of his love of so contriving a play that it should mean, to those who might choose to take it so, the precise opposite of what he knew it would mean to the multitude. For surely the most psychologically sound as well as the most delightful way of taking *The Taming of the Shrew* is the topsy-turvy one. Kate, in that case, is no shrew at all except in the most superficial sense. Bianca, on the other hand, is just what her sister is supposed to be. And the play ends with the prospect that Kate is going to be more nearly the tamer than the tamed, Petruchio more nearly the tamed than the tamer, though his wife naturally will keep the true situation under cover. So taken, the play is an early version of *What Every Woman Knows*—what every woman knows being, of course, that the woman can lord it over the man so long as she allows him to think he is lording it over her. This interpretation has the advantage of bringing the play into line with all the other Comedies in which Shakespeare gives a distinct edge to his heroine. Otherwise it is an unaccountable exception and regresses to the wholly un-Shakespearean doctrine of male superiority, a view which there is not the slightest evidence elsewhere Shakespeare ever held.

II

We must never for a moment allow ourselves to forget that *The Taming of the Shrew* is a play within a play, an interlude put on by a company of filling players at the house of a great lord for the gulling of Christopher Sly, the drunken tinker, and thereby for the double entertainment of the audience. For the sake of throwing the picture into strong relief against the frame—as in a different sense in the case of *The Murder of Gonzago* in *Hamlet*—the play within the play is given a simplification and exaggeration that bring its main plot to the edge of farce, while its minor plot, the story of Bianca's wooers, goes quite over that edge. But, even allowing for this, the psychology of the Katharine–Petruchio plot is remarkably realistic. It is even "modern" in its psychoanalytical implications. It is based on the familiar situation of the favorite child. Baptista is a family tyrant and Bianca is his favorite daughter. She has to the casual eye all the outer marks of modesty and sweetness, but to a discerning one all the inner marks of a spoiled pet, remade, if not originally made, in her father's image. One line is enough to give us her measure. When in the wager scene at the end her husband tells her that her failure to come at his entreaty has cost him a hundred crowns,

The more fool you for laying on my duty,

she blurts out. What a light that casts back over her previous "sweetness" before she has caught her man! The rest of her role amply supports this interpretation, as do the hundreds of Biancas—who are not as white as they are painted—in real life.

Apart from the irony and the effective contrast so obtained, there is everything to indicate that Kate's shrewishness is superficial, not ingrained or congenital. It is the inevitable result of her father's gross partiality toward her sister and neglect of herself, plus the repercussions that his attitude has produced on Bianca and almost everyone else in the region. Kate has heard herself blamed, and her sister praised at her expense, to a point where even a worm would turn. And Kate is no worm. If her sister is a spoiled child, Kate is a cross child who is starved for love. She craves it as a man in a desert craves water, without understanding, as he does, what is the matter. And though we have to allow for the obvious exaggeration of farce in his extreme antics, Petruchio's procedure at bottom shows insight, understanding, and even love. Those actors who equip him with a whip miss Shakespeare's man entirely. In principle, if not in the rougher details, he employs just the right method in the circumstances, and the end amply justifies his means.

It is obvious that his boast at the outset of purely mercenary motives for marrying is partly just big talk—at any rate the dowry soon becomes quite subsidiary to Kate herself and the game of taming her. In retrospect it seems to have been something like love at first sight on both sides, though not recognized as such at the time. Whatever we think of Petruchio's pranks in the scenes where farce and comedy get mixed, there is no quarreling with his instinctive sense of how in general Kate ought to be handled. When a small child is irritable and cross, the thing to do is not to reason, still less to pity or pamper, or even to be just kind and understanding in the ordinary sense. The thing to do is to take the child captive. A vigorous body and will, combined with good humor and a love that is not expressed in words but that makes itself felt by a sort of magnetic communication, will sweep the child off his feet, carry him away, and transform him almost miraculously back into his natural self. Anyone who does not know this knows mighty little about children. This is precisely what Petruchio does to Kate (and what Shakespeare does to his audience in this play). She is dying for affection. He keeps calling her his sweet and lovely Kate. What if he is ironical to begin with! The words just of themselves are manna to her soul, and her intuition tells her that, whether he knows it or not, he really means them. And indeed Kate is lovely and sweet by nature. (She is worth a bale of Biancas.) What girl would not like to be told, as Petruchio tells her; that she sits as sweetly as a nightingale and has a countenance like morning roses washed with dew? She knows by a perfectly sound instinct that he could never have thought up such lovely similes to be sarcastic with if he considered her nothing but a shrew. There is a poet within him that her beauty has elicited. What wonder that she weeps when the poet fails to appear for the wedding! It is not just humiliation. It is disappointed love.

And Kate is intelligent too. She is a shrewd "shrew." You can put your finger on the very moment when it dawns on her that if she will just fall in with her husband's absurdest whim, accept his maddest perversion of the truth as truth, she can take the wind completely out of his sails, deprive his weapon of its power, even turn it against him—tame him in his own humor. Not that she really wants to tame him, for she loves him dearly, as the delightful little scene in the street so amply proves, where he begs a kiss, begs, be it noted, not demands. She is shy for fear they may be overseen, but finally relents and consents.

> *Kath.*: Husband, let's follow, to see the end of this ado.
> *Pet.*: First kiss me, Kate, and we will.
> *Kath.*: What! in the midst of the street?
> *Pet.*: What! art thou ashamed of me?
> *Kath.*: No, sir, God forbid; but ashamed to kiss.
> *Pet.*: Why, then let's home again. Come, sirrah, let's away.
> *Kath.*: Nay, I will give thee a kiss; now pray thee, love, stay.
> *Pet.*: Is not this well? Come, my sweet Kate.
> Better once than never, for never too late.

How this little scene is to be fitted into the traditional interpretation of the play it is hard to see.

Everything leads up to Kate's long lecture at the end on the duty of wives to their lords. What fun she has reading it to those two other women who do not know what every woman knows! How intolerable it would be if she and Shakespeare really meant it (as if Shakespeare could ever have meant it!), though there is a deeper sense in which they both do mean it, a sense that ties the speech to Biron's on the complementary natures of man and woman. The self-styled advanced thinkers of our day, who have been for obliterating all distinctions between the sexes and leveling them to a dead equality, are just lacking enough in humor to think Kate's speech the most retrograde nonsense, as indeed it would be if it were the utterance of a cowering slave.

Though actresses in the past have edged in the direction of this interpretation of Kate, a triumph still remains for one who will go the whole distance and find in her a clear first draft and frank anticipation of Beatrice. Petruchio, too, must be made fine and bold, not just rough and bold, or crude and bold. And as for Bianca, you can pick up a dozen of her in the first high school you happen on, any one of whom could act her to perfection by just being herself.

The Taming of the Shrew, by slighting certain things like the tamer's begging for a kiss, is undeniably susceptible of the traditional rowdy interpretation whereby Petruchio becomes a caveman and Kate a termagant. It has been so acted down the years and there is little doubt that it was so acted in Shakespeare's time. Poets are under no obligation to spoil the popular success of their plays by revealing their secrets, even to stage directors. But unless *The Taming of the Shrew* is frankly taken as sheer farce, the primitive interpretation of it is utterly offensive to our sensibilities, saved only by its wit from being as brutal a spectacle as a bear-baiting. Indeed, the analogy that dominated the Elizabethan mind throughout must have been that of the taming of the female hawk. If, then, without distortion, the text is susceptible of another construction that both satisfies us better and at the same time deepens the psychological complexity and truth of the main characters, what, pray, is the authority of tradition that shall prevent our adopting it? If I find a key that fits a treasure chest and am about to open it, but am suddenly confronted with indisputable evidence that it is a key to an entirely different chest several hundred years old, I may defer to the authenticity of the historical documents that have proved the fact, but what a fool I would be not to go ahead in spite of them and open the chest! A work of art exists for what it says to us, not for what it said to the people of its "own" day, nor even necessarily for what it said, consciously, to its author. A work of art is an autonomous entity. So long as we do no violence to it, we may fit it to our own experience in any way we wish.

III

But, as it happens, there is something quite specific in this particular case to indicate that the author is giving us not just general but quite express leave to take his play in a subterranean sense. This due, if I may call it that, is found in the "Induction."

In a mathematical proportion, if three of the terms are known, the fourth unknown one (x) can easily be determined. Thus, if $(a/b) = (c/x)$, it follows that $x = (bc/a)$. The poet often proceeds from the known to the unknown by a similar procedure, but unlike the mathematician he does not meticulously put the x on one side and carefully label the other side of the equation "answer." He supplies the data rather and leaves it to the reader to figure out or not, as he chooses, what follows from them. This was plainly the method Shakespeare used in relating the story of Christopher Sly to the story of Petruchio.

It is generally agreed that the Induction to *The Taming of the Shrew* is one of the most masterly bits of writing to be found anywhere in Shakespeare's earlier works. Much as the authorship of the play has been debated, no one, so far as I recall, has ever questioned the authorship of the Induction. Shakespeare evidently bestowed on it a care that indicates the importance it had in his eyes. In *The Taming of a Shrew* (whose relation to *The Taming of the Shrew* has recently been widely discussed) the purpose of the Induction with reference to the play itself is made perfectly clear by a return to Sly at the end after the play within the play is over. Christopher Sly, the drunken tinker, has a wife who is a shrew. In the play that is acted before him he watches the successful subjugation of another woman to the will of her husband, and at the end of the performance we see him starting off for home to try out on his own wife the knowledge he has just acquired. Whatever part, if any, Shakespeare had in the earlier play, why did he spoil a good point in the later one by not completing its framework, by failing to return to Sly at the end of the Petruchio play? All sorts of explanations for the artistic lapse have been conjured up, the most popular being that the last leaf of the manuscript, in which he did so return, was somehow lost or that the scene was left to the improvisation of the actor; and so was never reduced to writing. But surely the editors of the *Folio* would have been aware of this and could have supplied at least a stage direction to clear things up!

I wonder if the explanation of the enigma is not a simpler and more characteristic one: that Shakespeare saw his chance for a slyer and profounder relation between the Induction and the play than in the earlier version of the story.

In the Induction to *The Taming of the Shrew*, Christopher Sly the tinker, drunk with ale, is persuaded that he is a great lord who has been the victim of an unfortunate lunacy. Petruchio, in the play which Sly witnesses (when he is not asleep), is likewise persuaded that he is a great lord—over his wife. Sly is obviously in for a rude awakening when he discovers that he is nothing but a tinker after all. Now Petruchio is a bit intoxicated himself—who can deny it?— whether with pride, love, or avarice, or some mixture of the three. Is it possible that he too is in for an awakening? Or, if Kate does not let it come to that, that *we* at least are supposed to see that he is not as great a lord over his wife as he imagined? The Induction and the play, taken together, do not allow us to evade these questions. Can anyone be so naïve as to fancy that Shakespeare did not contrive his Induction for the express purpose of forcing them on us? Either the cases of Sly and Petruchio are alike or they are diametrically opposite. Can there be much doubt which was intended by a poet who is so given to pointing out analogies between lovers and drunkards, between lovers and lunatics? Here surely is reason enough for Shakespeare not to show us Sly at the end when he no longer thinks himself a lord. It would be altogether too much like explaining the joke, like solving the equation and labeling the result ANSWER. Shakespeare wants us to find things for ourselves. And in this case in particular: why explain what is as dear, when you see it, as was Poe's *Purloined Letter*, which was skilfully concealed precisely because it was in such plain sight all the time?

There are two little touches in the first twenty-five lines of the Induction that seem to clinch this finally, if it needs any clinching. The Lord and his huntsmen come in from hunting. They are talking of the hounds and their performances:

> *Lord*: Saw'st thou act, boy, how Silver made it good
> At the hedge-corner, in the coldest fault?
> I would not lose the dog for twenty pound.
> *First Hunt.*: Why, Bellman is as good as he, my lord;
> He cried upon it at the merest loss,
> And twice today pick'd out the dullest scent:
> Trust me, I take him for the better dog.

Why, in what looks like a purely atmospheric passage, this double emphasis on the power to pick up a dull or cold scent? Why if not as a hint to spectators and readers to keep alert for something they might easily miss?

—————

1960—Bertrand Evans. "*The Taming of the Shrew,*" from *Shakespeare's Comedies*

Bertrand Evans taught at the University of California, Berkeley. His books include *Shakespeare's Tragic Practice* and *Gothic Drama from Walpole to Shelley*.

Last of the four widely divergent experiments, *The Taming of the Shrew* stands apart, in its own ways, as does each of the others. When it is examined from the point of view of the disposition and uses of awareness, its most conspicuous feature looms up at once: it is the profound contrast in the dramatic management of the two plots. One of these is developed on the lines of later romantic comedies, the other in a way that Shakespeare never used again.

Counting those of the Induction, *The Taming of the Shrew* has fourteen scenes, in nine of which our view of the situation is superior to that of some participants. Seven of the sixteen named persons (again including the Induction) stand occasionally in a condition of exploitable unawareness. Action and effects alike depend mainly upon the existence of multiple secrets, upon multiple discrepancies in awareness, and upon a remarkable throng of practisers, practices, and practisees. The stair-step structure of awarenesses, reared in several scenes, is once composed of three levels, once of five—with Baptista Minola, like Thurio of *The Two Gentlemen of Verona*—always at the bottom and Tranio–Lucentio at the top. Multiple blind spots afflict some persons occasionally, some frequently, some continuously: Baptista is wrong about everything that most concerns him—that 'Lucentio' is Tranio; that 'Cambio' is Lucentio; that 'Licio' is Hortensio; that both 'Tutors' are wooers; that 'Vincentio' is a Pedant; that Vincentio is in very fact Vincentio.

But it is most noteworthy that excepting one scene of the Induction all of the scenes that exploit discrepancies in awareness are in the sub-plot, none in the main plot of the taming of Kate. Though Petruchio is incidentally ignorant (I. ii), along with Gremio, Grumio, and Hortensio, of the right identities of Lucentio and Tranio, his unawareness is relevant only to the minor plot. So also, at the moment before the denouement begins (V. i), both Kate and Petruchio, returning to Padua to marvel at the mad confusion over the supposed Vincentio and the right Vincentio, the supposed Lucentio and the right Lucentio, are as much in the dark as Baptista and others who are directly concerned—but here, too, their unawareness is unrelated to the shrew story. Indeed, their separation from the frantic Padua situation is carefully marked: 'Prithee Kate, let's follow, to see the end of this ado.' Petruchio and Kate, like ourselves, are spectators, though with less than our advantage. *The Taming of the Shrew*, then, is unique among Shakespeare's comedies in that it has two distinct plots, one relying mainly on discrepant awarenesses, the other using them not at all. Moreover, the shrew plot is the only plot ever developed by Shakespeare without use of gaps between awarenesses, with the result that, in their dramatic character, its scenes are remote from the great body of his works. However successful was the comic action of the taming of Kate on Shakespeare's own stage, the dramatist never tried that dramatic way again.

But in this one trial he proceeded without compromise to unfold a comic plot in which no participant stands in a position of unawareness, none has a fuller view of the situation than another, and we ourselves occupy a vantage-point equal to that of the actors. The principal persons have no illusions about each other. Shakespeare appears to have taken pains not only to have each of the mad pair recognize the other's character, but to make it unmistakable to us that each does so. It is significant that none of the persons centrally involved—Hortensio, Gremio, Baptista—attempts to deceive Petruchio about Katherina, even though Hortensio and Gremio, as suitors of Bianca, would gain much by fooling him into marrying the older sister. Rather, far from practising on him, suitors and father alike seem determined that Petruchio shall know the worst. 'Katherine the curst', Hortensio begins, and goes on:

> Her only fault, and that is faults enough
> Is that she is intolerable curst
> And shrewd and froward, so beyond all measure
> That, were my state far worser than it is,
> I would not wed her for a mine of gold. (I. ii. 88–96.)

'Thou know'st not gold's effect', replies Petruchio, and assures Hortensio that he 'will board her, though she chide as loud / As thunder when the clouds in autumn crack'. Gremio, like Hortensio, and without his cause of friendship, goes out of his way in honesty, demanding at once on learning that Petruchio seeks Kate for wife, 'Hortensio, have you told him all her faults?' So also Baptista, long-suffering father with even more interest in getting Kate married off than have Bianca's suitors: 'But for my daughter Katherine, this I know, / She is not for your turn, the more my grief.' And more pointedly still:

> *Pet.* Pray, have you not a daughter
> Call'd Katherina, fair and virtuous?
>   *Bap.* I have a daughter, sir, call'd Katherina. (II. i. 41–43.)

Surely in the world of Shakespearian comedy, where the normal condition is to delight in deception, where almost everyone finds or makes occasion to practise on others, the villains for wicked purposes, the pranksters for the prank's sake, the heroines for the love of mockery and ultimate matrimony—in such a world the excessive concern of Hortensio, Gremio, and Baptista to see that Petruchio is not deceived about Kate is unique—is, in fact, curiously un-Shakespearian. And the dramatist's concern to have us understand that Petruchio knows all is curiously insistent also: he does not bring Katherina and Petruchio face to face until both we and Petruchio have had—besides the several verbal characterizations of Kate's shrewishness—an actual demonstration: *Re-enter* HORTENSIO *with his head broke.*

Nor is Kate allowed to mistake the nature of Petruchio. If her awareness of his quality lags briefly behind ours at first—since we hear much of him and see him in action before Kate even knows that he exists—yet she perceives clearly what he is in their very first encounter, when he returns insult for insult, roar for roar, and threatens blow for blow. Neither is there anything deceptive in the terms of Petruchio's proposal of marriage:

> For I am he am born to tame you, Kate,
> And bring you from a wild Kate to a Kate
> Conformable as other household Kates. (Ibid. 278–80.)

In this same openness, with equal vision shared by participants and ourselves, the entire action of the shrew plot is conducted.

In sharpest contrast is the management of the minor plot, which is all composed of false supposes and unperceived realities. Multiple exploitable gaps between participant and participant and between participants and ourselves are opened at once. In the latter half of I. ii the familiar stair-stepped structure of awarenesses rises with unusual abruptness—to endure through four acts as the machinery of action and source of comic effect. Its creation results from practices perpetrated by four principal practisers—each of whom is simultaneously the victim of others' practices; the four are Lucentio, Tranio, Hortensio, and Gremio. We are first advised of Lucentio's and Tranio's double-edged device; thus Lucentio:

> Thou shalt be master, Tranio, in my stead,
> Keep house and port and servants, as I should.
> I will some other be, some Florentine,
> Some Neapolitan, or meaner man of Pisa.
> 'Tis hatch'd and shall be so. (I. i. 207–10.)

Lucentio's practice is designed to deceive Baptista and gain admittance for himself to Bianca. Hortensio's practice, to the same end, briefly involves Petruchio also as a deceiver:

> Now shall my friend Petruchio do me grace,
> And offer me disguis'd in sober robes
> To old Baptista as a schoolmaster
> Well seen in music, to instruct Bianca;
> That so I may, by this device, at least
> Have leave and leisure to make love to her
> And unsuspected court her by herself. (I. ii. 131–7.)

The tangle of deceivers and deceived is complicated further when Gremio employs Lucentio, disguised as 'Cambio', to woo for him:

Hark you, sir; I'll have them very fairly bound,—
All books of love, see that at any hand;
And see you read no other lectures to her.
You understand me? (Ibid. 146–9.)

Gremio here holds the lowest rung on the ladder, knowing neither of his rival Hortensio's scheme to woo Bianca in person as her tutor nor of his own tutor's true identity and purpose. Hortensio, holding the edge over Gremio as proprietor of his own practice, is at the same time deceived by both Gremio and Lucentio. Lucentio, holding the highest place as deceiver of both Gremio and Hortensio, is himself ignorant of Hortensio's device. The entrance of Tranio, posing as Lucentio, puts the peak to the structure, above the levels of Gremio and Hortensio, who, ignorant that 'Cambio' is in fact Lucentio, are ignorant also that 'Lucentio' is in fact Tranio.

Such is the composition of the structure that the dramatist has established in our minds by the end of Act I. The action thereafter, through all scenes of the minor plot until the denouement, has meaning and produces effect only by reference to this structure. The structure remains essentially unchanged until the last, when it is further complicated by the arrival of the 'supposed' and the 'right' Vincentios. It is the most elaborate framework for foolery that Shakespeare had yet devised.

So far as the minor plot is concerned, then, the scenes that lie between the end of the first act and the denouement are given over to exploitation of the discrepant awarenesses of six persons. It is noteworthy that, whereas often Shakespeare's exploitation of such discrepancies makes a dazzling exhibition, with bold flashes of irony struck in line after line, throughout this action the exploitation is relatively subdued. The persons go about their business: Hortensio wooing Bianca as 'Licio', Lucentio wooing her as 'Cambio', and betraying his employer Gremio the while, Baptista promising Bianca to Tranio, supposing him to be Lucentio, unaware that all the while she is being wooed by false tutors under his own auspices. Merely the image in our minds of the true situation is allowed to suffice as interpreter of the action, without special comment in the lines themselves. Most often Shakespeare exploits discrepant awarenesses by centring attention on the unaware persons, giving them speeches which—sometimes by their remoteness from the truth that we perceive, sometimes by their accidental closeness to it—illuminate the chasm between the speakers' understanding and ours. But here the unawareness of Baptista, for example, is not the subject of exploitation when he is confronted in quick succession with several impostors: Petruchio presents 'Licio' as tutor when in fact he is Hortensio and a suitor; Gremio presents 'Cambio' as tutor when in fact he is Lucentio and a suitor, deceiving Gremio, Hortensio, and Baptista; Tranio presents himself as 'Lucentio', a suitor and a gentleman, when in fact he is Tranio, a servant, and no suitor. Baptista's unawareness is exploited only in that our view of the scene is controlled by the image of the true situation which was set in our minds earlier. In contrast, in Shakespeare's mature usage, when Malvolio in *Twelfth Night*, victim of the practices of Maria and Toby, is positive that Olivia loves him, it is he, in all his richly exploitable obliviousness, who is central, and the comments of bystanders as well as his own remarks serve to exploit his condition.

But in *The Taming of the Shrew*, with Shakespeare still feeling his way, the centre of attention is more often the deceiver than the deceived—or, more precisely, since most of the principal persons are both deceivers and deceived, attention is directed to them more often as deceivers than as deceived. During the bidding for Bianca that ends Act II, for example, while Tranio poses as 'Lucentio' and, in the name of the latter's father, Vincentio, outbids Gremio, the centre of attention is Tranio, as deceiver, rather than either Baptista or Gremio, each of whom is doubly deceived. So, too, in the very heart of the minor plot—the scene of the wooing of Bianca by Lucentio as 'Cambio' and Hortensio as 'Licio' (III. i)—it is as deceivers rather than deceived that the two suitors take turns as centre of attention; thus, while Lucentio 'construes' a Latin passage for Bianca and in the process reveals his identity to her, it is his practice rather than Hortensio's unawareness that holds the attention, and while Hortensio instructs Bianca in 'gamut in a briefer sort, / More pleasant, pithy, and effectual / Than hath been taught by any of my trade', and thus reveals his identity to her, it is his practice rather than Lucentio's unawareness that is central. Moreover, though each suitor continues ignorant of the other's identity, each immediately suspects the intentions of his rival tutor; thus Lucentio, aside:

> And watch withal; for, but I be deceiv'd,
> Our fine musician groweth amorous. (III. i. 62–63.)

And thus Hortensio:

> But I have cause to pry into this pedant.
> Methinks he looks as though he were in love. (Ibid. 87–88.)

Here, however, although Hortensio's ignorance of his rival's identity is little exploited for comic effect, it is the basis for action, since it motivates Hortensio's withdrawal from the race to win Bianca; and since Tranio, acting as 'Lucentio', has already outbidden Gremio, it is made apparent at this point that Lucentio must emerge victor. Thus says Tranio, summing up the situation:

We'll over-reach the greybeard, Gremio,
The narrow, prying father, Minola,
The quaint musician, amorous Licio,
All for my master's sake, Lucentio. (III. ii. 147–50)

It is not until Act IV that the exploitable unawareness of Baptista and other uninformed persons takes a central place. Tranio, needing an old man to pose as Vincentio and give 'assurances' to Baptista, deceives the newly arrived Pedant into supposing his life is in danger in Padua and prevails upon him to play the part. Baptista, from the beginning held to the bottom of the structure of awarenesses, is once more victimized, and his remarks on meeting 'supposed' Vincentio form a passage remarkably ribbed and studded—indeed, girt around—with the scraps of ignorance:

Your plainness and your shortness please me well.
Right true it is, your son Lucentio here
Doth love my daughter and she loveth him,
Or both dissemble deeply their affections;
And therefore, if you say no more than this,
That like a father you will deal with him
And pass my daughter a sufficient dower,
The match is made, and all is done.
Your son shall have my daughter with consent. (IV. iv. 39–47.)

Here Baptista addresses a false Vincentio about a false Lucentio and a non-existent love match, while the true Lucentio, whose love match is real, looks on as 'Cambio'. So, too, in his next speech every line throws into relief some aspect of Baptista's darkness:

Cambio, hie you home,
And bid Bianca make her ready straight;
And, if you will, tell what hath happened:
Lucentio's father is arriv'd in Padua,
And how she's like to be Lucentio's wife. (Ibid. 62–66.)

In the comedies it is always darkest just before the denouement. In the confusion at the opening of Act V, when Vincentio arrives at Lucentio's house, all except Lucentio and Tranio are deep-sunk in the condition of unawareness. Even Petruchio and Katherina are briefly affected, having encountered the true Vincentio on the road and brought him with them to Padua, knowing him to be Vincentio but supposing his son to be not the true Lucentio but the masquerading Tranio. As was earlier stated, however, the error is irrelevant to their own affairs; whether Tranio is Lucentio or Lucentio 'Cambio' interests them only as spectators. But for the others, their heads filled with half-truths or total falsities, all their illusions are relevant, exploitable, and exploited. First to bare his ignorance is Gremio, who, just after we have seen Lucentio and Bianca flee to the church to be married, arrives at Lucentio's house still expecting that his rival will fail to provide the 'assurances' demanded by Baptista and that therefore Bianca will be his by default. 'I marvel Cambio comes not all this while', he remarks from his pit of darkness, ignorant that 'Cambio' is a fiction, that Tranio is not Lucentio, that the false 'Lucentio' is even now inside the house giving assurances to Baptista—these being confirmed by a Pedant as 'Vincentio'—and finally that the true Lucentio, at this instant, is marrying Bianca. Next to have his ignorance exploited is the Pedant, who peers from the window at Vincentio's knock, ignorant that this is that very Vincentio whom he is impersonating, that the 'Lucentio' for whom he had agreed to provide assurances is really the servant Tranio, that the true Lucentio is now marrying Bianca, and, finally, that he need not have become involved in his present plight at all, there being in fact no danger to him in Padua as Tranio had made him think. Next is the 'right' Vincentio, father of the 'right' Lucentio, who has come suddenly in upon this bewildering world from outside, like Sebastian stepping into the Illyrian fog compounded by his sister in *Twelfth Night*; here Vincentio finds—he knows not what:

> *Ped.* What's he that knocks as he would beat down the gate?
> *Vin.* Is Signior Lucentio within, sir?
> *Ped.* He's within, sir, but not to be spoken withal.
> *Vin.* What if a man bring him a hundred pound or two, to make merry withal?
> *Ped.* Keep your hundred pounds to yourself; he shall need none, so long as I live.
> *Pet.* Nay, I told you your son was well beloved in Padua. Do you hear, sir? To leave frivolous circumstances, I pray you, tell Signior Lucentio that his father is come from Pisa and is here at the door to speak with him.
> *Ped.* Thou liest. His father is come from Padua and is here looking out at the window.
> *Vin.* Art thou his father?
> *Ped.* Ay, sir; so his mother says, if I may believe her. (V. i. 17–35.)

Though ignorant of particular aspects of the situation he has come into, Vincentio sees some facts more clearly than those involved in the tangle whose eyes are bleared with counterfeit supposes. He knows, at least, that he is in fact Vincentio, that 'Lucentio' is in fact Tranio, and that whatever the Pedant is, he is not Vincentio. He stands, therefore, a rung or two above Baptista, who remains, at the end as at the beginning, mistaken in his view of everything around him. In the last wild moments of confusion, he remains ignorant that Tranio and the Pedant are impostors, that 'Cambio' Lucentio has run off with Bianca to be married, and that the new arrival, whom he would have an officer drag away summarily—'Away with the dotard! To the gaol with him!'—is in fact Vincentio. The exploitation of his errors, long compounded, continues central until the 'right' Lucentio enters and dispels the fog.

The gaps between awarenesses of participants involved in the minor plot are all closed at the end of V. i. In V. ii we share with Petruchio a final advantage over all these persons. It is an advantage which has been long in preparation—indeed, the entire action of the shrew plot has moved toward this end. We have seen Katherina hailed up and down the road between Petruchio's house and Padua; at his command, we have heard her call the sun the moon, the moon the sun, indifferently, call old Vincentio a 'young budding virgin, fair and fresh and sweet', and finally, just before the last scene—for Shakespeare must always make assurance doubly sure—we have been given a clenching proof that the taming is complete:

> *Kath*. Husband, let's follow, to see the end of this ado.
> *Pet*. First kiss me, Kate, and we will.
> *Kath*. What, in the midst of the street?
> *Pet*. What, art thou asham'd of me?
> *Kath*. No, sir, God forbid; but asham'd to kiss.
> *Pet*. Why, then let's home again. Come, sirrah, let's away.
> *Kath*. Nay, I will give thee a kiss; now pray thee, love, stay.
> *Pet*. Is not this well? Come, my sweet Kate: Better once than never,
> for never too late. (V. i. 147–55.)

With Petruchio, therefore, we are well prepared to relish the exposure of all Padua's error, bluntly expressed by Tranio's remark: "'Tis thought your deer does hold you at a bay.' The exploitation of our enormous advantage is brief. It extends through only twenty-five lines and ends abruptly with Kate's cheerfully obedient entrance: 'What is your will, sir, that you send for me?'

On this proof the play closes; and with it closes also, until the first romances, Shakespeare's search for 'the way'.

1961—William Empson. "The Strengths of the Shrew," from the *Times Literary Supplement*

William Empson was a professor at Sheffield University, a poet, and one of the finest literary critics of his time. Two of his best-known books are Seven Types of Ambiguity *and* Some Versions of Pastoral.

A review of a recent production praised the actress of Katherina for putting Irony into her final sermon in favour of the wifely obedience which she has just been taught; obviously, it said, she could not have learned to recommend the nauseating doctrine by these high arguments, even if she would at all, after being shown only such a very seamy side of it. Another review, in a critical journal, was thrown into a scolding fit by the mere thought of this production gimmick, saying that it betrayed both the Elizabethan idealism and the primary duty of the historical approach. I am sorry not to have kept the references, but no doubt there is a regular crop of both types. My Shakespeare class at Sheffield voted to have the play discussed, or I would have continued to assume that it is low-minded, dull, and brutal; rewritten with little change by Shakespeare while he was first establishing his position, and perhaps merely an assignment set to test him.

It is more interesting than that. The inquiring mind at once meets the barbed-wire fence of the controversy whether *A Shrew* (1594) is an earlier play not by Shakespeare or a pirate's reconstruction of the Bard's very own bit of fun. I think it is an older play, because then Shakespeare has made the underplot rather less flat, whereas a pirate would hardly go out of his way to invent an even flatter one. *A Shrew* is in any case very badly reported, and perhaps there is not enough evidence to decide the question. What one can say is that the more interesting points of psychology come only in Shakespeare's version (*The Shrew*).

However, neither is so brutal as one is led to expect. The tamer does not beat the shrew in either version, though this would have been considered normal practice in real life; and in both her father tells him that all depends on his making her love him. This is natural, as the only purpose of the father is to get the shrew tolerably quiet and contented; but it is very unlike the standard comedy in which the audience is on the side of the young lovers while the mercenary parents scheme for the Arranged Marriage. Here it is the *jeune première* who says that, though he has money already, he doesn't care how much of a brute his wife is so long as she brings him more money. However, we are free to think that this is a boast, whereas really he positively wants to marry a woman of spirit. Even so, if his method of training is to break her spirit, how can she continue to give this kind of satisfaction? Shakespeare makes her raise the question when she says

I see a woman may be made a fool
If she had not a spirit to resist. (III.ii.218–19)

and

My tongue will tell the anger of my heart,
Or else my heart concealing it will break. (IV.iii.77–78)

The answer of the tamer is simply that they must have only one mind between them.

The shrew at first appears beating her younger sister, after binding her hands, to make her tell which of her suitors she prefers; the shrew is jealous, and thinks her father means to make her an old maid:

Talk not to me, I will go sit and weep,
Till I can find occasion for revenge. (II.i.35–36)

Thus she is not a man-hater, like one type of masculine woman; she wants a husband, but can't have one because she beats her suitors. She goes to the church to marry Petruchio, willingly we must suppose, and weeps when he does not come (III.ii.25). She hits him on their first meeting when after a pointless bit of duty talk he claims to be a gentleman, meaning apparently that she ought not to show contempt.

He that knows better how to tame a shrew,
Now let him speak: 'tis charity to show. (V.i.197–98)

This boast to the audience is I think sincere and confident in the claim to be doing the shrew a kindness.

Bernard Shaw is I think the only Shakespearean critic who has had the nerve to protest against his famous wit-combats, saying that they come from an appallingly callow and provincial craving to show off, and would have been torture to Shakespeare if he had ever read them over again after he had grown up. Shaw flourished in a time of unduly severe rules about what can be said in front of a lady, and he was quite ready to turn them against the Bard; for example, a lady ought not even to hear the name Sir Toby Belch. We may discount a good deal of this, but the Shrew actually does react to the pointless spiteful dirty-mindedness of her bully just as Shaw would want her to:

Kath. . . . and so farewell.
Pet. What, with my tongue in your tail? Nay, come again, Good Kate.
I am a gentleman—

> *Kath.* That I'll try. (*striking him*).
> *Pet.* I swear I'll cuff you, if you strike again.
> *Kath.* So may you lose your arms.
> If you strike me, you are no gentleman. (II.i.215–20)

I take it that she is on her way out when she hears the obscenity, and turns to look at him with contempt; this silent snub is what he is trying to answer when he claims to be a gentleman. She tests it with a blow, and he passes muster; there are no more blows on either side. The answer seems right as proving that he acts deliberately, not from bad temper; and indeed he is felt to be playing an artificial trick in turning a woman's weapons against her. Continuing the argument from heraldry, he offers (fatuously I expect) to be

> A combless cock, so Kate will be my hen.
> *Kath.* No cock of mine, you crow too like a craven. (II.i.225–26)

Here, apparently, she argues that he must be a coward merely because he is a bully. After badgering her and lying to her at some length, he says:

> Thus in plain terms: your father hath consented
> That you shall be my wife; your dowry greed on;
> And will you, nill you, I will marry you. (II.i.262–64)

There is a certain rough brotherly goodwill about it; as when he says this is the only way for her to become 'Conformable as other household Kates'. In fact, it is all right if she secretly wants to marry him; if his vanity is deluding him there, he is treating her badly.

The obedience owed by daughters to fathers was always short of the absolute at one point; a woman might refuse to marry—indeed, the reason why she says Yes in the Marriage Service is that even at the altar she is entitled to say No. She may not marry against her father's wishes, but she may choose to be an old maid, sometimes a nun; the point is by no means clear to Squire Western, admittedly, but he would come up against it if he took legal or moral advice. Indeed the situation of the *Lysistrata* has always been the basic weapon for Women's Rights, so that the demanding heroines of Jane Austen are more political than she would realize.

The question about the *Shrew* is whether it is morally a very sordid play, and we cannot acquit Petruchio of rape merely because he is vain. 'I know you have a craving for my body really, though you scream and kick in such an inconvenient way'—this may be true in the case before us; but if erected into a principle it would often be acted on, though false. It may be answered that, as he never hits her, he never forces her at all. But in their first meeting, as we have just seen, she calls his foul mouth a way of bullying her. He beats the priest at the wedding for dropping the prayer book (III.ii.161–62), and is always beating his servants in her presence. A pretence is kept up that this is done to honour her, but with such transparent untruth that the effect, as she says, is spiteful jeering (IV.iii.2). In the same way, immediately after the wedding, when he forces her to come home with him instead of eating the wedding feast, he pretends to be rescuing her from her relations:

> Grumio,
> Draw forth thy weapon, we are beset with thieves,
> Rescue your mistress if you be a man.
> Fear not, sweet wench, they shall not touch thee, Kate.
> I'll buckler thee against a million. (III.ii.233–37)

We might suppose that this saves her face, and lets her do what she prefers, but she is much more likely to go with him out of fright.

In law, a man could beat his wife 'without reason', as also his children and apprentices; but a gentleman was to some extent expected to be chivalrous. It seems natural to say that the play expresses the resentment of the rising bourgeoisie at finding themselves expected to gratify their women in this way. Making Kate miserable by pretending to treat her as a Lady is genuinely spiteful, and no doubt often occurred.

But then, when we try to estimate the reaction of the audience we must remember the firm moral delicacy of the observer Sly in *A Shrew*, who repeatedly calls the bully the Fool: 'Sim, when will the foole come againe?'

Katherina's sister comments, 'That being mad herself, she's madly mated' (III.ii.242); and the servant Peter at the tamer's country house says: 'He kills her in her own humour' (IV.i.67). Thus the male part of the audience may decently rejoice, not at seeing a woman beaten down by the superior strength of a man, but at seeing the offensive strength familiar in their wives overwhelmed by a man who can nag back just as unreasonably as a woman. Greater bodily strength is I suppose presumed in him, but her obedience to his whims hardly depends on it. There is indeed one passage, necessarily reported, where she seems to have the epic strength of (say) Britomart: it is reported by the servant who rode with the newly-wedded couple to Petruchio's country house:

> . . . hadst thou not crossed me, thou shouldst have heard how her horse fell, and she under her horse; thou shouldst have heard in how miry a place, how she was bemoiled, how he left her with the horse upon her, how he beat me because her horse stumbled, how she waded through the dirt to pluck him off me, how he swore, how she prayed that never

prayed before, how I cried, how the horses ran away, how her bridle was
burst, how I lost my crupper . . . (IV.i.64–73)

—all this in a frost so severe that it finally, he says, tamed both of them. To beat
the servant because her horse stumbled, instead of fetching the horse off her,
is his usual technique of pretended reverence for the lady; but in this case it is
much too dangerous, and would be murder if she died of it. However big and
strong she is, the horse is bigger. But we gather that she heaved it aside in her
craving to save the servant from his unjust punishment from the monster she
has married; she heaves her way on hands and knees towards him through the
icy mud. There must have been a lot of good in her somewhere. This splendid
picture would not be as prominent in acting as it deserves to be, but presumably
it is an indication to the producer of the overall intention. Indeed, come to think
of it, a man rather than a boy would presumably take the part of the shrew; thus
the joke is not so much that women are weak as that this character is unnaturally
strong for the part of a woman. I grant that Katherina speaks of her weakness in
her final sermon, but I think that this would raise a laugh.

The idea that anyone could laugh during the sermon needs separate defence.
The old Arden edition of the play, dated 1904 and breathing a vanished world
of good sense, reports that Fletcher wrote a continuation of it called *The
Woman's Prize: or The Tamer Tamed*, in which Petruchio tries again after the
death of Katherina and this time 'suffers defeat at every point'; the two plays
were acted before Charles I on successive nights. We must suppose then that,
although earnest about the Divine Right of Kings, the future martyr was not
as strong on the Divine Right of Husbands as our present literary mentors; he
thought the subject funny. Then again, most of the training in wifely behaviour,
as it is shown to us, consists in telling obvious frank lies—agreeing with the
husband in calling the sun the moon and suchlike. As soon as she does this,
he is jovial; what he wants is practically nothing, some wives might comment.
There is nothing in her training, at any rate, to keep her from preaching a
sermon on female subordination without believing a word of it, even that she
is physically weaker than he is. The author and the audience may be expected
to believe it all, and the great natural energy of the shrew will always give an
appearance of believing what she says; but a frank admission that she is just
repeating her lesson, while she upbraids the other two wives, would seem a
natural thing to admit into her tone of voice. It is only fair to Petruchio to
admit that her spirit does not seem broken at all; and if it is not I do not see
how she can believe that she ought [*words illegible*] her husband wrong when
she is anxious lest he be wrong.

The early Shakespeare strikes one chiefly as an energetic and searching mind,
inclined to say 'What's the point of this plot?' and to put the answer firmly on the
stage. This is enough to explain his making the converted shrew preach to the other

two wives. The parallel speech in *A Shrew*, though mangled and largely forgotten, must have started with the Creation and given an outline of the whole Chain of Being in support of the doctrine of female subordination; if it records an earlier pre-Shakespearean play, we have not to explain why Shakespeare introduced such a passage but why he cut it down to something much more homely and practical—introducing apparently the argument that women are physically weaker than men. Almost the only thing he retained, from what survives of the old speech, is the idea that women should spread their hands on the floor for their husbands to trample upon, 'to do them ease'. In both versions, her husband has just told her to trample on her hat, thus proving to the other two husbands her complete submission, and I suppose inviting him to trample on her fingers is a sort of hyperbole. It is a nasty fancy, as the only satisfaction it would give the husband is a spiteful one, and I should prefer to believe that Shakespeare copied it from an earlier play. None of the speech seems to me deeply felt, though it is easy and vigorous. On the other hand, the rejoicing of Petruchio before, as a matter of rhythm more than anything else, does seem to me to come from the heart of the author:

Marry, peace it bodes, and love, and quiet life,
An awful rule, and right supremacy,
And, to be short, what not that's sweet and happy. (V.ii.109–11)

This is echoed by Milton at the death of Samson, and Milton seems a good judge of the sincerity of the passage. Young men need to leave home, says the play (I.ii.50), and it is usual to guess that Shakespeare's marriage was unfortunate—I am inclined to the view that Anne was a Puritan, disapproving of plays, so that his whole career depended upon separation from her. We need not be surprised at his accepting the doctrine of female subordination, or even being rather spiteful in fancy about it; but his sense of reality carried him a long way on the topic. The other two wives do not seem to be presented as bad ones at all; thus the message of the widow is:

She says you have some goodly jest in hand.
She will not come. She bids you come to her. (V.ii.92–93)

When the men are sitting over their wine it is only prudent to leave them alone; surely, many ladies of the time would have thought this jokey answer the correct one. Thus the sermon of Katherina is not led up to with religious solemnity.

And finally of course one needs to consider the effect of the Induction, especially if allowed an Epilogue as in *A Shrew*. The world in which a man can tame his wife by nagging more than she does is a pure daydream, offered to the drunken Sly as like waking up and finding himself a lord; he believes it is the only part he can play in real life, but the audience is meant to be sure he is wrong.

Tapster. . . . you had best get you home,
For your wife will course you for dreaming here tonight.
    Sly. Will she? I know now how to tame a shrew;
I dreamt upon it all this night till now,
And thou hast wakt me out of the best dreame
That ever I had in my life, but Ile to my,
Wife presently and tame her too
And if she anger me.

The Elizabethan attitude to women, though complicated by the Chain of Being, and contrariwise the worship of Elizabeth, comes more naturally to us than the Victorian. Indeed our period is perhaps the first to feel at home with Shakespeare's women since his own (since all the critics in between are liable to be found simpering uneasily about the topic); and the reason for it is not the Suffragette Movement but simply the two World Wars. The ladies had to be let out of the drawing-room because there was so much they were needed to do; and when Lady Plumpton in the Plumpton correspondence, for example, acts as officer in command of the garrison of the beleaguered country house, while her husband tries to regain legal possession of it in London, she too is not leading a sheltered life. From 1660 to 1914 the ladies could be sheltered, and the gentlemen locked them up as a matter of pride. Thackeray is intelligent enough to realize that there is something queer about the tight-laced primness of the drawing-room, and keeps saying fretfully 'How disgustingly silly and feeble women are; I know we have got to manage to love them for it somehow, but how sick it does make us feel.' Now Spenser, especially in Book V of the *Fairie Queene*, has much more theoretical belief that women ought to be under the control of men, but regards their strength as obvious . . . ; in fact, he talks about them very much as if they were horses. If one has this clearly in mind, one of the main unpleasantness of *The Shrew* is removed; the lady is bullied not because she is weak but because she is strong.

⌐⌐⌐⌐⌐   ⌐⌐⌐⌐⌐   ⌐⌐⌐⌐⌐

1980—Ruth Nevo. "'Kate of Kate Hall,'" from *Comic Transformations in Shakespeare*

Ruth Nevo is Professor Emeritus at the Hebrew University of Jerusalem. She is the author of *Comic Transformations in Shakespeare* and *Shakespeare's Other Language*.

A more gentlemanly age than our own was embarrassed by *The Shrew*. G. B. Shaw announced it 'altogether disgusting to the modern sensibility'.[1] Sir Arthur Quiller-Couch of the New Shakespeare, judged it

> primitive, somewhat brutal stuff and tiresome, if not positively offensive
> to any modern civilised man or modern woman, not an antiquary. . . .
> We do not and cannot, whether for better or worse, easily think of
> woman and her wedlock vow to obey quite in terms of a spaniel, a wife
> and a walnut tree—the more you whip 'em the better they be.[2]

It will be noticed, however, that Q's access of gallantry causes him to overlook the fact that apart from the cuffings and beatings of saucy or clumsy *zanni* which is canonical in Italianate comedy, no one whips anyone in *The Taming of the Shrew*, violence being confined to Katherina who beats her sister Bianca, and slaps Petruchio's face. Anne Barton has done much to restore a sense of proportion by quoting some of the punishments for termagent wives which really were practised in Shakespeare's day. Petruchio comes across, she says,

> far less as an aggressive male out to bully a refractory wife into total
> submission, than he does as a man who genuinely prizes Katherina,
> and, by exploiting an age-old and basic antagonism between the sexes,
> manoeuvres her into an understanding of his nature and also her own.[3]

Ralph Berry reads the play rather as a Berneian exercise in the Games People Play, whereby Kate learns the rules of Petruchio's marriage game, which she plays hyperbolically and with ironic amusement. 'This is a husband–wife team that has settled to its own satisfaction, the rules of its games, and now preaches them unctuously to friends.'[4] In our own day, the wheel, as is the way with wheels, has come full circle and the redoubtable feminist, Ms Germaine Greer, has found the relationship of Kate and Petruchio preferable to the subservient docility of that sexist projection, the goody-goody Bianca.[5]

With all this fighting of the good fight behind us, we may approach the play with the unencumbered enjoyment it invites. As Michael West has excellently argued 'criticism has generally misconstrued the issue of the play as women's rights, whereas what the audience delightedly responds to are sexual rites'.[6] Nothing is more stimulating to the imagination than the tension of sexual conflict and sexual anticipation. Verbal smashing and stripping, verbal teasing and provoking and seducing are as exciting to the witnessing audience as to the characters enacting these moves. It is easy to see why *The Shrew* has always been a stage success, and so far from this being a point to be apologized for it should be seen as exhibiting Shakespeare's early command of farce as the radical of comic action, a mastery temporarily lost as he struggled to absorb more rarefied material in *The Two Gentlemen* and only later recovered. The mode, however, of the sexual battle in *The Shrew* is devious and indirect and reflects a remarkably subtle psychology. Petruchio neither beats his Kate nor rapes her—two 'primitive and brutal' methods of taming termagant wives, but neither is his unusual courtship of his refractory bride simply an exhibition of cock-of-the-walk male dominance to which in the end Katherina is forced to submit. Michael West's emphasis upon wooing dances and the folklore of sexual conquest is salutory, but Petruchio's conquest of Kate is far from merely a 'kind of mating dance with appropriate struggling and biceps flexing'. Nor is she simply 'a healthy female animal who wants a male strong enough to protect her, deflower her, and sire vigorous offspring' (p. 69).

Only a very clever, very discerning man could bring off a psychodrama so instructive, liberating and therapeutic as Petruchio's, on a honeymoon as sexless (as well as dinnerless) as could well be imagined. Not by sex is sex conquered, nor for that matter by the withholding of sex, though the play's tension spans these poles. Christopher Sly, one recalls, is also constrained to forgo his creature comforts, a stoic *malgré lui*, and thereby a foil and foreshadower of the self-possessed Petruchio.

In the Induction, the page Bartholomew plays his part as Lady Sly to such effect that Sly pauses only to determine whether to call the lovely lady 'Al'ce madam, or Joan madam?' (Ind. II. 110) or plain 'madam wife' before demanding 'Madam, undress you, and come now to bed' (Ind. II. 117). Bartholomew must think fast, of course, and does: '[I] should yet absent me from your bed', he says, lest '[you] incur your former malady', and hopes that 'this reason stands for my excuse' (Ind. II, 124). Sly clearly has his own problems: 'Ay, it stands so that I may hardly tarry so long. But I would be loath to fall into my dreams again. I will therefore tarry in despite of the flesh and the blood' (Ind. ii. 125–8). But Christopher Sly's 'former malady' is, of course, an imposed delusion: it is not as anamnesic lord that he is himself but as drunken tinker. Katherina's, we will finally learn to perceive, was self-imposed, and requires the therapies of comedy—'which bars a thousand harms and lengthens life'—not the tumbling tricks of a 'Christmas gambold' for its cure. This lower level functions as foil to the higher yardstick and guarantor of the latter's reality.

The play's formal *telos* is to supply that which is manifestly lacking: a husband for the wild, intractable and shrewish daughter of Baptista. But how shall Katherina herself not perceive that this husband is sought in order to enable her younger sister to be happily married to one of *her* numerous suitors? The situation of inflamed and inflammatory sibling rivalry which the good signor Baptista has allowed to develop between these daughters of his is suggested with deft economy. Her very first words:

I pray you, sir, is it your will
To make a stale of me amongst these mates? (I. i. 57–8)

speak hurt indignity, an exacerbated pride. Her response when Baptista fondles and cossets the martyred Bianca:

> A pretty peat! it is best
> Put finger in the eye, and she knew why. (I. i. 78–9)

indicates her opinion that if Bianca is long suffering she is also extracting the maximum benefit and enjoyment from that state. Nothing that Baptista says or does but will be snatched up and interpreted disadvantageously by this irascible sensitivity.

> Why, and I trust I may go too, may I not? What, shall I be appointed hours, as though (belike) I knew not what to take and what to leave? Ha! (I. i. 102–4)

These first glimpses already invite us to infer some reason for the bad-tempered, headstrong, domestic tyranny Kate exercises, but when we find her beating her cowering sister, screaming at her for confidences about which of her suitors she most fancies, and turning on her father with

> What, will you not suffer me? Nay, now I see
> She is your treasure, she must have a husband;
> I must dance barefoot on her wedding-day,
> And for your love to her lead apes in hell.
> Talk not to me, I will go sit and weep,
> Till I can find occasion of revenge. (II. i. 31–6)

we surely do not require inordinate discernment to understand what ails Katherina Minola. It is a marvellous touch that the pious Bianca, defending herself from the wildcat elder sister (with no suitor), says:

> Or what you will command me will I do
> So well I know my duty to my elders. (II. i. 6–7)

Bianca, it may be supposed, is not the only younger sister who has got her face scratched for a remark like that.

All of Padua, we are given to understand, is taken up with the problem of finding someone to take his devilish daughter off Baptista's hands, leaving the field free for the suitors of the heavenly Bianca. And this is precisely a trap in which Kate is caught. She has become nothing but an obstacle or a means to her sister's advancement. Even the husband they seek for her is in reality for the sister's sake, not hers. When she says: 'I will never marry' it is surely because she believes no 'real' husband of her own, who loves her for herself, whom she can trust, is possible. How indeed could it be otherwise since patently and manifestly no one does love her? Because (or therefore) she is not lovable. And the more unlovable she is the more she proves her point. Katherina of Acts I and II is a masterly and familiar portrait. No one about her can do right in her eyes, so great is her envy and suspicion. No one can penetrate her defences, so great her need for assurance. So determined is she to make herself invulnerable that she makes herself insufferable, and finds in insufferability her one defence. This is a 'knot of errors' of formidable proportions and will require no less than Petruchio's shock tactics for its undoing.[7]

The undoing begins with the arrival of Petruchio, to wive it wealthily in Padua. No doubts are entertained in Padua about the benefits of marriage where money is, but it will be noted that no one is banking on a rich marriage to save him from the bankruptcy courts. All the suitors are wealthy; Lucentio, potentially at least. The contrast that Shakespeare sets up between Petruchio and Lucentio is an interesting ironic inversion of that obtaining in the Terentian tradition. In Terence the second (liaison) plot entailed tricky stratagems for acquiring money in order to buy (and keep) the slave girl. The main (marriage) plot on the other hand hinged upon the fortunate discovery of a true identity, which meant both legitimizing the affair and acquiring the dowry. Here, in the case of Bianca and Lucentio the mercenary mechanics of match-making are masked by Petrarchan ardours on Lucentio's part (or Hortensio's, until the appearance of the widow):

> Tranio, I burn, I pine, I perish, Tranio,
> . . . let me be a slave, t'achieve that maid
> Whose sudden sight hath thrall'd my wounded eye. (I. i. 155; 219–20)

and by angelic docility on Bianca's part; while Petruchio's affairs are deromanticized by the unabashed, unmasked worldliness of his motivation:

> I come to wive it wealthily in Padua;
> If wealthily, then happily in Padua. (I. ii. 75–6)

and the formidable temper of Kate.

To Petruchio's incontinent and precipitate request to draw up the 'covenant' between them, Baptista demurs:

> Ay, when the special thing is well obtain'd,
> That is, her love; for that is all in all. (II. i. 128–9)

and the reply is unequivocal:

> Why, that is nothing; for I tell you, father,
> I am as peremptory as she proud-minded;
> And where two raging fires meet together,
> They do consume the thing that feeds their fury.
> Though little fire grows great with little wind,
> Yet extreme gusts will blow out fire and all;
> So I to her, and so she yields to me,
> For I am rough, and woo not like a babe. (II. i. 130–7)

And again: 'For I will board her, though she chide as loud / As thunder when the clouds in autumn crack' (I. ii. 95–6). Final recognitions will reverse these evaluations: the nakedly mercenary relationship will prove itself productive of affection and of spirit as well as sheer animal spirits; the romantic will prove hollow, its Petrarchanism a mere mask.[8]

In *The Shrew*, Shakespeare's characteristic handling of multiple levels is already to be discerned. The main protagonists are the agents of the higher recognitions, the middle groups function as screens on which are projected distorted mirror images of the main couples—images in a concave mirror; while the lower orders ridicule the middle by the parody of imitation, and act as foils for the higher by providing a measure of qualitative difference.

Though *The Shrew* fails to integrate Christopher Sly satisfactorily and indeed abandons him altogether after Act 1, such a function for him, as I have already indicated, is adumbrated. Shakespeare, it seems, felt more comfortable with the playlet-within-the-play of *Love's Labour's Lost* and *A Midsummer Night's Dream* for his clowns, or with the parenthetic internal comment of a cunning and a foolish servant combination like Grumio/Tranio or Launce/Speed than with the clown-frame, to which he does not return. But the flurry of disguisings and contrivings, 'supposes' and role-playings in Baptista's middle-class household, resolved finally by nothing more complex than natural selection and substantial bank balances, do set off admirably the subtler, more complex and interiorized transformations of the Petruchio–Katherina relationship.

Petruchio's first speech in reply to Katherina's haughty insistence on her full name, is richly expressive:

> You lie, in faith, for you are call'd plain Kate,
> And bonny Kate, and sometimes Kate the curst;
> But Kate, the prettiest Kate in Christendom,
> Kate of Kate-Hall, my super-dainty Kate,
> For dainties are all Kates, and therefore, Kate,
> Take this of me, Kate of my consolation—
> Hearing thy mildness prais'd in every town,

Thy virtues spoke of, and thy beauty sounded,
Yet not so deeply as to thee belongs,
Myself am mov'd to woo thee for my wife. (II. i. 185–94)

Ironic, mocking, amused and appreciative, it invites us to infer a certain relief, to
say the least. Though he has stoutly affirmed his priorities:

Be she as foul as was Florentius' love,
As old as Sibyl, and as curst and shrowd
As Socrates' Xantippe, or a worse . . .

I come to wive it wealthily in Padua;
If wealthily, then happily in Padua. (I. ii. 69–71; 75–6)

the spirited, bonny dark lass Baptista's terrible daughter turns out to be cannot
but cause him a lift of the heart. She, for her part, does not of course respond
immediately to his good-humoured teasing, but we may surely assume a certain
vibration to be caused by this note of a tenderness which her obsessive fear of not
finding has consistently put out of court. But she has built up sturdy bastions and
will certainly not imitate her conciliatory sister. Combat is her chosen defence,
and that these two are worthy opponents the set of wit which follows shows.
Then comes the cut and thrust of the clash between her proud-mindedness and
his peremptoriness. She misses no ploy, is outrageously provocative and brazenly
impolite, verbally and even physically violent. He trips her up with a bawdy pun,
she dares him to return a slapped face, and it is by no means certain to anyone
that he will not. His strategy of mock denial:

'Twas told me you were rough and coy and sullen,
And now I find report a very liar;
For thou art pleasant, gamesome, passing courteous . . . (II. i. 243–5)

contains an infuriating sting in its tail:

But slow in speech, yet sweet as spring-time flowers. (II. i. 246)

so that she is criticized for being what she most prides herself on not being, and
consoled by being told she is what she most despises. Again:

Why does the world report that Kate doth limp?
O sland'rous world! Kate like the hazel-twig
Is straight and slender, and as brown in hue

As hazel nuts, and sweeter than the kernels.
O, let me see thee walk. Thou dost not halt. (II. i. 252–6)

And poor Kate must be beholden to him for patronizing defence against the alleged detractions of a despised world, and finds herself judiciously examined for faults much as if she were a thoroughbred mare at a fair. It is no wonder that in reply to his

Father, 'tis thus: yourself and all the world,
That talk'd of her, have talk'd amiss of her.
If she be curst, it is for policy,
For she's not froward but modest as the dove;
She is not hot, but temperate as the morn;
For patience she will prove a second Grissel,
And Roman Lucrece for her chastity;
And to conclude, we have 'greed so well together
That upon Sunday is the wedding-day. (II. i. 290–8)

she can only splutter 'I'll see thee hanged on Sunday first'; a response which is immediately interpreted by Petruchio, for the benefit of the spectators, as a secret bargain between lovers:

'Tis bargain'd twixt us twain, being alone,
That she shall still be curst in company.
I tell you 'tis incredible to believe
How much she loves me. O, the kindest Kate,
She hung about my neck, and kiss on kiss
She vied so fast, protesting oath on oath,
That in a twink she won me to her love.
O, you are novices! 'tis a world to see
How tame, when men and women are alone,
A meacock wretch can make the curstest shrew. (II. i. 304–13)

Round one thus ends indeed with 'we will be married a'Sunday'.

Sunday, however, brings not the marriage that has been prepared for in the Minola household, but a mummer's carnival. Petruchio arrives inordinately late, and in motley. Of the uproar he produces in the church we hear from Gremio, in a lively description containing the shape of things to come:

Tut, she's a lamb, a dove, a fool to him!
I'll tell you, Sir Lucentio: when the priest

Should ask if Katherine should be his wife,
'Ay, by gogs-wouns,' quoth he, and swore so loud
That all amaz'd the priest let fall the book,
And as he stoop'd again to take it up,
This mad-brain'd bridegroom took him such a cuff
That down fell priest and book, and book and priest.
'Now take them up,' quoth he, 'if any list.'
    Tranio. What said the wench when he rose again?
    Gremio. Trembled and shook; for why, he stamp'd and swore
As if the vicar meant to cozen him.
But after many ceremonies done,
He calls for wine. 'A health!' quoth he, as if
He had been aboard, carousing to his mates
After a storm, quaff'd off the muscadel,
And threw the sops all in the sexton's face . . .

This done, he took the bride about the neck,
And kiss'd her lips with such a clamorous smack
That at the parting all the church did echo. (III. iii. 157–73; 177–9)

All of this is prologue to the first open clash of wills between these fiery newly-weds. He will instantly away, she 'will not be gone till I please myself':

The door is open, sir, there lies your way:
You may be jogging whiles your boots are green. (III. ii. 210–11)

Father, be quiet, he shall stay my leisure.

Gentlemen, forward to the bridal dinner.
I see a woman may be made a fool,
If she had not a spirit to resist. (III. ii. 217; 219–21)

This is Petruchio's cue:

They shall go forward, Kate, at thy command.
Obey the bride, you that attend on her.

But for my bonny Kate, she must with me.
Nay, look not big, nor stamp, nor stare, nor fret,
I will be master of what is mine own.
She is my goods, my chattels, she is my house,
My household stuff, my field, my barn,
My horse, my ox, my ass, my any thing;

And here she stands, touch her whoever dare,
I'll bring mine action on the proudest he
That stops my way in Padua. Grumio,
Draw forth thy weapon, we are beset with thieves;
Rescue thy mistress if thou be a man.
Fear not, sweet wench, they shall not touch thee, Kate!
I'll buckler thee against a million. (III. ii. 222–3; 227–39)

And he snatches her off, sublimely indifferent to anything she says, insisting upon his property rights, benignly protective, mind you, of his bonny Kate, turning all her protests to his own purposes and depriving her of any shred of self-justification by his indignant defence of her.

Stage-manager and chief actor, master of homeopathy—'He kills her in his own humour' as Peter says—Petruchio's play-acting, his comic therapy, provides the comic device. One of a long line of Shakespearean actor-protagonists he holds the mirror up to nature, and shows scorn her own image. The tantrums that she has specialized in throwing he throws in super-abundance, forcing her to see herself in the mirror he thus holds up.

Grumio's tale of the saga of the journey:

> . . . hadst thou not cross'd me, thou shouldst have heard how her horse fell,
> and she under her horse; thou shouldst have heard in how miry a place,
> how she was bemoil'd, how he left her with the horse upon her, how he
> beat me because her horse stumbled, how she waded through the dirt to
> pluck him off me; how he swore, how she pray'd that never pray'd before;
> how I cried, how the horses ran way, how her bridle was burst; how I lost
> my crupper, with many things of worthy memory, which now shall die in
> oblivion, and thou return unexperienc'd to thy grave. (IV. i. 72–84)

prepares for the continuing hubbub in the Petruchean dining-hall. That Petruchio's strategy has the additional advantage of an austerity regime as far as food and sleep and 'fine array' is concerned is all to the good. Petruchio is canny and will leave no stone unturned. Also, he has tamed hawks. But it is not physical hardship which will break Kate's spirit, nor does he wish it, any more than a spirited man would wish his horse or his hound spiritless. And Petruchio, we recall, wagers twenty times as much upon his wife as he would upon his hawk or his hound. Significantly, Kate's recurrent response to his carrying on is to fly to the defence of the cuffed and chivvied servants. Crossing her will, totally and consistently, under the guide of nothing but consideration for her desires, confuses and disorients her, as she complains to Grumio.

What, did he marry me to famish me?
Beggars that come unto my father's door
Upon entreaty have a present alms,

If not, elsewhere they meet with charity;
But I, who never knew how to entreat,
Nor never needed that I should entreat,
Am starv'd for meat, giddy for lack of sleep,
With oaths kept waking, and with brawling fed;
And that which spites me more than all these wants,
He does it under the name of perfect love; (IV. iii. 3–11)

Katherine gets the point; but fails to get from Grumio even one of the mouth-watering items from a hearty English menu with which he tantalizes her. When she, listening hungrily to Petruchio's 'sermon of continency', and knowing not 'which way to stand, to look, to speak,' is 'as one new-risen from a dream', she might well rub her eyes and say, with Christopher Sly, . . . 'do I dream? Or have I dream'd till now?' (Ind. ii. 69).

What subtle Dr Petruchio has done is to drive a wedge into the steel plating of Kate's protective armour, so that he speaks at once to the self she has been and the self she would like to be; the self she has made of herself and the self she has hidden. The exchange of roles, with herself now at the receiving end of someone else's furies, takes her, as we say, out of herself; but she also perceives the method of his madnesses. Petruchio's remedy is an appeal to Kate's intelligence. These are not arbitrary brutalities, but the clearest of messages. And they are directed to her with undivided singleness of purpose.

In Act IV the remedy comes to fruition and Kate enunciates it:

Then God be blest, it [is] the blessed sun,
But sun it is not, when you say it is not;
And the moon changes even as your mind.
What you will have it nam'd, even that it is,
And so it shall be so, for Katherine. (IV. v. 18–22)

And then it is enacted, with considerable verve, as she addresses Vincentio, on cue from Petruchio, as 'young budding virgin, fair, and fresh, and sweet' and then promptly again, on cue, undoes all. Kate has yielded to a will stronger than her own and to an intelligence which has outmanoeuvred her, but the paradoxical, energizing and enlivening effect of the scene is that the laughter is directed not against her as butt or victim, but, through her prim performance, towards the disconcerted Vincentio. The *senex* is made fun of, in effect, by a pair of tricksters in some subtle alliance with each other not clear to him, but clear to the audience. Partly this response is structured by New Comedy paradigms. As Grumio puts it in Act I: 'Here's no knavery! See, to beguile the old folks; how the young folks lay their heads together!' (I. ii. 138–9). But mainly I believe it is due to our sense of liberation from deadlock. Petruchio has enlisted Kate's will and wit on his side, not broken them, and it is the function of the final festive test to confirm and exhibit this. It is also to be noted that the arrival in Padua of Vincentio 'exhausts' Lucentio's wooing devices, just as Petruchio's taming device exhausts its function; and it is a dexterous turn of composition which balances the mock non-recognition of Vincentio on the way to Padua, and his encounter with his Mantuan proxy, with the unmasking and recognition of the true Katherina, and the true Bianca, at the banquet.

That Kate is in love by Act V, is, I believe, what the play invites us to perceive. And indeed she may well be. The man she has married has humour and high spirits, intuition, patience, self-command and masterly intelligence; and there is more than merely a homily for Elizabethan wives in her famous speech:

> A woman mov'd is like a fountain troubled,
> Muddy, ill-seeming, thick, bereft of beauty,
> And while it is so, none so dry or thirsty
> Will deign to slip, or touch one drop of it.
> Thy husband is thy lord, thy life, thy keeper,
> Thy head, thy sovereign; one that cares for thee,
> And for thy maintenance; commits his body
> To painful labor, both by sea and land;
> To watch the night in storms, the day in cold,
> While thou li'st warm at home, secure and safe;
> And craves no other tribute at thy hands
> But love, fair looks, and true obedience—
> Too little payment for so great a debt. (V. ii. 142–54)

She wins her husband's wager but the speech bespeaks a generosity of spirit beyond the call of two hundred crowns. We have just heard Bianca snap at Lucentio mourning his lost bet: 'The more fool you for laying on my duty', and it seems that the metamorphosis of folly into wisdom which the comic action performs makes an Erastian reversal. More fool the Paduans indeed, in their exploitative hypocrisies and meannesses, than this madcap pair.

The very un-Petrarchan Petruchio has been the initiator of remedies in *The Taming of the Shrew* as well as the temperamental suitor; Katherina largely a responder and a foil. These positions will be reversed in *As You Like It* but not without a number of intermediate moves. *The Two Gentlemen of Verona* which follows *The Shrew* allows very little scope for the presentation of independent action on the part of Julia (despite her notable independence) and no occasion for courtship at all. Nevertheless, the growth of perceptions which make later developments possible proceeds through this next play, and is positively advanced by its explorations in the ambivalent and mimetic rivalry of the gentlemen.

NOTES

1. *Shaw on Shakespeare*, ed. Edwin Wilson (1961; reprinted Penguin, 1969), p. 198.

2. Introduction, The New Shakespeare edn (Cambridge: Cambridge University Press, 192.8), p. xv.

3. The Riverside Shakespeare, ed. G. Blakemore Evans (Boston: Houghton Mifflin, 1974), p. 106.

4. Ralph Berry, *Shakespeare's Comedies* (New Jersey: Princeton University Press, 1972), p. 7.

5. Germaine Greer, *The Female Eunuch* (New York: McGraw Hill, 1971), pp. 220–1. 'The submission of a woman like Kate is genuine and exciting because she has something to lay down, her virgin pride and individuality: Bianca is the soul of duplicity . . .' (p. 221).

6. Michael West, The Folk Background of Petruchio's Wooing Dance: Male Supremacy in '*The Taming of the Shrew*', *Shakespeare Studies*, vol. vii (1974), p. 71.

7. This vicious circle of the psyche is strikingly similar in form, to those delineated by R. D. Laing in his 'anthology of human bondage' as he calls *Knots* (New York: Random House, 1970). For instance:

> She has started to drink
>> as a way to cope
>> that makes her less able to cope
>
> the more she drinks
> the more frightened she is of becoming a drunkard
>
> the more drunk
> the less frightened of being drunk
>
> the more frightened of being drunk when not drunk
>> the more not frightened drunk
>> the more frightened not drunk . . . (p. 29)

8. The contrast between hollow mercenariness, or the lower folly of ordinary existence and what Erasmus called the 'higher folly of the inner life' is further developed in *Much Ado*, and in *As You Like It*. See P. O. Kristeller, *The Classics and Renaissance Thought* (Cambridge, Massachusetts: Harvard University Press, 1955), pp. 62–3 and W. J. Kaiser, *Praisers of Folly* (Cambridge, Massachusetts: Harvard University Press, 1963).

———◁∿∿▷— —◁∿∿▷— —◁∿∿▷—

1989—Camille Wells Slights. "The Raw and the Cooked in *The Taming of the Shrew*," from *Journal of English and Germanic Philology*

Camille Wells Slights is a professor of English at the University of Saskatchewan, Canada. She is the author of *The Casuistical Tradition in Shakespeare, Donne, Herbert, and Milton* and *Shakespeare's Comic Commonwealths.*

'I must dance barefoot on her wedding-day.' (II.i.33)

Like *The Comedy of Errors, The Taming of the Shrew* creates humor by violating the decorum of social roles and resolves comic confusion with the recognition that the major characters have found places in the social order. Although these two early comedies share the assumption that people are social beings, they explore the contrast between wildness and civilization and between belonging and not belonging from significantly different perspectives. Egeon's narrative at the beginning of *The Comedy of Errors* fills in a background of harsh physical nature and capricious fate against which the drama of losing and recovering social identity will play itself out. The Induction to *The Taming of the Shrew* serves a similar purpose, but this time the contrast isn't between the human and non-human but between the cultivated and the brutish. Christopher Sly, the drunken tinker, is a portrait of human degradation—destructive, irascible, lawless, ignorant, and scurrilous. In obvious contrast, the Lord who plays an elaborate practical joke on Sly is a highly civilized man. He is introduced as a hunter, easily dominant over animal nature. His relations with his servants exhibit gracious familiarity on his part and respectful deference on theirs. His effortless authority is complemented by his attitude of protective care of his hounds; his desire to derive fun from the helpless drunk is controlled by concern that the joke not go to cruel extremes (Ind.i.66, 136–8), and his plans for deceiving Sly are interspersed with instructions to treat him gently (Ind. i.45, 66–8, 72, 94–9). While Christopher Sly bestializes himself, degrading his human form into a 'monstrous beast' lying in a drunken stupor 'like a swine' (Ind.i.34), the Lord lives in a world where men's physical needs are supplied with fine clothes and delicious foods and their senses gratified with delicate fabrics, sweet smells, music, and art. Although the Lord's practical joke is neither morally nor intellectually superior to Sly's form of self-indulgence, the contrast is undeniable. It is also evident that the aristocratic refinement and the vulgar coarseness are both forms of human culture. The success of the Lord's ruse—changing Sly's sense of social identity by changing his physical environment and by providing him with new relationships—stresses the artificiality of social identity and the power of social rank. The humor of the scene suggests the complexity of social manners and Sly's residual control of the situation. He is funnier after than before his transformation precisely because he insists on drinking small ale instead of sack and wants to know whether to call his wife 'Al'ce madam, or Joan madam' (Ind. ii. 110). In *The Comedy of Errors*, social identity is a birthright and its misapprehension produces confusion, but in *The Taming of the Shrew* social roles are arbitrary and must be learned.

While *The Comedy of Errors* emphasizes human dependence on social structure, *The Taming of the Shrew* focuses on the dynamics of human power and purpose. In *The Comedy of Errors*, being in a strange city means dangerous isolation. In *The Taming of the Shrew*, visitors have no such fears. Tranio indignantly and successfully challenges the rich citizen Gremio: 'Are not the streets as free / For me as for you?' (I.ii.231–2). A xenophobic law against foreigners, which in *The Comedy of Errors* imperils Egeon's life, in *The Taming of the Shrew* is a joke, part of Lucentio's amorous intrigue. By convincing an old man whom he finds on the road from Mantua that a quarrel with the Duke of Mantua has caused the Duke of Padua to proclaim 'death for any one in Mantua / To come to Padua' (iv.ii.81–2), Tranio persuades the old Pedant to masquerade as Lucentio's father. Petruchio and Tranio, of course, are even more eager than the Pedant to undertake the challenges offered by a new place. In *The Comedy of Errors*, Egeon and Antipholus come to Ephesus to search for their lost son and brother. In *The Taming of the Shrew*, visitors arrive in Padua anticipating new opportunities. Lucentio opens the play announcing that he has come to 'fair Padua, nursery of arts' to pursue a 'course of learning and ingenious studies' (I.i.2, 9), then immediately accepts Tranio's advice to mix study with pleasure, and before the scene is over falls in love. In the next scene Petruchio announces that he has come to Padua 'to wive and thrive as best I may' (I.ii.56). In the world of this play it is natural for young men to travel 'To seek their fortunes farther than at home' (I.ii.51), and being in a strange city means exhilaration rather than fear or bewilderment.

The wooing scenes in these two early plays also illustrate the contrast in their representation of attitudes towards social institutions. In both plays, humor depends on the existence of courtship conventions. The scene in which Antipholus of Syracuse declares his love to Luciana is comic not because his manner of courting is funny in itself but because he directs his eloquence to a woman who believes him to be her sister's husband. When his tender plea, 'Give me thy hand,' elicits the deflating response, 'O soft, sir, hold you still; / I'll fetch my sister to get her good will' (*CE*, III.ii.69–70), the effect is ludicrous. In contrast, Petruchio's wooing of Kate is comic not because of any misperception of social roles but because both Katherina and Petruchio intentionally flout the conventions of courtship.

The opening scene of *The Taming of the Shrew*, then, sketches the shape of the main action not only by demonstrating the artificiality of social roles and the extremes of civilized and uncivilized behavior but also by emphasizing intentional perversity and impudence rather than inadvertent error. The ruse that the Lord practices on Christopher Sly is potentially frightening. In *The Comedy of Errors* when Antipholus of Syracuse has a comparable experience of being assigned a strange new identity and an unknown wife, he doubts his own sanity, sees the people who claim to know him as witches and sorcerers, and plans to flee in terror from a place 'where every one knows us, and we know none' (III.

ii.152). Christopher Sly, on the other hand, enthusiastically accepts the new identity created for him by the Lord and his servants. For him, after some initial excitement, the experience is, as the Lord predicts, 'a flatt'ring dream' (Ind.i.44). When the play opens on Sly's altercation with the Hostess, he is as notable for his pretensions as for his ignorance, replying to the Hostess' threat of 'A pair of stocks, you rogue': 'Y' are a baggage, the Slys are no rogues. Look in the chronicles; we came in with Richard Conqueror. Therefore *paucas pallabris*, 'let the world slide' (Ind.i.2–6). The deception that transforms the poor tinker into a rich lord fulfills his fantasies of aristocratic rank as well as affording him the sensory gratification of fine clothes, food, and entertainment. Indeed, Sly is so delighted with the deception that his old life seems to him a dream 'he would be loath to fall into . . . again' (Ind.ii.126–7). And as a new identity is a dream-come-true for Christopher Sly in the Induction, in the main action most of the major characters (including Lucentio, Tranio, Hortensio, and the Pedant) put on new clothes and claim new identities for their own purposes. Most notably, Petruchio and Katherina achieve new social roles that satisfy their personal wishes. Both *A Comedy of Errors* and *The Taming of the Shrew* trace the achievement of secure social position, but while the former converts the nightmare of individual vulnerability into rollicking comedy, the latter dramatizes the dream of adapting society to one's own desires.

After the social extremes of the beggar and the aristocrat in the Induction, the major characters of *The Taming of the Shrew* are what contemporaries called the middling sort. The play has no lovelorn duke or legendary hero, no enchanted woods or fairy-tale castle, and no subplot involving characters of inferior social status: the action all involves a closely knit, materialistic, and conventional society. As a famous university town, Padua is an appropriate destination for Lucentio and Petruchio, who are looking for adventure, but so many commercial and personal ties bind the travelers to the native inhabitants that in no sense do they seem strangers to the culture they find there. Petruchio says that he has 'come abroad to see the world' (I.11.58), but he has come first to Padua to see friends, especially his 'best beloved and approved friend, / Hortensio' (I.ii.3–4). Although he hasn't met Katherina previously, his father was well known to her father, Baptista, who welcomes Petruchio for his father's sake (I.ii.101–2; II.i.68–70). Lucentio, who doesn't have old friends in Padua, can rely on his father's renown. When Tranio, disguised as Lucentio, asks permission to court Bianca 'upon knowledge of my parentage' (II.i.95), Baptista accepts him because Vincentio, Lucentio's father, is well known to him by reputation. Even the Pedant from Mantua is glad to accept protection from the son of a well-known merchant.

While this network of family and business connections enables the young men visiting Padua to combine adventure with security, it also seems almost suffocatingly restrictive. When Lucentio wants to adopt a disguise in order to be near Bianca and win her love, the main obstacle to his plan is that there must be someone to play the part of Lucentio. And his role is to

> be in Padua here Vincentio's son,
> Keep house and ply his book, welcome his friends,
> Visit his countrymen, and banquet them. (I.i.195–7)

Being his father's son and heir is undoubtedly useful, so that Lucentio finds it convenient to provide himself with a substitute father; still, he is severely embarrassed when his real father turns up unexpectedly. And if the emphasis on family connections is inconvenient for Lucentio, it is yet more troublesome for Katherina and Bianca, who are confined and frustrated by being thought of almost exclusively in terms of their familial roles. Katherina is publicly humiliated for being an unmarried and unsought-after elder daughter and understandably reacts with resentment towards her father and violent jealousy towards her sister. As younger daughter, Bianca is not free to marry until Katherina finds a husband. Even when Tranio/Lucentio urges that he be added to Bianca's list of suitors, he does so on the grounds that *her father* is 'a noble gentleman,' deserving multiple suitors for his daughter (I.ii.238). Unsurprisingly Bianca treats her apparently unmarriageable elder sister with veiled hostility. Subject to her father's authority in education and marriage—the only significant activities her society expects of her—Bianca subverts his will in both: secretly defying tutors he provides and making a clandestine marriage. The family unit, then, is not fragmented or threatened with dissolution as it is in such comedies as *The Comedy of Errors* or *As You Like It*,[1] but the very strength of the family generates hostility and hypocrisy.

While there is no real evil in *The Taming of the Shrew*, no malevolent villain or threat of death, there is considerable tension generated by the tightly knit, paternalistic social structures. The materialism of the play's world also contributes to an oppressive atmosphere. It is a world of objects: the luxurious objects evoked to convince Christopher Sly that he is a rich lord—'a couch, / Softer and sweeter than the lustful bed / On purpose trimm'd up for Semiramis,' horses with 'Their harness studded all with gold and pearl' (Ind.ii.37–9, 42), the expensive objects Gremio pledges to win Bianca—a house 'richly furnished with plate and gold, / Basins and ewers . . . Tyrian tapestry . . . ivory coffers . . . cypress chests . . . Costly apparel, tents, and canopies, / Fine linen, Turkey cushions . . . Pewter and brass . . . a hundred milch-kine . . . Six score fat oxen' (II.i.347–58); the homely, shabby things that constitute Petruchio's equipage on his wedding day—'a new hat and an old jerkin; a pair of old breeches . . . a pair of boots that have been candle-cases . . . an old rusty sword . . . his horse hipp'd' with an old mothy saddle and stirrups of no kindred' (III.ii.43–50). As a character in a novel by Umberto Eco exclaims, 'there is nothing more wonderful than a list, instrument of wondrous hypotyposis,'[2] and the lists in *The Taming of the Shrew* create this reassuring sense of reality, of warmth and security. But they also suggest a world almost too cluttered to move about in freely.

The language of the play not only fills the dramatic world with solid objects, it suggests that they are the determinants of human identity. While in *The Comedy of Errors* the confusions over the gold chain, the rope, and the bag of gold lead Antipholus of Syracuse to distrust his own perceptions, to Christopher Sly the testimony of his senses is irrefutable evidence of his new identity:

> I do not sleep: I see, I hear, I speak;
> I smell sweet savors, and I feel soft things.
> Upon my life, I am a lord indeed. (Ind.ii.70–2)

The multiple disguises in the body of the play—Tranio as Lucentio, Lucentio as Cambio, Hortensio as Litio, and the Pedant as Vincentio—focus attention on how much social identity depends on arbitrary conventions of costume. Of course, the power of disguise is a dramatic convention assumed in many of the comedies, but while Rosalind's female identity continues to function dramatically in spite of her doublet and hose, in *The Taming of the Shrew* we are directed to believe that there are no perceptible differences among men except those of costume. All that is necessary for Tranio to bear Lucentio's part in Padua is to put on his master's hat and cloak, for they cannot 'be distinguish'd by [their] faces / For man or master' (I.i.200–1). And, although the Pedant no more resembles Vincentio than an 'apple doth an oyster' (IV.ii.101–2), he is the right age and 'In gait and countenance surely like a father' (IV.ii.65), so that, as Tranio tells him, it is necessary only 'to clothe you as becomes you' (IV.ii.121) for him to play Vincentio.

Shakespeare's Padua is also materialistic in the sense that the characters are preoccupied with wealth and possessions. Almost invariably they identify themselves and describe others in terms of their economic status. Petruchio assures Hortensio that he has 'Crowns in [his] purse . . . and goods at home' (I.ii.57) and more formally assures Baptista that he has inherited his father's entire fortune and increased that inheritance (II.i.117–18). Baptista welcomes Lucentio not simply because he has heard of Vincentio but because he has heard of him as a 'mighty man of Pisa' (II.i.104); similarly the Pedant remembers him as a 'merchant of incomparable wealth' (IV.ii.98). Bianca's suitors are conscious that her father is 'very rich' (I.i.124), and the inducement Hortensio uses to interest Petruchio in Katherina is that she will be 'very rich' (I.ii.63). Petruchio notoriously announces that he has come 'to wive it wealthily in Padua' (I.ii.75), and Hortensio, when he becomes disillusioned with Bianca, his 'treasure' and his 'jewel' (I.ii.118–19), decides immediately to marry 'a wealthy widow' (IV.ii.37).

The metonymical identification of people with their possessions is a salient characteristic of the play's farcical hilarity. In the noisy quarrel where Katherina has bound Bianca's hands and then berates her about her suitors, Bianca offers to take off 'these other gawds . . . Yea, all my raiment' (II.i.3, 5) in return for her release. Bianca clearly understands that her finery symbolizes to Katherina her value on the marriage market. Bianca is their father's 'treasure, she must have a husband,' while poor Kate fears that she 'must dance barefoot on [Bianca's] wedding-day' (II.i.32–3). When Baptista announces that he will give Bianca to the highest bidder, he explains even more explicitly that the human deeds he cares about are the deeds to land and property:

'Tis deeds must win the prize, and he of both
That can assure my daughter greatest dower
Shall have my Bianca's love. (II.i.342–4)

Characters so universally equate personal with economic worth and so unabashedly declare their economic motives that the effect is not individual characterization so much as the establishment of the values and mores of an acquisitive society.

Finally, perhaps the most striking feature of Shakespeare's Padua is the conventionality of its inhabitants. The characters are all thoroughly imbued with the ideology of a patriarchal society and assume that men have power over their wives, children, and servants. The dramatic action rests on the unquestioned assumption that marriage is right for everyone, and the plot develops from Baptista's determination that his daughters' marriages follow the usual pattern, his elder daughter marrying before her younger sister. The conflict arises from the universal abhorrence of Katherina's refusal to conform to conventional ideas of femininity.

The play does not, however, simply pit rebellious youth against aged conventionality. On the whole, the young lovers defer to the values and opinions of the group as automatically as do their elders. If Baptista's auctioning of his younger daughter satirizes the way the old sacrifice love to social and financial considerations, Hortensio's snobbish outrage when he believes he has discovered Bianca making love with her tutor also reveals the timid conventionality of a man who adheres unquestioningly to dominant social values. He announces himself as

one that scorn[s] to live in this disguise
For such a one as leaves a gentleman,
And makes a god of such a cullion, (IV.ii.18–20)

and he renounces Bianca because she has lost value by favoring a social and economic inferior. Lucentio is less of a prig as a suitor, but he is just as obviously controlled by literary conventions as Hortensio is by social ones. When Lucentio first sees Bianca, he confesses his love in conventional Petrarchan language:

Tranio, I burn, I pine, I perish, Tranio,
If I achieve not this young modest girl. (I.i.155–6)

He expresses his rapture in the clichéd images Shakespeare satirizes also in Sonnet 130.

Tranio, I saw her coral lips to move,
And with her breath she did perfume the air. (I.i.174–5)

The young women too are directed by the norms of their society. Bianca's fulfillment of the conventional ideal of feminine docility and modesty and her later imperiousness together testify to the importance she attaches to the approval of others. She tries to evade the disadvantages of a subordinate position, but she never challenges the principle of subordination or disregards public opinion. Despite Katherina's rebellious refusal to adopt the role of feminine passivity, she too desires above all the approval of her society. Her outbreaks of temper, indeed, arise directly from resentment that she is not valued by others. She berates Baptista for neglecting his parental duties by exposing her to derision (I.i.57–8), by failing to provide her with a husband (II.i.31–4), and by matching her with an unconventional suitor (II.i.285–9). And when Petruchio is late for the wedding, Baptista's horror at 'What will be said? What mockery will it be . . .!' (III.ii.4) is echoed by Katherina: 'No shame but mine . . . Now must the world point at poor Katherine' (III.ii.8, 18). The reactions of the rich merchant and his rebellious daughter are the same: anger and fear at what people will say.

The 'happy gale' (I.ii.48) that blows Petruchio to Padua brings a gust of uncomfortably bracing air to this stultifyingly tightly knit, materialistic, and conventional community. In the early scenes his brashness is a major source of humor. Within a few lines of his first appearance he is beating his servant for failing to understand and comply immediately with his orders. In the next scene, Gremio twice rebukes him for being 'too blunt' and 'marvellous forward' (II.i.45, 73). But despite his temper and impatience with social proprieties Petruchio does not provoke serious hostility. Unlike Katherina, whose reactions to social constraints are anti-social and self-defeating, Petruchio tempers his assertiveness with engaging frankness and friendliness and acts effectively in personal and social relationships, demonstrating that society's rules are flexible enough to be shaped to fit individual needs.

The most important demonstration of Petruchio's combination of self-assertion and sociability is his marriage. At first he doesn't challenge conventional matrimonial practices but brushes aside the cant surrounding them. When he bursts on the scene in Padua, he is an energetic young man eager to participate fully in whatever life has to offer. No longer a student like Lucentio, he has some travel, business, and military experience behind him and is ready to take his place in society as a married man. Common sense tells him that financial considerations are the normal basis for matrimony in his society, and his habitual honesty prevents his draping his intentions in robes of sentiment. He unapologetically announces that he means to wed wealthily and 'If wealthily, then happily' (I.ii.76), and briskly sets about arranging financial terms with Baptista. His startling frankness makes him a natural target for Grumio's sarcasm: 'Nay, look you, sir, he tells you flatly what his mind is. Why, give him gold enough, and marry him to a puppet or an aglet-baby, or an old trot with ne'er a tooth in her head, though she have as many diseases as two and fifty horses. Why, nothing comes amiss, so money comes withal' (I.ii.77–82). But Petruchio is not trying to be what others expect or desire him to be. He insists on making his own decisions and is impervious to both ridicule and solicitous advice.

Petruchio's honesty about his economic motives is refreshing, but it is his response to Katherina herself that clearly shows his independent spirit. While his original intention to marry a rich woman reflects the materialism of his society, his assumption that the character of his wife will be totally irrelevant to his marital happiness shows that he is relatively inexperienced with women. While he may have 'heard lions roar' and 'heard the sea . . . Rage like an angry boar' (I.ii.200, 201–2), there is something comically naive in the breezy self-confidence with which he contemplates marriage with a shrew:

> Have I not in a pitched battle heard
> Loud larums, neighing steeds, and trumpets' clang?
> And do you tell me of a woman's tongue,
> That gives not half so great a blow to hear
> As will a chestnut in a farmer's fire?
> Tush, tush, fear boys with bugs. (I.ii.205–10)

Petruchio obviously has never been in love and, unlike Lucentio or the young lovers in *A Midsummer Night's Dream*, has not been attracted by the poets' accounts to want or expect the experience Lucentio calls 'love in idleness' (I.i.151). His brash assumption that his affections will not alter whether his wife is 'as foul as was Florentius' love, / As old as Sibyl, and as curst and shrowd / As Socrates' Xantippe' (I.ii.69–71) is not cynicism or misogyny so much as the comic hubris of inexperience. Katherina forces Petruchio to rethink his assumptions about women, and his transformation convinces the audience that he is indeed the man capable of taming her.

While the other eligible men desire Bianca because she fits the stereotypical ideal of femininity and despise Katherina because she so emphatically does not, Petruchio is excited by Katherina's spirit. After he hears about her forthright way of dealing with an unwanted music teacher, he is intrigued:

> Now by the world, it is a lusty wench!
> I love her ten times more than e'er I did.
> O, how I long to have some chat with her! (II.i.160–2)

At this point he gives some thought as to how to 'woo her with some spirit' (II.i.169) and decides to smother her shrewishness under the banalities of conventional courtship:

> Say that she rail, why then I'll tell her plain
> She sings as sweetly as a nightingale;
> Say that she frown, I'll say she looks as clear
> As morning roses newly wash'd with dew. (II.i.170–3)

When he actually meets Katherina, he modifies this plan considerably.

She seizes the initiative with her first words, haughtily rebuking his informality in addressing her familiarly as Kate: 'They call me Katherine that do talk of me' (II.i.184). Petruchio is thrown off balance and retorts, 'You lie, in faith, for you are call'd plain Kate' (II.i.185). Kate's combativeness and verbal dexterity force Petruchio to abandon his plan of ignoring what she actually says and provoke him into a verbal battle in which both participants intentionally flout courtship conventions. Kate responds to Petruchio's proposal of marriage by warning him that she is 'Too light [quick] . . . to catch' (II.i.204) and 'dangerously waspish' (210), by rudely calling him a join'd-stool (198), an ass (199), a jade (201), a buzzard (206), a crab (229), and a fool (212, 257), and even by striking him. Clearly her sharp-tongued belligerence deliberately repudiates the gentle modesty expected in a young woman waiting to be wooed and won by an eligible suitor. Petruchio is equally far from the conventional lovesick swain, but while Katherina's language is consistently abusive, Petruchio's is notable for its variety. He not only joins in the wordplay Kate initiates ('*Kath.* What is your crest? a coxcomb? / *Pet.* A combless cock, so Kate will be my hen' [II.i.225–6]), but the song accompanying his wooing dance also includes sarcastic flattery ('thy mildness prais'd in every town' [191]), obscenity ('What, with my tongue in your tail?' [217]), praise ('sweet as spring-time flowers' [246]), and unembellished literal statement—to threaten ('I swear I'll cuff you, if you strike again' [220]), to inform ('your father hath consented / That you shall be my wife; your dowry greed on' [269–70]), and to invite ('Now, Kate, I am a husband for your turn' [272]).

Petruchio's verbal flexibility makes his victory in the battle of wits appear both credible and desirable. As audience, we can laugh at their mutual travesty of courtship rituals, delight in their sexual and intellectual energy, sympathize with this variation of the traditional comic material of young love, and yet see that Kate's knee-jerk shrewishness is no match for Petruchio's more varied responses. We see that, although Petruchio decided to marry Kate sight unseen because she was rich, when he meets her he in fact responds to the actual woman. Engaging in this combat of wits shows Petruchio that a shrewish wife cannot simply be ignored, determines him to tame Katherina, and convinces him that she is worth taming. The bawdy puns that are his chief weapon suggest that Petruchio, who boasted earlier that if his bride is rich enough she cannot be too foul for him, is sexually excited by the exchange with Kate. It may be worth remembering in this connection the Lord's 'wanton pictures' (Ind.i.47) offered to Christopher Sly: Adonis pursued by Venus, Io 'beguiled and surpris'd' by Jupiter, and Daphne fleeing from Apollo (Ind.ii.55). Petruchio's exuberant ribaldry is a far cry from the aristocratic Lord's decadent taste for sexual violence among the Olympians, but it does show that he finds the battle of the sexes erotically provocative.

In the course of the scene with Kate, Petruchio converts from an eagerness to marry any rich woman to a determination to marry and win the love of a particular woman. And he stops talking about her wealth. When he returns to the plan of meeting her shrewishness with the softness of love, his language—more personal and original than the intended clichés about roses and nightingales—expresses genuine admiration and tenderness:

> Kate like the hazel-twig
> Is straight and slender, and as brown in hue
> As hazel-nuts, and sweeter than the kernels. (II.i.253–5)

Using a strategy similar to that in Sonnet 130 ('My mistress' eyes are nothing like the sun'), Shakespeare here convinces us of Petruchio's sincerity by the contrast between what he intended to say and what he does say, between Lucentio's stale Petrarchisms and Petruchio's homely similes. When Petruchio brings their private interview to a close, he does so in terms of such a linguistic contrast:

> And therefore setting all this chat aside,
> Thus in plain terms: your father hath consented
> That you shall be my wife; your dowry 'greed on;
> And will you, nill you, I will marry you.
> Now, Kate, I am a husband for your turn,
> For by this light whereby I see thy beauty,
> Thy beauty that doth make me like thee well,
> Thou must be married to no man but me. (II.i.268–75)

Dismissing their contest of wits as chat, Petruchio speaks in plain terms that acknowledge economic and social reality and also speak his admiration and affection convincingly. This contrast between verbal games and plain honest statement suggests that Petruchio's idea of taming Kate is not to enforce a narrow, rigid conformity but to replace constricting formulas with mutual responsiveness.

Petruchio falls in love with Kate's vivacity and nimble wit, but he is dismayed that she thinks and acts in terms of unexamined social conventions. Her rebellion is not free and spontaneous but a performance as the stereotypical shrew. Insecure and resentful but always painfully aware of how others see her, she is afraid of Petruchio's heterodoxy. Ignoring Petruchio's offer of affection, she primly reproves her father for wishing to marry her to a 'madcap ruffian' (II.i.288). In the courtship scene, Petruchio responds to Kate's underlying conventionality by teasing her with patently false accounts of what people say about her, reporting that he heard her 'mildness prais'd in every town' (II.i.191) and indignantly wondering 'Why does the world report that Kate doth limp?' (II.i.252). Then he begins his program for taming her by flouting social decorum. First, he firmly wards off outside interference with his announcement of their wedding date: 'I choose her for myself. / If she and I be pleas'd, what's that to you?' (II.i.302–3). Next he carefully plans their wedding as a social event, explicitly making arrangements for food, clothing, and guests, and then deliberately turns the occasion into a fiasco—arriving late dressed in outlandish clothes, interrupting the ceremony with bizarre behavior, and finally carrying his bride off before the wedding feast in a hilarious parody of a knight-errant rescuing a damsel-in-distress. While Petruchio's earlier *faux pas* were by-products of energetic spontaneity ('O, pardon me,' he apologizes at Gremio's chiding, 'I would fain be doing' [II.i.74]), his 'mad marriage' (III.ii.182) is a deliberate repudiation of social decorum. Whether Petruchio is a boorish brute or a wise and benevolent teacher and whether he breaks Kate's spirit, rescues her from a repressive society, or teaches her civility by negative example are hotly contested critical questions, but unquestionably he forces Kate to think consciously about the norms of acceptable behavior in her community.

His program for taming 'wild Kate' (II.i.277) obviously does not include high culture. Hortensio and Lucentio in their roles as tutors discover to their dismay Kate's resistance to the fine arts. Indeed, her reaction to the lute is even less gratifying than Christopher Sly's to Shakespearean comedy. While he is bored and in most productions falls asleep, she breaks the lute over Hortensio's head. At first, Petruchio's method of modifying Kate's behavior seems like a replication of the Lord's practice on Christopher Sly, changing her identity by changing her external environment. He provides her with a new image of herself: instead of hearing her sister's suitors reject her as a whore and a devil (I.i.55, 66), she hears her husband insist that she is 'patient, sweet, and virtuous' (III.

ii.195). By denying her food, clothing, and sleep, he forces her out of the role of selfish aggressor into that of suffering victim. Like Sly, Kate is disorientated by a radically changed environment that supplants familiar reality: she seems to Curtis 'as one new risen from a dream' (IV.i.186). And like Sly, Kate finds herself adopting unfamiliar modes of behavior: she 'who never knew how to entreat' (IV.iii.7) and who asserted the freedom to say and do whatever she wished, usually at others' expense, learns to ask for help, to express gratitude and compassion, to conciliate and accommodate.

But Kate's experience is fundamentally different from Sly's. While he does not have to discover the fragility of a personal identity based on external trappings, Kate learns that personal worth does not depend on deferential servants and fashionable clothes. When Baptista charges that marrying Katherina in disreputable clothes is shameful, Petruchio replies that clothes do not make the man: 'To me she's married, not unto my clothes' (III.ii.117). After tantalizing Kate with promises of 'silken coats and caps, and golden rings' (IV.iii.55) and then capriciously denying her the proposed finery, he expounds the moral even more explicitly:

> For 'tis the mind that makes the body rich;
> And as the sun breaks through the darkest clouds,
> So honor peereth in the meanest habit.
> What, is the jay more precious than the lark,
> Because his feathers are more beautiful?
> Or is the adder better than the eel,
> Because his painted skin contents the eye?
> O no, good Kate; neither art thou the worse
> For this poor furniture and mean array. (IV.iii.172–80)

Kate's transformation, then, must be internal, not external like Sly's.

What Petruchio teaches Kate is not simply a sense of proportion which subordinates surfaces to substance or the conventional piety that exalts immaterial virtue over material wealth (his objections to the cut of the gown are at least as arbitrary and as superficial as the vagaries of fashion for gentlewomen). The most important lesson Kate learns is that 'it is the mind that makes the body rich' (IV.iii.172)—the human power of understanding and choice that values the song of the lark more highly than the plumage of the jay. Although Kate is spirited and rebellious, she reacts to conventions with thoughtless, puppetlike predictability. Her shrewishness fulfills a socially defined stereotype as much as Bianca's docility does. By usurping Kate's role of aggressive ill-temper and subjecting her to a bewildering mixture of harshness and tenderness, Petruchio forces her to abandon her customary modes of perception and behavior. She learns to exercise choice instead of conforming automatically to the expectations of the people she lives with and to select ways to act from among alternatives rather than to react with habitual shrewishness.

Petruchio challenges conventions governing time as well as costume. In *The Comedy of Errors*, as we saw earlier, time, both as natural phenomenon and as social convention, is men's master. In *The Taming of the Shrew*, Petruchio asserts his mastery over time. His lack of punctuality, like that of Antipholus of Syracuse, is cause for complaint, but while Antipholus' tardiness makes his wife shrewish, Petruchio's is part of the cure for shrewishness. In Act III he defies social convention by deliberately arriving late for his wedding. In Act IV when he makes the return to Baptista's house contingent on his version of time, he enunciates the principle clearly:

> I will not go to-day, and ere I do,
> It shall be what a' clock I say it is. (IV.iii.194–5)

Hortensio's response—'Why, so this gallant will command the sun' (IV.iv.196)— is prophetic. On the journey, when Katherina objects to his calling the moon the sun, Petruchio claims the power not only to name the intervals of time as he chooses but to impose his own meaning on the natural phenomena by which people measure time: 'It shall be moon, or star, or what I list' (IV.v.7). By finally agreeing—'be it moon, or sun, or what you please' (IV.v.13)—Katherina acknowledges the arbitrariness of the human order imposed on the natural world and Petruchio's independence of that conventional order. She also shows her understanding that she too can control the world she lives in. In the next episode, where she gaily addresses old Vincentio as a 'Young budding virgin' (IV.v.37), she exercises her power to interpret age and sex to suit her needs. The fun, of course, depends on the limits of that power—there would be no joke if Vincentio were young and female, but Kate's ability to parody Petruchio is a measure of her mastery of his strategy. The old Katherina could only chafe against temporal conventions ('What, shall I be appointed hours, as though (belike) I knew not what to take and what to leave?' [I.i.103–4]) or feel humiliated at their breach by Petruchio ('Who woo'd in haste, and means to wed at leisure' [III.ii.11]). By the time she returns to her father's house with Petruchio, she can cheerfully assert a personal view of a timeless world where 'every thing I look on seemeth green' (IV.v.47), and can also acknowledge common reality and social propriety by apologizing for her 'mad mistaking' (IV.v.49).

In contrast to Kate's unorthodox marriage, Bianca's reveals the absurd contradiction between literary convention and social convention by literalizing both. Lucentio, following the romantic tradition in which a woman is a sought-after ideal, puts on a disguise to get access to Bianca and defeats a rival for her love, while his stand-in, Tranio, outbids another suitor in a parody of sixteenth-century matrimonial custom in which a woman is a man's property. Although

the contrast between the unconventionality of the Petruchio–Katherina plot
and the conventionality of the Lucentio–Bianca plot has received considerable
critical attention,[3] the differences are variations within a parallel movement from
confinement to freedom through marriage. Petruchio indirectly helps to liberate
Bianca as well as Kate. At the beginning of the play Bianca's father has 'closely
mew'd her up' (I.i.183), and Petruchio's courtship of the elder sister is initiated as
a means to 'set the younger free' (I.ii.266).[4] More directly, Bianca, like her sister,
gains her independence through a lover who overcomes the social conventions
that confine her. Lucentio usurps the authority of both fathers, supplanting
his own father with a substitute and defying Bianca's by marrying her 'without
asking [his] good will' (V.i.134).[5] The two bridegrooms' language of defiance
marks their similar stances toward society. Lucentio anticipates how, once he is
married, 'let all the world say no, / I'll keep mine own, despite of all the world'
(III.ii.141–2); a few lines later Petruchio challenges the same social world: 'I
will be master of what is mine own . . . touch her whoever dare' (III.ii.229,
233). Moreover, just as Petruchio's wedding costume and his attack on the tailor
symbolize his disruption of social decorum, improprieties in clothing compose a
striking visual image of Lucentio's overturning of social order. For example, when
Vincentio turns up unexpectedly and is denounced as an impostor by Biondello
and Tranio, it is Tranio's clothing that Vincentio finds most upsetting:

> O immortal gods! O fine villain! A silken doublet, a velvet hose, a scarlet
> cloak, and a copatain hat! O, I am undone, I am undone! (V.i.66–8)

Bianca, like Kate, is a strong-willed young woman determined to have her own
way in spite of social coercion: 'I'll not be tied to hours, nor 'pointed times'
(III.i.19). By proceeding at her own rate, marrying first and securing parental
approval afterwards, she achieves her goal. Like her sister, she accepts the role
defined for her by society only in her own good time and her own fashion. While
current audiences admire Katherina's rebellion more than Bianca's outward
conformity and find Kate's overcoming of internalized barriers more interesting
than Bianca's eluding of external ones, we shouldn't regard Bianca as Kate's
villainous antithesis. Kate surpasses her sister, but Bianca is not much wide of
the mark, as Petruchio's last speech reminds Lucentio: ''Twas I won the wager,
though you hit the white' (V.ii.186).

For all their neglect of social amenities and their assertion of personal rights
against paternal authority, neither Lucentio nor Petruchio is a radical social critic.
Lucentio defies the social convention of arranged marriages to court Bianca,
but once he is safely married, far from hurling defiance at an outraged world,
he kneels submissively begging his father's pardon and moves immediately to
conciliate Bianca's father. Petruchio talks of freeing Bianca but of taming Kate;
his aim is not to produce a rebel but 'a Kate / Conformable as other household

Kates' (II.i.277–8). He sees himself as a member of the community, and he shares its basic values. His success in gaining a rich bride, in having his courtship expenses paid by others, and in winning a wager on his wife's obedience all testify to his ease and facility in an acquisitive, materialistic society. His preference for 'a lusty wench' as a bride is exceptional, but his desire for 'peace . . . and love, and quiet life' (V.ii.108) in marriage is entirely usual. He is unconventional in a conventional society not because he minimizes the importance of social usages but because he asserts his power to control them. When he contends that Kate is marrying him and not his clothes, he is not demanding that she come to terms with unaccommodated man as 'a poor, bare, fork'd animal' but rather asserting his right to wear what clothes he chooses.

In contrast, Kate at the beginning of the play has neither the critical detachment nor the understanding of herself as a social being that could help her to control social customs. She has absorbed the assumptions that the admiration and deference of others guarantee social acceptance and that becoming a wife is the only desirable goal for a woman. Her resentment at being undervalued creates hostility and aggression that paradoxically threaten to produce the fate she most fears: a future as that social anomaly, an old maid. Shakespeare's Padua, of course, is not unusual in its abhorrence of a mature, unmarried woman. Sixteenth-century England displayed a similar attitude. Marriage was the normal condition for both sexes, and women derived their social and economic position from their husbands. The few women who remained unmarried suffered from an ambiguous social status and humiliating economic dependence.[6] Moreover, such customs as the English tradition requiring a bride's unmarried elder sister to dance barefoot on the wedding day or the French one requiring an unmarried elder brother or sister to eat raw vegetables suggest that the uneasiness about unmarried women was not caused solely by practical economic considerations.[7] In Claude Lévi-Strauss' interpretation, 'dancing barefoot' is equivalent to 'dancing raw,' and these and other related customs all depend on a contrast between 'the raw' (equivalent to nature) and 'the cooked' (equivalent to culture) and reflect the idea that the person who remains celibate too long is not fully socialized. Shakespeare's apparently unmarriageable shrew with her fear that she 'must dance barefoot on [her sister's] wedding day' (II.i.33) dramatizes not only a psychological but a social problem, the presence within society of the raw or uncivilized, someone not fully integrated into the community. When Petruchio denies Kate food, insisting that the meat is too burned to eat (IV.i.161), he implicitly tells her that she is not civilized enough to eat the food cooked for civilized people. Although Lévi-Strauss says that, in cultures where magical thought is vestigial, customs based on the equivalence of 'the cooked' with 'the socialized' are not intended to change but to describe a situation,[8] Petruchio clearly intends to change Katherina's behavior. When she tries to counter similar objections to the fashionable clothing she wants by arguing that 'gentlewomen wear such caps as these,' he makes the point explicitly: 'When you are gentle, you shall have one too' (IV.iii.70–1).

In the Induction, the Lord and Christopher Sly portray the civilized and the uncivilized in terms of social rank. In Kate we see similar extremes within a single person. Kate the shrew is aggressive, destructive, abusive, and self-defeating. By the end of the play she is a respected, socially secure wife. In *The Taming of the Shrew* belonging to a human community is not simply a birthright as it is in *A Comedy of Errors*; it depends instead on the acquisition of civilized values and manners. Kate's transformation from despised shrew to happily married woman suggests that civilization depends on people with a critical attitude towards it.[9] By suffering deprivation of the necessities of food and clothing that she can't provide for herself, Kate learns that she depends on other people. From Petruchio's iconoclastic attacks on conventional forms and rituals, she learns to see social institutions and practices not as threatening and intractable givens but as human constructions amenable to human control. By examining social customs critically, she learns not to reject society but to live comfortably within it.

As Petruchio confides to the audience, he also has 'Another way . . . to man [his] haggard' (IV.i.193), a way that involves intimacy and affection as well as deprivation. G.R. Hibbard quotes Gervase Markham's *Country Contentments* (1615) to elucidate the falconry metaphor: 'All hawks generally are manned after one manner, that is to say, by watching and keeping them from sleep, by a continual carrying of them upon your fist, and by a most familiar stroking and playing with them . . . and by often gazing and looking of them in the face, with a loving and gentle countenance, and so making them acquainted with the man.'[10] So too the necessary complement to Petruchio's program of harshness and deprivation is constant attention and affection: he does it all 'in reverend care of her' (IV.i.204). Subjected to unremitting offers of affection and demands for acquiescence, Kate discovers not only how much she owes but how much she can give to other people. When she tells Vincentio that she mistook him for a young girl because her eyes had been 'so bedazzled with the sun' (IV.v.46), she is ironically alluding to Petruchio's identification of himself as 'my mother's son' (IV.v.6) and to his insistence that she call the sun the moon. Her playfulness demonstrates that she understands Petruchio not as a man unable to tolerate a wife with a mind of her own but as a loving husband asking her to show that she wants to please him. Kate, who originally thought that the mark of maturity was knowing 'what to take and what to leave' (I.i.104), has learned that living harmoniously with other people is a matter of knowing when to take and when to give.

The understanding and cooperation between Kate and Petruchio in the last act has prompted several of the play's most perceptive critics to comment on their creation of a separate world, what Marianne Novy calls 'a private world, a joke that the rest of the characters miss' or what J. Dennis Huston calls 'a select society, which includes themselves, the playwright, and perhaps a few members of his audience.'[11] I believe that this emphasis on a exclusive community in collusion against the rest of the world assumes a twentieth-century opposition between public and private worlds that distorts the play's conceptual and structural dynamics.[12] Unlike Christopher Sly, who remains suspended in his dream of aristocratic splendor, Kate returns to her old environment.[13]

The action rises to a climax in Act III with the farcical violence of Petruchio rescuing his bride from her family and friends, but neither Kate nor Petruchio expresses any wish to remain isolated in Petruchio's country house. Acts IV and V dramatize Kate's gradual reintegration into society. Certainly the play works against Norbert Elias' thesis that the civilizing process depends on the coercive power of a strong central government:[14] the basis of Kate's transformation is the self-understanding she develops in her relationship with her husband. But her domestication is complete only when it is made public. Hortensio assures Petruchio that 'the field is won' (IV.v.23) as soon as Kate yields to him over what to call the sun, but Petruchio arranges a series of increasingly public demonstrations of Kate's new civility. The incident with Vincentio adds a stranger to the audience that already includes Hortensio and the servants. Next, Petruchio demands a kiss in the public street. Finally, Kate wins the wager on whose wife is most obedient before the assembled group of family and friends. Her education culminates, then, not in achieving intimacy with Petruchio but in winning recognition and approval from the social group. The pattern of interrupted feast, solitary fast, and celebratory feast marks the stages of her separation from and return to society. Significantly her final speech explaining the rationale of her obedience is not a private act of submission to Petruchio but a public demonstration of her full acceptance of her position as Petruchio's wife and a public reprimand of the Widow and Bianca for their failures 'to serve, love, and obey' (V.ii.164) their husbands.

Kate's demonstration of obedience is presented as a victory, not a humiliation. Her offer to place her hand under Petruchio's foot acknowledges her subordination in a hierarchical relationship, but the gesture also expresses gratitude at being cherished and pride at fulfilling her husband's desires. Petruchio certainly demands that Katherina submit to his will, but we know, as she does, that he won't step on her hand. Shakespeare, then, does not ironically subvert the patriarchal power structure portrayed in *The Taming of the Shrew*. As David Underdown has demonstrated, in the period between 1560 and 1640 a perceived threat to patriarchal order from unruly women produced a widespread fascination with literary shrews as well as a marked increase in legal proceedings against assertive women.[15] The representation of Kate's domestication as a paradigm of the civilizing process responds to that cultural anxiety by affirming women's subordination. Readings of Kate's endorsement of patriarchy as ironic are, I think, unconvincing.[16] Unlike Petruchio's claim that Kate is 'My horse, my ox, my ass, my any thing' (III.ii.232), which is qualified by the farcical context, Kate's exposition of wifely submission stands unqualified and unrefuted. Similarly, in *The Comedy of Errors* the Abbess' lecture to Adriana on how a nagging wife can drive a man mad (V.i.68–86) is consonant with the view of marriage in the play as a whole. Neither play is designed merely to teach uppity women their places. Both suggest that husbands and wives should be subject to each other in love, but both also endorse a hierarchical view of marriage in which wives owe obedience to husbands that husbands do not owe wives.

As tempting as it is to explain away Kate's final speech, such revisionism deflects needed attention from the patriarchal ideology the play enacts. As Lynda Boose convincingly argues, 'the impulse to rewrite the more oppressively patriarchal material in this play serves the very ideologies about gender that it makes less visible by making less offensive.'[17] Similarly, to ignore the play's consistent exclusion of physical brutality also obstructs the feminist project of writing the history of the construction of gender in Western society. While endorsing women's subordination within patriarchal marriage, *The Taming of the Shrew* mitigates the violence used to control unruly women in the real world and in the shrew-taming literary tradition. Although sparring verbally with Katherina excites Petruchio in their pre-marital battle of the sexes, his goal is 'peace . . . love, and quiet life' (V.ii.108), and he puts a stop to the violence she initiates. His use of physical and economic force to deprive Katherina temporarily of food and sleep is relatively mild compared with the horrifying brutalities of actual social practice and with the sadism of earlier versions of the shrew story.[18] For example, in contrast to the hero of *A meery Jeste of a Shrewde and curste Wyfe lapped in Morrelles skin*, who subjects his bride to a brutal sexual initiation, Petruchio on their wedding night lectures Kate on continence. Not only do the methods employed in Petruchio's taming-school appear humane in the context of a society that tortured women judged to be scolds with cucking stools and scold's bridles, the play also demystifies the patriarchal authority it confirms. Discussions of unruly women in the years around 1600 usually represent female insubordination as a perversion of natural order and a symptom of an incipient breakdown of all social order. In contrast, Kate's shrewishness is a danger to no one but herself. Although Kate invokes the familiar analogy between familial and political order in her final speech, her subjection to Petruchio is presented not as an inevitable alignment with the natural relations between men and women but as the result of protracted negotiations between two people, anticipating Locke's theory of a contractual basis for marriage rather than reinscribing the family as the divinely instituted origin of political power.[19] Kate's exposition of a wife's duties is general and normative rather than personal, but she justifies wifely obedience on the basis not of the religious sanctity of the conventional sexual hierarchy but of its justice and convenience. The only inherent superiority she attributes to men is their greater physical strength, and she describes a wife's duties of 'love, fair looks, and true obedience' (v.ii.153) as just recompense to a husband who endures 'painful labor' to care for her (149).[20]

The Taming of the Shrew offers Kate and Bianca no alternative to the limited choice between spinsterhood and patriarchal marriage. In the context of contemporary discussions of domestic relations, it supports the ideal of marriage based on mutual love within the framework of masculine authority.[21] Petruchio's announced desire for a rich wife and Baptista's offer of his youngest daughter to the highest bidder allude unmistakably to the practice among the propertied classes of arranging marriages on an economic basis, and the play explicitly subordinates these financial motives to the emotional responses of the female characters. Petruchio's success consists not in winning a rich wife but in winning the love and obedience of a shrewish one and is proved not by Kate's humiliation but by her triumph. Her prompt response when Petruchio sends for her and her long final speech demonstrate to the community she lives in and to the audience that she is no longer wild but self-assured, self-controlled, and considerate—a civilized woman who understands human relationships as a balance of duties and privileges. By her public submission to her husband and her dominance over the Widow and Bianca, she simultaneously acknowledges her dependence and asserts her personal worth. Kate, in short, achieves what she has always wanted: a dominant place as a valued member of society.

The comedy's happy ending embodies the achievement of mutual love and understanding recommended by the proponents of companionate marriage who insist also on husbands' authority over their wives. *The Taming of the Shrew* is distinctive not in its unresolved tension between mutuality and inequality but in its uncompromising acknowledgment of the demand that women choose their own subordination. The play exposes the inequities and potential brutality of male power, the patriarchal attitudes and institutions only temporarily disguised by courtship rhetoric such as Lucentio's, and the voluntary subjection required of women by love within a framework of gender inequality. At the same time it shows men and women achieving happiness by actively asserting control over those structures. By the last scene all the major characters have been able to fulfill their personal desires through their relationships with each other. Petruchio has a rich and spirited wife as well as 'peace . . . and love, and quiet life, / . . . and right supremacy' (V.ii.108–9). Lucentio has Bianca, and Bianca has parental approval for the husband she has chosen for herself; moreover, she is still learning her lessons as she pleases. Baptista and Vincentio have seen their children married to their social equals with appropriate financial settlements. Even Gremio and Hortensio, who lose Bianca to Lucentio, have the satisfaction of watching their successful rival's discomfort with his wife. In spite of—or better, because of—the tensions and rivalries of personal relationships, the conclusion of *The Taming of the Shrew* presents us with an image of a society that conforms to all the members' individual desires. And the supreme example of eating his cake and having it too is Shakespeare: by transforming the traditional shrew story of a struggle for domestic mastery into a process of domestication, he manages to satirize the absurdities of social convention while simultaneously celebrating the human capacity to shape society to express individual values. By presenting Kate's transformation in a play-within-a-play, he also allows the unsettling implication that this happy reconciliation of individual freedom with repressive communal values is possible only in a work of art.

NOTES

1. As is usual in the comedies, the absence of a wife and mother is not commented on.

2. Umberto Eco, *The Name of the Rose*, trans. William Weaver (San Diego: Harcourt, Brace, Jovanovich, 1983), 73. Puttenham calls hypotyposis *'the counterfait, otherwise called the figure of representation.'* George Puttenham, *The Arte of English Poesie*, intro. Baxter Hathaway (Kent, Ohio: Kent State University Press, 1970), 320.

3. See Alexander Leggatt, *Shakespeare's Comedy of Love* (London: Methuen, 1974), 46–9, and Peter G. Phialas, *Shakespeare's Romantic Comedies* (Chapel Hill: University of North Carolina Press, 1966), 28–30. Bertrand Evans and George R. Hibbard emphasize the contrast between the deception and disguise of the subplot and Petruchio's lack of subterfuge in the main plot. Evans, *Shakespeare's Comedies* (Oxford: Oxford University Press, 1967), 26; Hibbard, *'The Taming of the Shrew: A Social Comedy'* in *Shakespearean Essays*, ed. Alwin Thaler and Norman Sanders (Knoxville: University of Tennessee Press, 1964), 22.

4. Images of Bianca as confined or imprisoned and of her accessibility to suitors as freedom are recurrent; see I.i.87, 138; I.ii.19–19; I.i.138; I.ii.262.

5. Shakespeare has emphasized the rebelliousness of Bianca's and Lucentio's courtship by adding the clandestine marriage that does not appear in Gascoigne's *Supposes*, his source for the subplot.

6. According to Lawrence Stone, because the system of primogeniture fostered a growing reluctance to provide marriage portions, the proportion of the daughters of landed families who never married increased dramatically during the seventeenth century, rising to nearly 25 per cent in 1700. In the sixteenth century, however, more than 95 per cent of the daughters of the upper class married, a nuptial rate slightly higher than among the rest of the population. *The Family, Sex and Marriage in England, 1500–1800* (London: Weidenfeld & Nicolson, 1977), 43–5, graph 3 and 380. See also Miriam Slater, *Family Life in the Seventeenth Century* (London: Routledge & Kegan Paul, 1985), 84–90.

7. Claude Lévi-Strauss, *The Raw and the Cooked*, trans. John Weightman and Doreen Weightman (New York: Harper & Row, 1969), 334–6.

8. Ibid., 338.

9. Kate's coming to terms with her society can be seen as an exploration of the self-conscious forging of human identity in the context of Renaissance culture described by Stephen Greenblatt in *Renaissance Self-Fashioning: From More to Shakespeare* (Chicago: University of Chicago Press, 1980). We should notice, however, that whereas Greenblatt describes Renaissance culture wholly in terms

of its official cultural institutions, *The Taming of the Shrew* presents three distinct cultures—the plebeian world of the Hostess and Christopher Sly, the aristocratic world of the Lord and his retinue, and the middle-class world of Baptista's daughters and their suitors. In *The Taming of the Shrew*, emphasis on how a particular culture shapes individual identities is balanced by acknowledgment of the variety of cultures existing simultaneously and of the possibility of controlling cultural conventions whatever they are. Greenblatt's assumption of a monolithic Renaissance culture is criticized and supplemented by Michael Bristol in *Carnival and Theater: Plebeian Culture and the Structure of Authority in Renaissance England* (New York: Methuen, 1985).

10. Gervase Markham, *Country Contentments* (1615), 4th ed. (London, 1631), 36–7, as quoted in *The Taming of the Shrew*, ed. G.R. Hibbard (Harmondsworth: Penguin Books, 1968), n. to IV.i.176–82.

11. Marianne L. Novy, *Love's Argument: Gender Relations in Shakespeare* (Chapel Hill: University of North Carolina Press, 1984), 61; J. Dennis Huston, *Shakespeare's Comedies of Play* (New York: Columbia University Press, 19811, 64.

12. In early modern England the family was usually thought of as the fundamental social unit rather than as a refuge from society. See Susan Amussen, 'Gender, Family and the Social Order, 1560–1725,' 196–217, in *Order and Disorder in Early Modern England*, ed. Anthony Fletcher and John Stevenson (Cambridge: Cambridge University Press, 1985), and Amussen, *An Ordered Society: Gender and Class in Early Modern England* (Oxford: Basil Blackwell, 1988).

13. In *The Taming of a Shrew*, which most scholars now see as a bad quarto or memorial reconstruction of *The Taming of the Shrew*, Sly falls asleep after commenting on the play several times and in an epilogue awakes in his own clothes and interprets his experience as a dream. Some scholars have argued that Shakespeare intended *The Taming of the Shrew* to include similar scenes and have proposed various explanations for their loss. Other hypotheses are that Shakespeare deliberately dropped Sly from later scenes for artistic reasons or that Sly's expanded role is an unauthorized addition by those responsible for *The Taming of a Shrew*. For a discussion of the relationship of the texts see Brian Morris' 'Introduction' to the Arden edition (London: Methuen, 1981), 12–50.

14. Norbert Elias, *The Civilizing Process*, trans. Edmund Jephcott, 2 vols. (Oxford: Basil Blackwell, 1978 and 1982).

15. David Underdown, "The Taming of the Scold: the Enforcement of Patriarchal Authority in Early Modern England," in Fletcher and Stevenson, 116–36, and Underdown, *Revel, Riot, and Rebellion: Popular Politics and Culture in England, 1603–1660* (Oxford: Clarendon Press, 1985), 38–40.

16. On the development of the ironic reading of Kate's speech see Robert Heilman, 'The *Taming* Untamed, or the Return of the Shrew,' *Modern Language Quarterly*, 27 (1966), 147–61. Linda Woodbridge presents a sensible critique of ahistorical attempts to exonerate Shakespeare from the charge of sexism in *The Taming of the Shrew in Women and the English Renaissance: Literature and the Nature of Womankind, 1540–1620* (Urbana: University of Illinois Press, 1984), 221–2.

17. Lynda E. Boose, 'Scolding Brides and Bridling Scolds: Taming the Woman's Unruly Member,' *Shakespeare Quarterly*, 42 (1991), 181–2.

18. For the literary tradition, see Woodbridge, 201–7; for historical practices of controlling women, see Underdown, 'The Taming of the Scold,' and Boose, 179–213.

19. On the analogy between familial and political power and on Locke's undermining of the organic theory of patriarchal power, see Amussen, *An Ordered Society*, 37–66.

20. See John C. Bean, 'Comic Structure and the Humanizing of Kate in *The Taming of the Shrew*' in *The Woman's Part: Feminist Criticism of Shakespeare*, ed. Carolyn Ruth Swift Lenz, Gayle Green, and Carol Thomas Neely (Urbana: University of Illinois Press, 1980), 65–78, especially 68–71; Juliet Dusinberre, *Shakespeare and the Nature of Women* (London: Macmillan, 1975), 78–9; Morris, 148–9; Novy, 58–60.

21. Some historians attribute a growing emphasis on marriage as an affective rather than an economic relationship to the influence of Puritan ideas of spiritual equality. See Stone, *The Family, Sex and Marriage, 1500–1800*. Others stress that the ideal of marriage based on love appears throughout the period. See, for example, Ralph A. Houlbrooke, *The English Family, 1450–1700* (London: Longman, 1484). Ann Jennalie Cook, whose useful study of marriage in Shakespeare's society appeared after I had completed this book, provides references on this controversy. *Making a Match: Courtship in Shakespeare and His Society* (Princeton: Princeton University Press, 1991), 13.

THE TAMING OF THE SHREW
IN THE TWENTY-FIRST CENTURY

❧

In recent years commentary on *The Taming of the Shrew* has taken some new paths, especially regarding Kate's troubling "obedience" speech at the end of the play. The critic Carolyn E. Brown wrote in reaction to a number of past critics, including some included in this volume. Brown stated that Kate, in the course of the play, is transformed from a "straight-speaking rebel to a subversive shrew." Unlike many commentators, Brown saw Kate's final speech as subversive; by pretending to be excessively subservient, Kate gets revenge on the other new wives and tricks her new husband to boot.

2004—Carolyn E. Brown. "Bianca and Petruchio: 'The Veriest Shrew[s] of All,'" from *Re-Visions of Shakespeare: Essays in Honor of Robert Ornstein*

Carolyn E. Brown is an associate professor at the University of San Francisco. Her work has been published in *Re-Visions of Shakespeare* and in the journal *Shakespearean Criticism*.

For years I avoided *The Taming of the Shrew*. It seemed so different from the rest of the comedies in which Shakespeare shows appreciation for the woman's situation and compellingly, even affectionately, characterizes his female protagonists as strong, admirable, and self-sufficient. I found it troublesome to read the play as many scholars had read it, with Katherine as a monstrous virago who requires severe taming measures to transform her into a functional wife and member of society, and Petruchio as the only man brave and wise enough to accomplish such an unenviable mission. It was distressing to me to view Petruchio in such laudable terms, as a kind of Dr. Freud, a psychotherapist whose therapy includes temporarily adopting the stance of shrewishness himself to cure Katherine of her bad temperament.[1] I could not join with other scholars when they celebrated Petruchio's miraculous transformation of the violent, unhappy, bitter shrew into a strong, happy, and graceful woman by the play's end. What bothered me was that Katherine seems so unshrewish and so crushed by the treatment Petruchio shows her. She seems anything but happy and more emotionally adjusted by the play's end. Moreover, Petruchio offended me and seems to fit Katherine's delineation of him as a "mad-brain rudesby, full of spleen"[2] more than he does some scholars' tributes to him as a brilliant shrew tamer.

The turning point came for me when I participated in a conference on Shakespeare's comedies at the University of San Francisco in 1990, at which Robert Ornstein was also a participant. He spoke of how Shakespeare had modified the shrew tradition by coarsening Petruchio and softening Katherine until she bears little resemblance to the quintessential shrew, so prevalent in medieval and early modern literature. He described his perceptions of Petruchio as a bully, whose treatment of Katherine is cruel and gratuitous, far in excess of Katherine's actions and far beyond a point of justification. He went so far as to imply that Katherine did not need to be tamed. This discussion sent me to Ornstein's book on the comedies. There I found what I still regard as one of the most incisive analyses of the play, a reading that contends that Katherine is not an "overbearing termagant" but a sympathetic, psychologically complex heroine who is "courteous" and "capable of kindness to servants" and whose "behavior at her wedding is remarkably restrained given the anxiety and humiliation she suffers from Petruchio's behavior." There I also found a condemnation of Petruchio as an "unregenerate boor" who abuses a woman under the guise of reforming her.[3] Ornstein's compelling defense of Katherine and censure of Petruchio was such an eye-opening, intellectually exciting experience that I returned to Shakespeare's play and discovered a reading that I had never seen before. The play would never be the unrewarding reading experience it had been before. Ornstein's insights prodded me to analyze the play more closely and to publish an article that argues that Katherine is not modeled after the typical shrew but, rather, after the Griselda figure, a woman who needlessly endures physical and mental torture at the hands of a domestic tyrant.[4]

Others have also viewed Katherine more sympathetically and the play less comically. In recent years, the play has been read as more of a "problem" play than a romantic comedy, and as more of a troubling exploration of domestic violence than a comical portrayal of the maturation of a compassionate union. Scholars have argued that the play can be funny only if one reads it as a farce, minimizes and justifies the violence, and identifies with the tamer. Otherwise, the play "loses its humor."[5] Shakespeare has been seen to portray Katherine in psychologically rich terms as a woman whose shrewishness has resulted from the cruelty and oppressiveness of a patriarchal society, the mockery of a spoiled sister, and the neglect of an indifferent father.[6] Yet another body of critics argues that Katherine is not a shrew at all and that her ostensible shrewishness is a defensive strategy adopted to protect herself from further hurt in a misogynistic world.[7] Critics have viewed Petruchio's actions as excessive, disproportionate to Katherine's behavior, unjustifiably cruel, and inhumane.[8] In reading Petruchio in less benign dimensions and Katherine in more compassionate terms, I have been grappling with the issue of identifying the real shrew in the play. I returned again to Ornstein's book for guidance, discovering that he identifies a "latent shrewishness" in Bianca.[9] I began to explore Bianca's character more fully and realized that while appearing to be an insignificant, minor character, she, in fact, is a seminal figure, instrumental to the audience's understanding of another character—Petruchio. While Bianca is a shrew and Katherine is not, Bianca is not the only shrew and not the worst one by far. The shrew who is far worse than any of the others is Petruchio. I realized that Ornstein is correct: Petruchio is, indeed, a bully who subjects Katherine to unnecessary humiliation and torture. He is a bully because he is a shrew, just like Bianca. This essay argues that Shakespeare heightens Petruchio's shrewishness by having his behavior duplicate that of the other shrew, Bianca. Two plots develop simultaneously—the maturation of Petruchio and Katherine's relationship and that of Bianca and Lucentio, both of which end in marriage. What I discovered is that Shakespeare consistently juxtaposes the two plots and, more particularly, the characters Petruchio and Bianca, who can be seen as doubles, a paralleling device well-established in Shakespeare that mirrors two similar characters and, thus, delineates the delicate nuances of characterization in both.

Petruchio can be read as not pretending to be a shrew but, rather, as indulging his genuine shrewish nature under the guise of taming Katherine, who does not need to be tamed. Shakespeare's depiction of a man as a shrew was nourished largely by the more enlightened attitudes toward women and marriage of this time, and it was possible because of the etymological ambiguity associated with the word "shrew." In the medieval period the word applied primarily to men and designated a "wicked, evil-disposed, or malignant man."[10] Chaucer applied it to both sexes, but by the end of the sixteenth century it applied primarily to women. Shrews were so prevalent in the cultural context of the medieval and early modern periods that a whole body of literature developed around them.[11] In this widespread literature, certain qualities and behaviors became associated with shrews—characteristics that Shakespeare's audience would have recognized in Bianca and Petruchio, not Katherine. The latitude in the word's designation allowed Shakespeare to play on its equivocation and make one of his shrews a man, according to the original definition, and his heroine a spirited woman who has been mislabeled a shrew.

Shakespeare contrives his play so that the multitude could interpret it as a comedy in which a wise man tames a shrewish wife and, in turn, creates a peaceful marriage for himself. But he also allows for those who might choose to take the opposite interpretation to read his play as a less comical work about a strong-willed woman tormented by two shrews in her life—her sister and husband—and trying to find a way to endure both of them. The play can be viewed from a feminist perspective, with Shakespeare sympathetically exploring the dilemma of an honest, intelligent, outspoken woman who tries not to compromise her integrity and manipulate others by dissembling, as her sister does. The play records Katherine's protest against an unloving father and sister and a misogynistic society, and the gradual squelching of her vitality, identity, and voice. The play embodies Katherine's descent from an honest speaking rebel to a "conformable" "household Kate" (2.1.271).

Shakespeare begins 1.1 by giving us some hints about Bianca's shrewish nature, which becomes clearer as the play progresses. When her father asks her to leave the scene, Bianca appears to be obedient to her father's every command:

> Sister, content you in my discontent.
> Sir [father], to your pleasure humbly I subscribe.
> My books and instruments shall be my company,
> On them to look and practice by myself. (1.1.80–83)

But Shakespeare makes us suspicious of Bianca: her submissiveness is overdone, and she has no reason to be "discontent[ed]" since all of the men, including her father, have expressed their adoration of her. It is Katherine who gives us a clue that there is a less pleasing side to her sister that few get to witness: "A pretty peat! it is best put finger in the eye, and she knew why" (78). Katherine's intimations about her sister make us suspect that Bianca is not what she appears to be, that she adopts a "gentler, milder mold" (60) in public, assuming such meekness that she deludes everyone into thinking that she is the embodiment of "mild behavior and sobriety" (71). Even in this early scene, though, Shakespeare gives us an inkling of Bianca's coarse, unkind nature. Under a guise of gentleness, Bianca mocks Katherine, slyly making her sister look like the evil one and taunting her by declaring that Katherine is happy in Bianca's misery—"content you in my discontent"—of which there is no textual evidence. Shakespeare allows for a sympathetic reading of Katherine as the truly discontented, isolated one—not the pampered and spoiled Bianca. Katherine is the one who is mocked and ostracized because she dares to speak her mind and openly defy male characters, while Bianca disguises her defiance.

Shakespeare presents the public Bianca in her first appearance and allows us only to suspect she is different in private. But he permits us in 1.2—Petruchio's first appearance—to see both the public and private Petruchio and to detect a stark contrast between the two, as we will detect in Bianca in the next scene. Because Petruchio is a much more egregious shrew and because he is male, Shakespeare makes him more violent and physically dangerous than Bianca in private, as he bullies and beats Grumio. Petruchio plays with language: he vexes his servant, making the unsophisticated Grumio think that his master wants him to hit him, and refuses to clear up Grumio's misunderstanding. He, for example, orders Grumio to "knock me here soundly" (8), "knock me at this gate / And rap me well" (11–12), and "now knock when I bid you" (19). Petruchio is provoking Grumio to "knock" him or hit him so that he can beat Grumio more severely. Grumio suggests the game playing and beating are chronic: "I should knock you first, / And then I know after who comes by the worst" (13–14). The scene is coarse also in that both Petruchio and Grumio irresistibly play with the bawdy, indecent designation of "knock me."[12] So much din is created by Petruchio's threats and by Grumio's complaints at having his ears wrung that the peace is disturbed outside of Hortensio's door and Hortensio comes to inspect the commotion. The designations of Katherine as a "brawling scold" who raised "loud alarums" (1.1.127) and "began to scold and raise up such a storm / That mortal ears might hardly endure the din" (1.1.172–73)—all of which are behaviors associated with shrews but are grossly exaggerated references to Katherine's demeanor in 1.1—accurately describe Petruchio's first appearance.

Luckily for Grumio, Hortensio breaks up the "fray" and saves him from further abuse. Petruchio and Grumio, then, give an accounting to Hortensio of what has just transpired. Petruchio tries to make Grumio look like a disobedient servant who has not followed directly stated instructions and himself a good master, vindicated in administering the "knocks" that Hortensio was not meant to witness: "I bade the rascal knock upon [Hortensio's] gate, / And could not get him for my heart to do it" (37–38). Grumio rightly protests that Petruchio never clearly said "knock at the gate" (39). When shrews bother to justify their unprovoked violence, they sound like Petruchio. They are "shrewd," a word related to the word "shrew" and suggesting not just malignancy and evil, but also cunning and artfulness (*OED* 13). Shrews are good at manipulating words and situations to suit their needs, and they are often described as "wily" and "tricky." Petruchio fabricates excuses for abusing Grumio by making his servant look surly and disobedient. Shrews also engage in deception, appearing to be other than what they are. The shrew Valeria of John Dickenson's "Greene in Conceipt" (1598), for example, was shrewd at "cloking of hir crime [of wantonness], with the spew of holynesse and religion"; she adopted a "smoth habit of hipocrisie" and is described as a "wily Dame [accomplished at] dissembling."[13] Petruchio, likewise, dissembles. Once Hortensio enters the scene and observes the "fray," Petruchio immediately tries to cover his indiscreet, coarse behavior, which he thought no one was witnessing. He, consequently, greets Hortensio with civilities, projecting a sophisticated pose by speaking in Italian and appearing to be a gentleman, and silences Grumio's complaints of abuse with an implicit threat: "Sirrah be gone or talk not, I advise you" (43).

Shakespeare has Petruchio do what we are suspicious the other shrew, Bianca, is doing: in public both conceal their unkind natures and assume a "gentler, milder" demeanor. Just as Petruchio fools the public (and Hortensio, in particular) into perceiving him as a gentleman, Bianca, like the shrew Valeria, dupes everyone, especially her father, into thinking she is an innocent, ingenuous, submissive maiden. The wily Petruchio and Bianca misrepresent their situations, accusing their victims—Grumio and Katherine, respectively—of being vile, and presenting themselves as benign. Grumio warns Hortensio, though, that "you know him not, sir" (115), alluding to the less pleasing, possibly malevolent, side to Petruchio, to which only a few are privy. Both Grumio and Katherine know that the shrews are less civil in private.

Act 2, scene 1 parallels the previous scene in that just as Shakespeare offers us a private view of Petruchio, he permits us to observe Bianca when she is alone with her sister. Moreover, he allows us to contrast the private Bianca with the public one, once her father enters the scene, and to detect the dissembling. In this meeting with Bianca, isolated Katherine reaches out for a meaningful, genuine conversation with her sister, addressing Bianca in all seriousness and beseeching her to speak from her heart and to drop her shrewish game playing: "Of all thy suitors here I charge thee tell / Whom thou lov'st best. See thou dissemble not" (8–9). Unlike her shrewish sister, Katherine is forthright and ingenuous, not a game player. To Katherine's repeated entreaties that Bianca tell her of her heart—"Is't not Hortensio [whom you love]" and "You will have Gremio to keep you fair" (13, 17)—Bianca will not drop her games and, instead, never misses an opportunity to tease and antagonize Katherine about her own more privileged status.

Bianca repeatedly distorts her sister's words into their contrary meaning or pretends not to understand her sister. She refuses to acknowledge Katherine's serious message and, instead, acts as if her sister makes frivolous requests. She, for example, accuses Katherine of being jealous of her "raiment" and envious of her superfluity of suitors: "Is it for [Gremio] you do envy me so?" (18). The final indignity is her nullifying Katherine's serious intent by accusing Katherine of being playful: "Nay then you jest, and now I well perceive / You have but jested with me all this while" (19–20). The more earnest Katherine becomes, the more flippant Bianca becomes and the more evasive about her "love" interests. Katherine knows that her sister is teasing her and tells her "Minion, thou liest" (13). We have just seen the other shrew "lie" when Petruchio refuses to be straightforward with Hortensio about his mistreatment of Grumio. Shrews' tricky shrewdness often takes the form of lies. Although Bianca continually rebuffs and provokes her sister, Katherine each time attempts to ignore the mockery and the equivocation until she can ignore it no longer and finally lashes out in frustration. While Petruchio is more physically violent than Bianca, they both provoke their victims, mentally tormenting and taunting them by playing with words until their victims want to "knock" them. The epithet of "irksome scold" (1.2.186) applies more to them than to Katherine, for they are the ones who display shrewish behavior of delighting in annoying others with their troublesome and wearisome taunts (*OED* "irksome" a.2). Although in 1.1, Bianca accuses Katherine of shrewishly deriving "content" from her "discontent," Bianca reveals here that she, like Petruchio with Grumio, is the one, not her sister, who enjoys causing others anguish.

Bianca is adept and "shrewd" at turning situations to her advantage, especially at making herself look like the victim and the good sister, as Petruchio makes himself look like the good master. Once Baptista enters and Bianca has an audience, she enhances her playacting by appearing as the hurt, silent, and meek one, just as she did in 1.1: "Poor girl, she weeps" (24). She shrewdly traps Katherine into looking like the "insolent" one who has been "crossing [her] with a bitter word" (28) or contradicting her with cutting, harsh words when it is the other way around just as Petruchio made Grumio look like the "cross" one who has wronged him. Katherine rightly protests that "her silence flouts me" (29) as she describes her sister's passive aggressive behavior. Although characters accuse Katherine of being "shrewd" or crafty (1.1.180; 1.2.59; 1.2.88–89), their accusations ironically apply more to Bianca and Petruchio than to Katherine, who is not "shrewd" and, thus, does not resort to trickery or cunning but is straightforward.

Shakespeare continues to juxtapose Bianca's behavior to that of Petruchio, who enters in 2.1 as Bianca leaves the scene. Petruchio's behavior in this scene mirrors both Bianca's two previous appearances and her next one in the following scene (3.1). Petruchio's actions are like Bianca's previous ones in that he, too, behaves differently when he is alone with Katherine and when he is in public with her father. His appearance is parallel to that of Bianca in the next scene in that they conduct a similar wooing process. Like Bianca, Petruchio projects a mild exterior when he is in public and is negotiating with Baptista for his daughter. Part of shrews' tricky nature is that they often appeared as doves before marriage and turned into beasts after the ceremony. Like Bianca, John Dickenson's shrewish Valeria, for example, appeared sweet and obedient before the wedding so that she could dupe a mild man into marrying her and so that she could "raign as Mistresse of all" after the ceremony.[14] Petruchio, likewise, projects an affable pose as a wooer when he first addresses Baptista:

> I am a gentleman of Verona, sir,
> That hearing of [Katherine's] beauty and her wit,
> Her affability and bashful modesty,
> Her wondrous qualities and mild behaviour,
> Am bold to show myself a forward guest
> Within your house. (2.1.47–52)

He proclaims himself a "gentleman" and seems the embodiment of good manners. His pose, though, is as saccharine and disingenuous as is his excessive description of Katherine. His civility is as excessive and false as Bianca's mildness and obedience to her father's "pleasure" in 1.1.

Once Petruchio is alone, though, awaiting Katherine's arrival, he changes his tone:

> Say that she frown, I'll say she looks as clear
> As morning roses newly wash'd with dew.
> Say she be mute and will not speak a word,
> Then I'll commend her volubility,
> And say she uttereth piercing eloquence.
> If she do bid me pack, I'll give her thanks,
> As though she bid me stay by her a week. (2.1.172–78)

Although some critics read this passage as evidence of Petruchio's taming strategy of presenting Katherine with an ideal image of the woman she can become, it can also be read as a description of shrewish contrary and "irksome" behavior. Petruchio states that he will do exactly what we have just seen Bianca do: if Katherine is upset and pensive, he will act as if she is content and humorous; if she makes a request, he will not honor it. It certainly sounds like the shrew's method of mocking and teasing someone and molesting someone's mind.[15]

Once Petruchio is alone with Katherine, he behaves in a similar fashion to Bianca when in 2.1 she, too, was alone with her sister. He drops the mild, courteous facade and unveils his real nature, immediately vexing Katherine. When she requests that he maintain decorum and accord her dignity by calling her by her full name "Katherine," he does the opposite, repeatedly trivializing her and her request. Like Bianca, he responds to her seriousness with jesting, insulting behavior. Although he was the embodiment of social graces and polite speech when he was speaking with her father, he in private reveals his obscene and wanton nature, speaking in language surfeited with bawdy subtext, as he did in the "knock me" scene with Grumio. He refers to Katherine's "bearing" him during intercourse and gets more and more obscene until he reaches his most offensive point of speaking of putting his "tongue in [her] tail" (2.1.216), an expression that can refer to sodomy, heterosexual intercourse, or cunnilingus.[16] Scolds typically resort to shameful language, which shocks their listeners. Like Bianca earlier in the scene, Petruchio keeps taunting, provoking, and insulting Katherine until she slaps him, a reaction that Shakespeare once again makes understandable since Petruchio's sexual harassment is so offensive. Shakespeare makes Katherine's violence look like that of shrews only on the surface. Shrews are violent just for the pure love of causing turmoil; Katherine lashes out only when mercilessly provoked.

Petruchio is forced to feign courtesy if he is to prevent the offended Katherine from leaving the scene until her father arrives and if he is to prevent himself from losing a stab at her dowry. His behavior mirrors that of Bianca, who can be charming one moment, and vexatious the next; who can play the hurt one with her father and the devilish one with her sister. Shrews can turn the charm on and off to suit their purposes. Petruchio adopts shrewd dissembling, assuming the same pose he did with Katherine's father, and becoming excessively complimentary, excessively sweet—like the public Bianca: "For thou art pleasant, gamesome, passing courteous, / But slow in speech, yet sweet as springtime flowers" (2.1.239–40). Katherine realizes that Petruchio is partially disingenuous, for she speaks of his "stud[ied]" "goodly speech" (2.1.256), recognizing he is adopting a "calculated performance" of a shrew.[17]

Once he, nonetheless, puts Katherine off her guard and distracts her from leaving, he betrays that his previous cordiality was a ruse, for he tells her that he will have his will, no matter what she says: "And will you, nill you, I will marry you"; "Never make denial; / I must and will have Katherine to my wife" (2.1.264; 272–73). He correctly characterizes himself as "peremptory" (2.1.131) in his wooing, for he will admit no contradiction or denial of his will. He "must" have his way—as shrews always do. Petruchio characterizes himself as a wooer: "For I am rough, and woo not like a babe" (2.1.137). He is not a "babe" or an inexperienced suitor, and he is not a gentleman, as he projects in public, but a "rough" (*OED* a.7) or a rude, ungentle suitor, who does not waste time on delicate formalities.

Once Baptista and the other men enter, Petruchio's behavior parallels that of Bianca with her sister. At the beginning of 2.1, we saw Bianca privately torment Katherine, but once her father entered, we saw her play the innocent role. Likewise, Petruchio bullies and toys with Katherine in private, but once the others appear, he projects the false image of the mild mannered, loving, successful suitor, her most avid supporter, when, in fact, he has insulted her throughout their meeting:

> Father, 'tis thus: yourself and all the world
> That talk'd of her have talk'd amiss of her.
> If she be curst it is for policy,
> For she's not froward, but modest as the dove;
> She is not hot, but temperate as the morn. (2.1.283–87)

Shakespeare has Petruchio speak the truth and declare that Katherine is not a shrew as she is falsely reported to be. Being a shrew himself, he can see that Katherine is not the real thing.

Just as Bianca traps Katherine into seeming the opposite of what she is—the offensive one—so does Petruchio, projecting the opposite image of what has actually transpired, negating Katherine's voice and making her seem to be what she is not—in love with him and a willing partner in the forthcoming marriage: "And to conclude, we have 'greed so well together, / That upon Sunday is the wedding day"; "She hung about my neck, and kiss on kiss / She vied so fast, protesting oath on oath, / That in a twink she won me to her love" (2.1.290–91; 301–3). Petruchio, like Bianca, shows his tricky nature, which allows him to turn the truth upside down. To put it bluntly, he lies, just as Katherine earlier accused Bianca of lying. Petruchio tricks Katherine into marriage; the other cunning shrew Bianca tricks Lucentio into thinking he is marrying a mild-mannered maiden. Like typical shrews, Petruchio and Bianca are knavish—dishonest and crafty.[18] Even Katherine's reaction is paralleled in her meeting with Bianca and Petruchio. Both shrews have so consummately frustrated, angered, and trapped Katherine that she verbally lashes out, vowing retaliation: she vows that she will "be revenged" on Bianca and she will "see [Petruchio] hang'd on Sunday first" (2.1.292) before she will have anything romantically to do with him. Petruchio's game playing leaves her in the "dumps" (2.1.277), dejected, isolated, and tricked into silence; Bianca tricked her into the same helpless despondency: "Talk not to me, I will go sit and weep" (2.1.35). Shakespeare mirrors the scene between Bianca and Katherine with that between Petruchio and Katherine to underscore the similar sly shrewishness of Bianca and Petruchio and the deplorable condition of the tricked and tormented Katherine, whose honesty and directness result in her loss of freedom.

Shakespeare parallels this mock-wooing between Petruchio and Katherine with the next scene, 3.1, and 4.2, in which Bianca, likewise, is alone with her suitors. Like Petruchio, who deceives Baptista into thinking he is a loving wooer who has won his daughter's heart, Bianca deceives her father into thinking she is an obedient daughter when, in fact, she is secretly entertaining wooers behind his back. Just as Petruchio in his private "wooing" of Katherine begins to reveal that he actually is no gentleman but, rather, a bawdy, disrespectful shrew, Bianca begins to uncover that she actually is no lady or chaste maiden but a wanton flirt. Just as Petruchio brags that he is "not a babe," Bianca vaunts that she is not a beginning student in the school of love: she is "no breeching scholar in the schools" (3.1.18). When Hortensio begins with the "rudiments of art" (63) and with teaching her "the order of [his] fingering" "before [she] touch[es] the instrument" (61–62), she snaps back that she is "past [her] gamut long ago" (68). The double entendre implies that she is sexually experienced, that she does not need to be taught the basics of how to "finger an instrument," which she learned "long ago."[19] Like Petruchio, she is devoted exclusively to her own pleasures: she will "learn my lessons as I *please myself*" (3.1.20, italics mine). Although Katherine is accused of embodying shrewish "hot[ness]" (2.1.287) or lasciviousness, it is Bianca who betrays she is a "hot" shrew in her receptiveness to her suitors' advances. Shakespeare allows for the reading that Katherine breaks the lute over Hortensio's head not because she is uncontrollably violent but because she will not let him take sexual liberties with her as her sister allows.

Although the men are arguing about who will get to woo Bianca fast, the truth is that neither one of them has any input in the process—no more input than Katherine with Petruchio. While seeming shy and reserved in public, Bianca is like Petruchio in that she dominates the wooing in private and is "peremptory": "Why, gentlemen, you do me double wrong / To strive for that which resteth in my choice" (3.1.17). She, like Petruchio, will be the one to decide who will be her spouse; she will make the "choice." When Hortensio attempts to take the initiative in the wooing, she proclaims, "I'll not be tied to hours nor pointed times" (3.1.19). The wooing will be at her pace, not his, as she reasserts control. Like a shrew, she is not told when to come and go. In refusing to decide between her suitors, she keeps them all under her control and keeps them all waiting until she makes up her mind whom she will wed. Lucentio reconciles himself to the fact that "he must wait" (3.1.59) upon her wishes. Like Petruchio, she is "rough" and betrays no delicacy during the wooing process. Although Katherine is said to have a "headstrong humour" (4.1.196), an attitude associated with shrews, she shows none of the characteristics associated with the word "headstrong"—willfulness, obstinacy, determination to have one's own way (*OED* 1). Katherine never gets her way; rather, it is Petruchio and Bianca who are stubbornly self-willed.

These two appearances of Bianca (3.1 and 4.2) reflect on two other adjoining scenes (3.2 and 4.1), both dominated by Petruchio. Just as Bianca becomes more and more amorously aggressive, Petruchio proves to be more and more physically aggressive as the play proceeds, with both coming closer to revealing their shrewishness as their wedding days approach. Petruchio in 3.2 echoes Bianca's previous appearance in 3.1 in that he will not "be tied to hours nor 'pointed times." Petruchio is in no hurry to marry, and he, consequently, keeps all of the guests waiting until he feels like appearing at the ceremony, as we have just seen Bianca keep her wooers waiting upon her fickleness. Katherine knows that Petruchio, like Bianca, is dedicated to acting only when it brings him pleasure: she exclaims that he will arrive "'if it would *please him* come'" (3.2.20, italics mine).[20] Once he arrives for the wedding, he behaves uncivilly, cursing, insulting the guests, and becoming violent. It is not Katherine who betrays shrewish "rough[ness]"; rather, it is Petruchio who is violent, uncivil, and rude (*OED* "rough" a.5, 6). There is no indication that Katherine behaves like a shrew: she arrives at the "'pointed" time for the ceremony and in the "'pointed" attire and patiently waits for Petruchio; she does not deceive her father or demand to have her will but, instead, obediently follows her father's wishes and marries Petruchio against her heart; and Grumio does not suggest that she behaves uncivilly during the ceremony.

Shrews are particularly offensive at dinners, and much of the activity in shrew literature centers around eating occasions. Shrews inevitably upset dinners because meals are symbolic of social community, order, and harmony, while shrews are antisocial and discordant elements. They refuse to attend meals, behave disrespectfully, or create havoc at the dinner table if they do agree to dine. Petruchio does all of this. Petruchio leaves his wedding reception before it begins, acting as ungraciously as when he entered the scene and telling his guests that they "can go hang [them]selves" (3.1.224). He betrays that he is the "froward" (1.1.69, 5.2.184) shrew, refractory, ungovernable, and disposed to go counter to what is demanded or is reasonable (*OED* "froward" 1). Katherine, in contrast, does not behave in shrewish fashion: she is accommodating and wants to stay for the social occasion and tries to persuade her new husband to be civil.

Once Petruchio gets further removed from civilized company and once he sees no need to feign even a modicum of sociable behavior, he, like a shrew, only becomes more of a beast after marriage (as will Bianca) and after he has achieved what he wants—Katherine's dowry and Bianca's suitors' contributions. In 4.1, Shakespeare shows us the complete transformation as Petruchio requires that his servants wait on him hand and foot, and he physically abuses them nonetheless. He reveals his brutal nature, to which Shakespeare allowed us to be privy in Petruchio's first scene with Grumio. He is perpetually dissatisfied and unjustifiably finds fault with the servants' slavish behavior, with the food they serve him, and with the clothing that the Haberdasher and Tailor present to him. He subjects his victims to a constant barrage of undeserved abusive epithets, displaying the shrewish characteristic of scolding. The clothes are either too small or too big, too fashionable or not enough.[21] Both Petruchio and Bianca "lik'st it not" (4.3.83, 3.1.77), incapable of being pleased and displaying "curst[ness]" (1.1.180; 1.2.88, 128; 2.1.186, 285)—a word associated with shrews and meaning not just deserving a curse but also perversely disagreeable or cross (*OED* 2, 4) and contradictory (*OED* 14). Katherine, on the other hand, behaves civilly, not shrewishly: she likes the meat, the service, and the clothing, and she pleads for Petruchio's patience. He, not Katherine, is the shrew with the "impatient humor" (3.2.29), the "brawling scold" and "chide[r]" (1.2.225).

Once Bianca is married, Shakespeare parallels her behavior with that of Petruchio after the wedding ceremony. While Petruchio marries early in the play and Shakespeare lets us witness his complete transformation into his shrewish nature after the wedding, Bianca marries late in the play and Shakespeare gives us only an inkling of Bianca's transformation. The parallels between Bianca and Petruchio up to this point in the play, however, assure us that her behavior after marriage will be similar to that of Petruchio and that Lucentio is in store for some rough times. In the beginning of 5.2, Bianca is married to Lucentio, and everyone sits down for a banquet, which seems very much like a wedding reception for Bianca and Lucentio. Lucentio tries to be a cordial host, welcoming his guests and bidding his wife to be accommodating, especially to his father (4–8). There is no textual indication that Bianca extends felicitations to Vincentio or, for that matter, any guest. She no longer dissembles nor suppresses the full extent of her shrewishness. She, like Petruchio, only gets worse after marriage.

During the repartee, Bianca is conspicuously silent, and soon we realize why: she has fallen asleep. She awakens only when the guests begin to insult each other and the atmosphere gets rowdy. The previous cordial interchanges bore her, just as Petruchio was bored at the prospect of attending his own wedding reception. When she finally speaks, it is in order to utter a crass, indelicate remark: "Head and butt! An hasty-witted body / Would say your head and butt were head and horn" (5.2.40–41). Making her coarse words resemble those of Petruchio during his "wooing" of Katherine when he speaks of putting his "tongue in [her] tail," Shakespeare has Bianca elicit similar sexual puns, referring to "heads of penises" or the testes and buttocks.[22] Like Petruchio, Bianca is adept at "ropetricks" (1.2.111) or indecent jests. She subsequently leaves the dinner prematurely and refuses to engage in the communal process, preferring to "please herself" and mirroring Petruchio's previous impoliteness in leaving his wedding reception early. When the men decide to wager on their wives coming when they are called, Bianca's actions parallel those of Petruchio. In several previous instances, Petruchio betrayed that he would not "be tied to hours nor pointed times," as when he refused to come when he was called for his wedding at a designated time, to stay for the wedding reception, and to leave for Baptista's house unless he has "'pointed" the appropriate hour. Likewise, when the husbands bid their wives to come to them, Bianca and the Widow—yet another shrew—refuse to budge and to be told when to come and go. Earlier Bianca betrayed her recalcitrance to leave the scene at the time "appointed" by her father (1.1.75, 91; 2.1.25, 30). Bianca and Petruchio disrupt the social harmony and betray shrewish "rough[ness]"—rudeness, lack of refinement and civility (OED "rough" 13, 14)—and impatience with social graces.

Just as Bianca and Petruchio's actions are paralleled throughout the play to underscore the similarities in their character, so too are the attempts to tame them. Katherine tries to tame both of them with comparable strategies. After futilely trying direct tactics, which enlist reason, affection, resistance, and self-assertion with both of them, Katherine resorts to less straightforward means, embodied in the "sun moon" scene (4.5) and her last speech (5.2.137–80), both of which have perplexed critics. Some critics argue that Shakespeare uses her last speech to pay tribute to patristic conceptions of marriage in which the husband is the head of his wife. But Shakespeare allows her last speech to be read as ironic, sarcastic, and subversive. One of the lines in Katherine's last speech most poignantly describes her covert tactics: she tells the women that she and they must "seem" "to be most which we indeed least are" (176). Certainly, this line characterizes Bianca's behavior throughout much of the play, with her seeming to be excessively meek and mild in public when in reality she is anything but this. It is my contention that in order to try to tame the shrews in her life, Katherine, ironically, must become what everyone mistakenly judged her to be in the first place—a shrew. Shakespeare, then, enlists parallelism one last time in the play, making Katherine's behavior duplicate that of Bianca and Petruchio in order to emphasize her new shrewishness. She must learn to practice "seeming" or dissembling, and it is the "most[ness]" or the excessiveness of her later behavior— the extreme obedience and subservience—that betrays her disingenuousness. She becomes as, if not more, accommodating and compliant as Bianca when in 1.1 she publicly feigned dedication solely to her father's "pleasure." At the play's end Katherine, in other words, practices artfulness and cunning and prevaricates, as do the other shrews, engaging in a "goodly speech" or a calculated performance meant to deceive.

Her performance serves several purposes. Katherine gets "revenge" on her sister and the Widow, both of whom have insulted her. Just as Bianca used her public pose of extreme meekness to trap Katherine into looking like the insolent one, Katherine practices shrewish trickiness and turns the tables, using her even more severe pose to make her sister look disobedient in comparison. Now it is Katherine who takes control with her shrewish stance, chiding and scolding the other women, deriving "content from [their] discontent" and "triumph[ing] thus upon [their] misery" (4.3.34). Her other purpose is to outsmart Petruchio as well, feigning obedience and gratitude as excessive as Petruchio's earlier public gentlemanliness, and trapping and deceiving him into thinking she is a compliant wife, just as he trapped Katherine into marriage and Baptista into believing in his cordial facade. Like Petruchio, she speaks the opposite of what she means and mocks him behind his back. Like a shrew, she has learned to couch and conceal her hostility and sarcasm, to disguise the fact that she, like Bianca and the Widow, would like "to offer war" rather than "kneel for peace," "to wound [her] lord," and to be "a foul contending rebel, / And graceless traitor" to Petruchio (5.2.163, 139, 160–61).

For some critics, then, Katherine is triumphant at the play's end. In some ways she does win: for the first time she, for example, dominates a scene, imitating the shrewish Petruchio and Bianca by making others wait upon her as she delivers one of the longest speeches in the play. But while she has learned to play the part of the shrew, her last speech lodges more than sarcasm, and dissembling has more personal consequences for her than it does for Petruchio and Bianca. Her last speech also contains the tone of a lament, with the imagery of domination and battle denoting another meaning: while she may have won the battle, she, unfortunately, has lost the war. She delivers a speech of surrender, "kneel[ing] for peace" and offering her words as a "tribute" (5.2.153) or as a peace offering to a superior force (*OED* 1)—to Petruchio in particular, and the male-dominated culture in general, whom she is "bound to serve." The imagery of invasion presents her as a prisoner of war, being held against her will and forced to do, say, and be what she "indeed least" feels—the situation of women in a misogynistic world. While prevaricating and adopting a "smoth habit of hipocresie" may not distress Bianca and Petruchio, it has deep significance for Katherine, who has been shown to have more integrity than either of her tormentors and to be a proponent of forthrightness. Although she has told Bianca to "dissemble not," now she must compromise her beliefs and dissemble. Earlier she articulated the importance of "say[ing] her mind" and directly expressing her anger:

> My tongue will tell the anger of my heart,
> Or else my heart concealing it will break,
> And rather than it shall, I will be free
> Even to the uttermost, as I please, in words. (4.3.77–80)

While in her last words she may vent her anger, she does not speak her ire "free[ly]" but must couch it. In some sense, then, her "headstrong humour" has been "curb[ed]," and she becomes as "conformable as other household Kates" (2.1.271), behaving like the other women in the play and like a "puppet," who compromises her voice and says what is expected of her—in public at least. That she "conceal[s]" "the anger of [her] heart" must give us pause and make us wonder if her "heart" is "break[ing]" at the play's end. In getting revenge on her sister and Petruchio, she has confined herself. Shakespeare inverts the shrew tradition to underscore this confinement: whereas Bianca and Petruchio conceal their natures before marriage but come to exercise them after marriage, Katherine expresses herself throughout the play, but at the end she must put on a mask. There is no indication that she will ever have the freedom to be herself again.

Moreover, there is no indication that her sacrifice has helped to tame the shrews. Certainly, neither Bianca nor Petruchio shows any sign of being subdued. Katherine has lost more than she has gained, for she ends the play with the prospect of "vail[ing] [her] stomach," which the Arden edition glosses as abasing one's pride and adopting a pose of submission.[23] Katherine, in other words, has had to compromise her integrity and "proud-minded[ness]," which have been her most defining qualities. Lucentio ends the play with an equivocal statement: "'Tis a wonder, by your leave, [Katherine] will be tam'd so" (5.2.190). His remark can be interpreted as an expression of admiration for Petruchio's miraculous transformation of his wife into a tamed shrew ("wonder" *OED* sb. 1, 2, 3). But with the word "wonder" also denoting something so disgraceful or horrible that it causes astonishment (*OED* 5), Shakespeare is suggesting that the changed Katherine is a distressing sight. Shakespeare, likewise, has Baptista deliver an ambiguous line: "She is changed, as she had never been" (5.2.115). While Baptista means to pay tribute to Petruchio's skills in so transforming his daughter into a pleasant "Kate" that he no longer recognizes her, Shakespeare has his line denote the annihilation of Katherine's being: she has lost so much of herself that it is as if she no longer exists. Her spiritedness has been squelched, and she has become what she has despised most—a dissembling shrew, a parody of her sister.

The Taming of the Shrew records the toll of a misogynistic society on young women—throughout time. The play can be viewed in allegorical dimensions, with Katherine representing everywoman, and Petruchio embodying the male power base. Shakespeare has Petruchio clarify his symbolic significance, identifying himself as the upholder of the oppressive hegemonic code: "For I am he am born to tame you, Kate, / And bring you from a wild Kate to a Kate / Conformable as other household Kates" (2.1.269–71). Like Katherine, young women begin their lives as strong-willed, assertive, and confident, idealistically thinking they can lodge a direct assault and resist the influence of the oppressive system on their lives: "My mind hath been as big as one of yours, / My heart as great, my reason haply more, / To bandy word for word and frown for frown" (5.2.171–73). But such women are immediately identified as threats, refusing to stand in adoration of men and determined to place their own desires and needs above those of men. Petruchio lodges a systematic attack on Katherine's individuality and becomes an example for the other men to emulate as they attend the "taming school" (4.2.54). Katherine's journey becomes that of everywoman, her individuality and resolve being chiseled away with each assault by a hostile culture. By the end, she conforms, discarding her rebellious stance and behaving as society prescribes—appropriate to her gender. What Shakespeare shows is that women cannot afford to be openly defiant; they must learn to play the system to their advantage or else be crushed into submission and defeat. Like Bianca, the smart ones go underground, outwardly appearing meek and vulnerable but secretly finding cunning methods to achieve their ends and ultimately posing more danger to the patriarchy than the outwardly hostile women. Bianca becomes the model of female behavior in a world unkind to women. It is her duplicity and cunning that ensure her success—marriage to a wealthy man whom she chooses and overpowers. We come to realize that it is Katherine's honesty, integrity, and straightforwardness that are her greatest liabilities. Once she transforms into an indirect and shrewish deceiver, she is far more successful. Ironically, society forces women to become what it condemns them for being—shrews. The play records Katherine's transformation from a straight-speaking rebel into a subversive shrew, the precursor to some of Shakespeare's other strong heroines, who have also learned the valuable lesson—Portia, Rosalind, Viola, and Juliet.

NOTES

1. For example, consult the following: Maynard Mack, "Engagement and Detachment in Shakespeare's Plays," in *Essays on Shakespeare and Elizabethan Drama in Honor of Hardin Craig*, ed. Richard Hosley (Columbia: University of

Missouri Press, 1962), 280; Cecil C. Seronsy, "'Supposes' as the Unifying Theme in *The Taming of the Shrew*," *Shakespeare Quarterly* 14 (1963): 18–19; Robert Heilman, "*The Taming* Untamed, or, The Return of the Shrew," *Modern Language Quarterly* 27 (1966): 160–61; Hugh Richmond, *Shakespeare's Sexual Comedy: A Mirror for Lovers* (New York: Bobbs-Merrill, 1971), 90–98; G. R. Hibbard, introduction to *The Taming of the Shrew* (New York: Penguin, 1980), 20–22; Brian Morris, introduction to the New Arden edition of *The Taming of the Shrew* (New York; Methuen, 1981), 124, 131–32; Ann Thompson, introduction to *The Taming of the Shrew* (Cambridge: Cambridge University Press, 1985), 32–34; Valerie Wayne, "Refashioning the Shrew," *Shakespeare Studies* 17 (1985): 171, 173; Joel Fineman, "The Turn of the Shrew," in *Modern Critical Interpretations of The Taming of the Shrew*, ed. Harold Bloom (New York: Chelsea House, 1988), 97; Ruth Nevo, "Kate of Kate Hall," in *Modern Critical Interpretations of The Taming of the Shrew*, 36–37; Maurice Hunt, "Homeopathy in Shakespearean Comedy and Romance," *Ball State University Forum* 29 (1988): 47–50.

2. 3.2.10. All textual citations will be from the New Arden edition of *The Taming of the Shrew* and will be included in the body of the essay.

3. Robert Ornstein, *Shakespeare's Comedies: From Roman Farce to Romantic Mystery* (Newark: University of Delaware, 1986), 66, 67, 72.

4. Carolyn E. Brown, "Katherine of *The Taming of the Shrew*: 'A Second Grissel,'" *Texas Studies in Literature and Language* 37 (1995): 285–313.

5. Shirley Nelson Garner, "*The Taming of the Shrew*: Inside or Outside of the Joke," in *"Bad" Shakespeare: Reevaluations of the Shakespeare Canon*, ed. Maurice Charney (Teaneck, N.J.: Fairleigh Dickinson University Press, 1988), 114. See also Emily Detmer, "Civilizing Subordination: Domestic Violence and *The Taming of the Shrew*," *Shakespeare Quarterly* 48 (1997): 273–94.

6. For example, consult the following: Harold C. Goddard, *The Meaning of Shakespeare* (Chicago: University of Chicago Press, 1960), 1:69–70; Nevill Coghill, "The Basis of Shakespearian Comedy," in *Shakespeare Criticism 1935–60*, ed. Anne Ridler (London: Oxford University Press, 1963), 207; Coppélia Kahn, "*The Taming of the Shrew*: Shakespeare's Mirror of Marriage," in *The Authority of Experience: Essays in Feminist Criticism*, ed. Arlyn Diamond and Lee R. Edwards (Amherst: University of Massachusetts Press, 1977), 84, 91; Morris, introduction, 114; H. J. Oliver, introduction to *The Taming of the Shrew* (Oxford: Clarendon, 1982), 47–51; Peter Saccio, "Shrewd and Kindly Farce," *Shakespeare Survey* 37 (1984): 36.

7. For example, see the following: John Masefield, *William Shakespeare* (New York: Henry Holt, 1911), 108; Charles Brooks, "Shakespeare's Romantic Shrews," *Shakespeare Quarterly* 11 (1960); 351–56; George R. Hibbard, "*The Taming of the Shrew*: A Social Comedy," in *Shakespearean Essays*, ed. Alwin Thaler and Norman Sanders (Knoxville: University of Tennessee Press, 1964), 23; Anne Barton, introduction to *The Taming of the Shrew* in *The Riverside Shakespeare*, ed. G. Blakemore Evans (Boston: Houghton Mifflin 1974), 107; James P. McGlone, "Shakespeare's Intent in *The Taming of the Shrew*," *Wascana Review* 13 (1978): 82, 87; Marilyn French, *Shakespeare's Division of Experience* (New York: Ballantine, 1981), 77.

8. For example, look at the following: William Hazlitt, *Complete Works of William Hazlitt*, ed. P. P. Howe (London: J. M. Dent, 1930), 4:343; Dennis Huston, "'To Make a Puppet': Play and Play-Making in *The Taming of the Shrew*," *Shakespeare Studies* 9 (1976): 74; Thomas MacCary, *Friends and Lovers: The Phenomenology of Desire in Shakespearean Comedy* (New York: Columbia University Press,

1985), 127, 128; and Jeanne Addison Roberts, "Horses and Hermaphrodites: Metamorphoses in *The Taming of the Shrew*," in *Modern Critical Interpretations of The Taming of the Shrew*, 60.

9. Ornstein, *Shakespeare's Comedies*, 70.

10. *Oxford English Dictionary* (New York: Oxford University Press), sb² 1a. All further citations from the *OED* will be noted in the text.

11. Some of the shrew literature includes the following: John Heywood, *A Merry Play between John John the Husband, Tyb his Wife, and Sir John the Priest*, in *The Dramatic Writings of John Heywood*, ed. John S. Farmer (Guildford: Charles Traylen, 1966), 67–89; *Tom Tyler and his Wife*, *PMLA* 15 (1900): 253–89; Thomas Ingelend, *The Disobedient Child*, in *The Dramatic Writings of Richard Wever and Thomas Ingelend*, ed. John S. Farmer (Guildford: Charles Traylen, 1966), 45–92; *The Taming of a Shrew*, in *Narrative and Dramatic Sources of Shakespeare*, ed. Geoffrey Bullough (New York: Columbia University Press, 1957), 1:69–108; "How the Devil, though Subtle, was Guld by a Scold," in *Humour, Wit, and Satire of the Seventeenth Century*, collected by John Aston (London: Chatto and Windus, 1883), 87–90; "The Farmer's Curst Wife," in *English and Scottish Popular Ballads*, ed. Helen Child Sargent and George Lyman Kittredge (New York: Houghton Mifflin, 1904), 605–6; *A Merry Jest of a Shrewd and Curst Wife Lapped in Morel's Skin, for her Good Behaviour*, in *Shakespeare's Library: A Collection of the Plays, Romances, Novels, Poems and Histories Employed by Shakespeare in the Composition of his Works*, ed. William C. Hazlitt (London: Reeves and Turner, 1875), 4:415–48; "The Patient Husband and the Scoulding Wife" (#100) and "Simple Simon's Misfortunes and his Wife" (#406), in *Roxburghe Ballads*, vol. 2, collected by Robert Earl of Oxford (London: n.p., 1774).

12. Frankie Rubinstein, *A Dictionary of Shakespeare's Sexual Puns and their Significance*, 2d ed. (London: Macmillan, 1989), 142.

13. "Greene in Conceipt: New raised from his grave, to write the Tragique storie of faire Valeria of London" (1598), in *Prose and Verse by John Dickenson*, ed. Rev. Alexander B. Grosart (Manchester: Charles E. Simms, 1878), 125. This work depicts the egregious shrew Valeria as behaving as cunningly as Petruchio in distorting situations and words so that she can justify her abuse of her servant: the servant "neuer wanted blowes, nor she a cause, though faulse, yet seeming iust, hauing a write so rich to coyne occasions . . . to vse them" (138).

14. Ibid., 113.

15. Shakespeare makes Petruchio's description of his behavior echo that of shrews in other literature of the period. In "How the Devil, though Subtle, was Guld by a Scold," one shrewish wife boasts that "by fine meanes or by foule, the contrary He doe" (88), and the description of her behavior sounds similar to Petruchio's delineation of his own:

> Had [her husband] bid her goe homely, why then she would goe brave,
> Had he cal'd her good wife, she cal'd him rogue and slave;
> Bade he, wife goe to Church, and take the fairest pew,
> Shee'd goe unto an Alehouse, and drinke, lye down and spew. (89)

16. See Rubinstein, *Dictionary of Shakespeare's Sexual Puns*, 278, and Eric Partridge, *Shakespeare's Bawdy* (New York: Routledge, 1990), 196.

17. *The Taming of the Shrew*, Cambridge edition, 90.

18. The shrew's trickery in the wooing process is an established characteristic as she devises "sundrie sleights in her minde" to trap her unsuspecting spouse, as illustrated by the shrewish wife in Thomas Deloney's *Jack of Newbury* in *The Novels of Thomas Deloney*, ed. Merritt E. Lawlis (Bloomington: Indiana University, Press, 1961), 13. Because she is determined to marry Jack, who wants to live a single life, the wife does something quite similar to Petruchio: she distorts Jack's words into an assent to marry her. She tricks him into following her to church and into thinking that she intends to marry another man. But, of course, when the fictitious groom does not arrive, she tells the priest to marry her to Jack, as she reminds him that he once said that he would never hinder her marriage. These words certainly do not constitute a marriage proposal, but she traps Jack into seeming to say something he never has.

19. Partridge, *Shakespeare's Bawdy*, 127, records the obvious sexual meaning of "instrument" as penis, and glosses the sexual meaning of "finger" as to "caress intimately" or, in vulgar terms, to "finger-fuck" (105).

20. Petruchio is behaving, for example, like the notorious shrew Uxor, Noah's wife, who appears in numerous medieval shrew texts. In *The Wakefield Pageants in the Towneley Cycle*, ed. A. C. Cawley (Manchester: Manchester University Press, 1958), 19–24, the flood water is approaching, everyone is on board the ark, and Noah has explained the dangers to his wife, but nothing can happen because Uxor will not get on the ark. She endangers everyone's life because they must all wait for her, as she decides she will spin for a while.

21. "The Scold" (#27), in *Ballads: Salisbury* (Press of Fowler of Salisbury: n.d.) in The British Museum, presents a shrew who is similar to Shakespeare's Petruchio:

> Too fat, too lean, too hot, too cold,
> I ever am complaining;
> Too raw, too roast, too young, too old,
> Each guest at table paining;
> Let it be fowl, or flesh, or fish,
> Tho' of my own providing,
> I yet find fault with ev'ry dish,
> Still every servant chiding.

The shrewish Valeria in Dickenson's "Greene in Conceipt" resembles Petruchio in her "difficulty to be pleased" with clothing: "For were the least stitch in hir Atyre not as shed would haue it, though the garment most fayre and costly, the Tailor most rare and cunning, yet would shee furiously fling it from hir, with purpose neuer to weare it; so that the sillye workeman set at his NON PLUS, lost both his custome and the creedit of his workmanshippe" (124).

22. James T. Henke, *Renaissance Dramatic Bawdy (Exclusive of Shakespeare): An Annotated Glossary and Critical Essays*, Salzburg Studies in English Literature under the Direction of Professor Erwin A. Sturzl, *Jacobean Drama Studies*, ed. James Hogg (Salzburg: Universitat Salzburg, 1974), 2:102, 174; Rubinstein, *Dictionary of Shakespeare's Sexual Puns*, 122.

23. *The Taming of the Shrew*, Arden edition, 297.

BIBLIOGRAPHY

Abate, Corinne S. "Neither a Tamer Nor a Shrew Be: A Defense of Petruchio and Katherine," from *Privacy, Domesticity, and Women in Early Modern England* (Aldershot, England: Ashgate, 2003), pp. 31–44.

Anderson, Linda, and Janis Lull, eds. *"A Certain Text": Close Readings and Textual Studies on Shakespeare and Others in Honor of Thomas Clayton* (Newark, Del.: University of Delaware Press; London and Cranbury, N.J.: Associated University Presses, 2002).

Aspinall, Dana, ed. *The Taming of the Shrew: Critical Essays* (New York: Routledge, 2002).

Babula, William. "*The Taming of the Shrew* and the New Historicism," from *Journal of the Wooden O Symposium* 4 (2004), pp. 1–8.

Bailey, Amanda. "Livery and Its Discontents: 'Braving It' in *The Taming of the Shrew*," from *Renaissance Drama* 33 (2004), pp. 87–135.

Bate, Jonathan, Jill L. Levenson, and Dieter Mehl, eds. *Shakespeare and the Twentieth Century* (Newark, Del.: University of Delaware Press; London and Cranbury, N.J.: Associated University Presses, 1998).

Berry, Edward I. *Shakespeare and the Hunt: A Cultural and Social Study* (Cambridge: Cambridge University Press, 2001).

Blake, Ann. "*The Taming of the Shrew*: Making Fun of Katherine," from *Cambridge Quarterly* 31, no. 3 (2002), pp. 237–252.

Bloom, Edward A. *Shakespeare, 1564–1964: A Collection of Modern Essays by Various Hands* (Providence, R. I.: Brown University Press, 1964).

Bloom, Harold, ed. *William Shakespeare's* The Taming of the Shrew (New York: Chelsea House, 1988).

———. *Shakespeare's* The Taming of the Shrew (New York: Riverhead Books, 2005).

Bradbrook, M. C. *Muriel Bradbrook on Shakespeare* (Brighton, Sussex: Harvester Press; Totowa, N.J.: Barnes and Noble Books, 1984).

Bretzius, Stephen. *Shakespeare in Theory: The Postmodern Academy and the Early Modern Theater* (Ann Arbor: University of Michigan Press, 1997).

Carroll, William C. *Fat King, Lean Beggar: Representations of Poverty in the Age of Shakespeare* (Ithaca, N.Y.: Cornell University Press, 1996).

Charlton, H. B., ed. *The Taming of the Shrew* (Folcroft, Pa.: Folcroft Library Editions, 1970).

Charney, Maurice. *All of Shakespeare* (New York: Columbia University Press, 1993).

Collins, Michael J. *Shakespeare's Sweet Thunder: Essays on the Early Comedies* (Newark, Del.: University of Delaware Press; London and Cranbury, N.J.: Associated University Presses, 1997).

Conaway, Charles. "'Thou'rt the Man': David Garrick, William Shakespeare, and the Masculinization of the Eighteenth-Century Stage," from *Restoration and 18th Century Theatre Research* 19, no. 1 (summer 2004), pp. 22–42.

Crosman, Robert. *The World's a Stage: Shakespeare and the Dramatic View of Life* (Bethesda, Md.: Academica Press, 2005).

Culpeper, Jonathan. "A Cognitive Approach to Characterization: Katherina in Shakespeare's *The Taming of the Shrew*," from *Language and Literature: Journal of the Poetics and Linguistics Association* 9, no. 4 (November 2000), pp. 291–316.

Dolan, Frances E., ed. The Taming of the Shrew: *Texts and Contexts* (Boston: Bedford Books of St. Martin's Press, 1996).

Free, Mary. "Hortensio's Role in Closing *The Taming of the Shrew*'s Induction," from *Renaissance Papers* (1999), pp. 43–53.

Friedman, Michael D. "'I'm Not a Feminist Director, but . . .': Recent Feminist Productions of *The Taming of the Shrew*," from *Acts of Criticism: Performance Matters in Shakespeare and His Contemporaries: Essays in Honor of James P. Lusardi*, edited by Paul Nelsen and June Schlueter (Madison, N.J.: Fairleigh Dickinson University Press, 2006), pp. 159–174.

Gabriner, P. J. "Hierarchy, Harmony and Happiness: Another Look at the Hunting Dogs in the 'Induction' to *The Taming of the Shrew*," from *Reclamations of Shakespeare*, edited by J. J. Hoenselaars (Amsterdam: Rodopi, 1994), pp. 201–210.

Gay, Penny. *As She Likes It: Shakespeare's Unruly Women* (London and New York: Routledge, 1994).

Gilbert, Miriam. "Performance Criticism," from *An Oxford Guide to Shakespeare*, edited by Stanley Wells and Lena Cowlin Orlin (Oxford, England: Oxford University Press, 2003), pp. 550–67.

Greetham, D. C., ed. *The Margins of the Text* (Ann Arbor: University of Michigan Press, 1997).

Hallett, Charles A. "'For She Is Changed, as She Had Never Been': Kate's Reversal in *The Taming of the Shrew*," from *Shakespeare Bulletin: A Journal of Performance Criticism and Scholarship* 20, no. 4 (fall 2002), pp. 5–13.

Hamilton, Sharon. *Shakespeare's Daughters* (Jefferson, N.C.: McFarland, 2003).

Haring-Smith, Tori. *From Farce to Metadrama: A Stage History of* The Taming of the Shrew, *1594–1983* (Westport, Conn.: Greenwood Press, 1985).

Henderson, Diana E. *Collaborations with the Past: Reshaping Shakespeare Across Time and Media* (Ithaca, N.Y.: Cornell University Press, 2006).

Holderness, Graham. "Text and Performance: The Taming of the Shrew," from *New Casebooks: Shakespeare in Performance*, edited by Robert Shaughnessy (New York: St. Martin's, 2000), pp. 123–141.

Hudson, the Reverend Henry N., ed. *The Complete Works of William Shakespeare* (Boston: Ginn and Heath, 1880–1881).

Martindale, Charles, and A. B. Taylor, eds. *Shakespeare and the Classics.* (Cambridge: Cambridge University Press, 2004).

Marvel, Laura, ed. *Readings on* The Taming of the Shrew (San Diego: Greenhaven, 2000).

McDonald, Russ, ed. *Shakespeare Reread: The Texts in New Contexts* (Ithaca, N.Y.: Cornell University Press, 1994).

McEvoy, Sean. *Shakespeare: The Basics* (London and New York: Routledge, 2000).

Miola, Robert S. *Shakespeare and Classical Comedy: The Influence of Plautus and Terence* (Oxford, England: Clarendon Press; New York: Oxford University Press, 1994).

Rebhorn, Wayne A. "Petruchio's 'Rope Tricks': *The Taming of the Shrew* and the Renaissance Discourse of Rhetoric," from *Modern Philology: A Journal Devoted to Research in Medieval and Modern Literature* 92, no. 3 (February 1995), pp. 294–327.

Schneider, Gary. "The Public, the Private, and the Shaming of the Shrew," from *SEL: Studies in English Literature, 1500–1900* 42, no. 2 (spring 2002), pp. 235–58.

Schulz, Max F., William D. Templeman, and Charles R. Metzger, eds. *Essays in American and English Literature Presented to Bruce Robert McElderry, Jr.* (Athens, Ohio: Ohio University Press, 1967).

Scott, Mark W. *Shakespeare for Students: Critical Interpretations* (Detroit: Gale Research, 1992).

Siberry, Michael. "Petruccio in *The Taming of the Shrew*," from *Players of Shakespeare 4: Further Essays in Shakespearian Performance by Players with the Royal Shakespeare Company*, edited by Robert Smallwood (Cambridge: Cambridge University Press, 1998), pp. 45–59.

Soule, Lesley Wade. "Tumbling Tricks: Presentational Structure and 'The Taming of the Shrew,'" from *New Theatre Quarterly* 20, no. 2 [78] (May 2004), pp. 164–179.

Sugiura, Yuko. "A Reconsideration of the 'Incomplete' Sly-Framework in *The Taming of the Shrew*," from *Shakespeare Studies (Tokyo, Japan)* 40 (2002), pp. 64–92.

Thompson, Ann. "Feminist Theory and the Editing of Shakespeare: *The Taming of the Shrew* Revisited," from *Shakespeare, Feminism and Gender*, edited by Kate Chedgzoy (Basingstoke, England: Palgrave, 2001), pp. 49–69.

Williams, Gwyn. *Person and Persona: Studies in Shakespeare* (Cardiff: University of Wales Press, 1981).

Wynne-Davies, Marion, ed. Much Ado about Nothing *and* The Taming of the Shrew (Basingstoke, England: Palgrave, 2001).

Yachnin, Paul. "Personations: *The Taming of the Shrew* and the Limits of Theoretical Criticism," from *Early Modern Literary Studies: A Journal of Sixteenth- and Seventeenth-Century English Literature* 2, no. 1 (April 1996).

Ziegler, Georgianna, Frances E. Dolan, and Jeanne Addison Roberts. *Shakespeare's Unruly Women* (Washington, D.C.: Folger Shakespeare Library; Seattle: Distributed by University of Washington Press, 1997).

Acknowledgments

Twentieth Century

Richard G. Moulton, "Personality and Its Dramatic Expression in Intrigue and Irony," from *The Moral System of Shakespeare* (New York and London: Macmillan Company, 1903), pp. 209–222.

Charlotte Carmichael Stopes, "*The Taming of the Shrew*," from *The Atheneum* (June 11, 1904), pp. 762–764.

Alice Meynell, "Introduction," from *The Complete Works of William Shakespeare*, with annotations and a general introduction by Sidney Lee, vol. 4 (Boston and New York: Jefferson Press, 1907), pp. ix–xx. © 1907 by the University Press.

William Winter, "Characters of Katharine and Petruchio," from *Shakespeare on the Stage*, second series (New York: Moffat, Yard, and Company, 1915), pp. 516–520. © 1915 by William Winter.

Edmund K. Chambers, "*The Taming of the Shrew*," from *Shakespeare: A Survey* (New York: Oxford University Press, 1926), pp. 40–48.

Harold C. Goddard, "*The Taming of the Shrew*," from *The Meaning of Shakespeare* (Chicago and London: University of Chicago Press, 1951), pp. 68–73. © 1951 by the University of Chicago.

Bertrand Evans, "*The Taming of the Shrew*," from *Shakespeare's Comedies* (London: Oxford University Press, 1960), pp. 24–32. © 1960 by Oxford University Press.

William Empson, "The Strengths of the Shrew," essay drafted in 1961, from the *Times Literary Supplement*. Reprinted in *The Strengths of Shakespeare's Shrew: Essays, Memoirs and Reviews*, by William Empson, edited by John Haffenden (Sheffield, England: Sheffield Academic Press, 1996), pp. 27–33. © 1996 by Sheffield Academic Press. By kind permission of Continuum International Publishing Group.

Ruth Nevo, "'Kate of Kate Hall,'" from *Comic Transformations in Shakespeare* (London and New York: Methuen and Company, 1980), pp. 37–52. © 1980 by Ruth Nevo.

Camille Wells Slights, "The Raw and the Cooked in *The Taming of the Shrew*," from *Journal of English and Germanic Philology* 88 (1989). Reprinted in *Shakespeare's Comic Commonwealths* (Toronto and Buffalo: University of Toronto Press, 1993), pp. 32–54. © 1993 by the University of Toronto Press. Reprinted with permission of the publisher.

Twenty-first Century

Carolyn E. Brown, "Bianca and Petruchio: 'The Veriest Shrew[s] of All,'" from *Re-Visions of Shakespeare: Essays in Honor of Robert Ornstein,* edited by Evelyn Gajowski (Newark, Del.: University of Delaware Press, 2004), pp. 35–56. © 2004 by Rosemont Publishing and Printing.

INDEX